Acclaim for TIMOTHY EGAN *'s*

Lasso the Wind

"Egan again demonstrates his considerable skills. . . . [This is] an immensely entertaining and informative tour. . . . He has a dazzling ability to capture a place or a person in telling words and details."   —*Seattle Post-Intelligencer*

"Egan does it better than almost anyone. . . . [His] artistry with the English language is in full flower here."   —*Seattle Weekly*

"An often startling study of how and why the West became what it is. . . . Egan is outspoken and passionate."   —*The Oregonian*

"Egan is a lively writer with an unabashed love for his native West and a gift for describing its natural landscape."
—*Santa Fe New Mexican*

"A freewheeling, deeply meditative journey. . . . [Egan's] love for the land is tangible and his erudition impressive."
—*Publishers Weekly*

"Egan's easy, humorous style . . . ties the pieces together and gives

TIMOTHY EGAN

Lasso the Wind

Timothy Egan, a third-generation Westerner, is
the author of *The Good Rain* and *Breaking Blue*.
The Pacific Northwest correspondent for *The
New York Times*, he lives in Seattle with his wife,
Joni Balter, and their two children.

ALSO BY TIMOTHY EGAN

Breaking Blue

The Good Rain

Lasso the Wind

VINTAGE DEPARTURES
Vintage Books
A Division of Random House, Inc.
New York

Lasso the Wind

Away to the New West

TIMOTHY EGAN

FIRST VINTAGE DEPARTURES EDITION, NOVEMBER 1999

Copyright © 1998 by Timothy P. Egan
Map copyright © 1998 by David Lindroth, Inc.

All rights reserved under International and Pan-American Copyright Conventions. Published in the United States by Vintage Books, a division of Random House, Inc., New York, and simultaneously in Canada by Random House of Canada Limited, Toronto. Originally published in hardcover in the United States by Alfred A. Knopf, Inc., New York, in 1998.

Vintage is a registered trademark and Vintage Departures and colophon are trademarks of Random House, Inc.

Grateful acknowledgment is made to Tom Lehrer for permission to reprint an excerpt from "The Wild West Is Where I Want to Be" by Tom Lehrer, copyright © 1953 by Tom Lehrer.

The Library of Congress has cataloged the Knopf edition as follows:
Egan, Timothy.
Lasso the wind: away to the New West / Timothy Egan. —Ist ed.
p. cm.
Includes index.
ISBN 0-375-40024-9
I. West (U.S.)—Description and travel. 2. West (U.S.)—History, Local. I. Title
F595.3.E43 1998
978—dc21   97-50556
CIP

Vintage ISBN: 978-0-679-78182-0

Author photograph © Marek Zaranski
Book design by Cassandra J. Pappas

www.vintagebooks.com

To Ash Green,

who escaped the curse of Rocky Colavito,
and passed his good fortune West

Painted on one side of our Sunday school wall were the words, God Is Love. We always assumed that these three words were spoken directly to the four of us in our family and had no reference to the world outside, which my brother and I soon discovered was full of bastards, the number increasing rapidly the farther one gets from Missoula, Montana.

—NORMAN MACLEAN
A River Runs Through It

Contents

Lasso the Wind

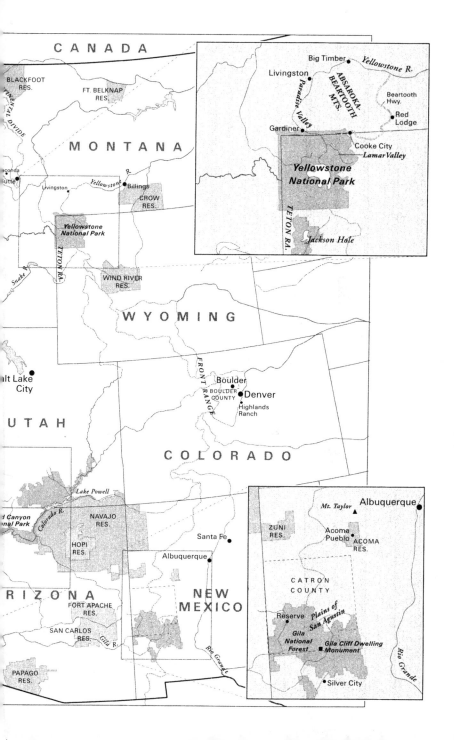

Jackson Hole, Wyoming

I n early November, snow muffled the Teton Range, forcing the elk down into the valley and a sudden intimacy on all of us. Outside, a whisper worked in place of a shout and the great peaks had fresh personality, bold and showy in the coat of the coming season. It was that best of all times to be breathing air at eight thousand feet in the Rockies: the few weeks when life is on the cusp of doing something else and the money has yet to arrive and put everything out of balance.

I spent the morning trying to get closer to Grand Teton, and the evening gathered in a circle of people who agreed on nothing about the American West except that we all loved it. The morning had me feeling bouncy, kind of infatuated. I dropped into Jackson Hole—the old trapper and Indian refuge, the place where men who smelled of a three-month affair with campfire smoke would scrub the creosote from their backsides in a thermal pool—by Boeing 727. Grand Teton is the only national park that has a large-runway jet airport inside its borders. You don't come over the rim or through the valley or past a gateway of gray-shirted park rangers as you enter this home of the natural heritage. It is strictly "Thank you for flying Delta" when you arrive in the Hole, as many of us do, falling from thirty thousand feet in an aluminum cylinder carrying a year's supply of yellow goldfish crackers.

But from there, the generic and interchangeable are left behind. No billboards. No hotel ads. No digital traffic reminders. Fences around meadows are made of wood, split and quartered. The signs just outside the airport are of cedar, with the words carved into the grain; they are polite and trusting in a way that only the National Park Service among all government agencies can still get away with. Please do not feed the animals. Stay on the existing trails. Enjoy your stay. A cynic is paralyzed. Animals? Trails? Enjoy? Are you talking to me?

I found a trailhead at sixty-seven hundred feet, the ground covered by seven inches of snow as light as a tuft of bear grass. Wilderness can cleanse the toxins from a tarred soul, but it takes several days, at least, for the antidote to work. I was in the instant-immersion phase, trying to recalibrate, to forget sea level and the mean politics of the season. I had been around too many county commissioners on rental horses, the cul-de-sac cowboys mending fences for the cameras with their soft hands. I had seen enough senators wearing creased jeans, and ministers blessing snow-making machines. I had heard too many lies about the "Real West," flimflam and fraud retold as gilded narrative by people whose grandparents took the land by force and have been draining the public trough ever since to keep it locked in a peculiar time warp of history. I needed a land without filter or interpretation—the West, unplugged.

THE SKIES, now clear, were cluttered with ravens, magpies, and the occasional red-tailed hawk looking for easy prey in the impressionable snow. Jackson Hole seemed to have everything that has been enshrined in Indian petroglyph form or frozen on canvas by Charles Russell. The place was full of charismatic megafauna, as biologists say in moments of attempted clarity. Bighorn sheep, moose, and mule deer were just starting to congregate at the lower elevations, joining an occasional bison. And elk, after six weeks of bugling and strutting, the males with harems of a dozen cows or more, the females shameless in their provocations, were ready to put their sexual appetites aside in search of winter range. The celebrity lawyers, ski country socialites, and cowboy industrialists had yet to follow a similiar migratory pattern; they awaited a signal that it was time for the herd to move.

The Snake River runs through it, gathering snowmelt from the high

Yellowstone plateau just a spit distance west of the Continental Divide and sending it all on a slow ride to the Pacific. The ribbons of life, from the Gros Ventre, Flat Creek, and other streams, support beaver, muskrat, trout, and the ever-stylish-looking herons, strutting the watery runways with those pencil-thin legs.

I could see flashes of icy gold down below, where the cottonwoods still held a few leaves. Above me, the great temperamental bulk of Grand Teton, just under fourteen thousand feet, came out again, lashed by the wind, and then disappeared behind a cloud wrap. The West is full of mountains imprinted with pedestrian names. But the French-Canadian fur trappers, openly lustful, had it right when they named the Tetons for their wet dreams.

Looking for a little meadow at the base of the upper Tetons, I got tangled in my thoughts, and wandered. I came upon a ghost forest from a fire, black skeletons against the snow. The tips of new growth, saplings barely a foot high, looked up beneath the standing dead. Clouds swooshed up and over the summits and then settled in—a hint of menace in a shroud of mist. I was chilled. My pulse quickened as the wind bristled. Snow fell. I was lost. And I was home.

INDOORS, we argued. We came from big cities and ranches, reservations and universities, downtown apartments and desert split-levels. Some of us rode horses, some of us rode mountain bikes. A few people wore bolo ties around their necks; others used them for shoelaces. We were Westerners from Connecticut and Westerners from Wyoming. We were from moss country and saguaro land. We had among us the strains of nationality and blood conflict that form the West, the long-conquered and the uneasy victors: Blackfoot Indians who once dominated a broad swath of north country; Italian and Irish urbanites whose ancestors were the conscripts that shot native bison herds as their introductory chore in the West and then deserted the Army for homesteads or gold; Hispanos with traces of conquistadors and Zunis in their family lines; Mormons who are still curious.

The topic was "The Next Hundred Years in the American West." We were the storytellers, unsure to a person what the last hundred years had been all about. But fenced in by dated metaphors, we were struggling to find a new story to inhabit, a way to live in a West closer to the truth, neither fairy tale nor a barren replacement. One side was fantasy; the other was a pit of guilt and banality—Western ho-hum. Where was the sense of wonder? Whether we spoke of the West of the imagination, the West of open spaces, or the West of mythology, this region's hold on the American character never seemed stronger. A person puts on a cowboy hat anywhere in the world, even if alone in a room, and starts acting differently—sometimes stupidly, sometimes nobly, but it is a new personality. The land west of the 100th meridian is full of tombstones under which are buried people who lived longer than any doctor ever gave them a chance to do. "It's the air," they used to say, arriving in the desert pallid and hacking up blood. Yes. And much more.

What is the West, beyond an incongruous grouping of eleven American states holding basin, range, and plenty of room to hide, a place where people think that geography alone makes them different? It was, until recently, a process instead of a place. Teddy Roosevelt's four-volume history of the West never even got beyond the Mississippi River until the end of the last book. And the essay that rerouted a caravan of American historians, Frederick Jackson Turner's 1893 thesis on the death of the frontier, was all about homesteads and perpetual movement. By that reasoning, the West died more than a century ago. The Prairie States are flat lands with a separate personality, but they are not the West. Nor is Texas, the blood of its violent past coursing through its boundaries; part of the old Confederacy, it is a state and region unto its own.

If land and religion are what people most often kill each other over, then the West is different only in that the land is the religion. As such, the basic struggle is between the West of possibility and the West of possession. On many days it looks as if the possessors have won. Over the past century and a half, it has been the same crew, whether shod in snakeskin boots or tasseled loafers, chipping away at the West. They have tried to tame it, shave it, fence it, cut it, dam it, drain it, nuke it, poison it, pave it, and subdivide it. They use a false view of history to disguise most of what they are up to. They seem to be afraid of the native West—the big, cloud-crushing, prickly place. They cannot stand it that green-eyed wolves are once again staring out from behind aspen groves in Yellowstone National Park. They cannot live with the idea that at least one of the seventeen rivers that dance out of the western slopes of the Sierra Nevada remains undammed. They are disgusted that George Armstrong Custer's name has been removed from the name of the battlefield memorial, the range of the Sioux and Crow and Arapaho, replaced by a name that gives no special favor to either side: the Little Bighorn Battlefield. Worse, the person now in charge of the memorial is an Indian.

But, given a chance, the West will leave most people feeling a sense of light-headed exuberance. The mountains, the space, the distance from anywhere that "counts." Who can look at rivers that boil out of the ground, or Las Vegas at dawn, or the hunchbacked, flute-playing Kokopelli incised on a side of sandstone, and not laugh? I could not get Grand Teton and those cartographically incorrect trappers out of my head. Was there still a place in the next hundred years for someone smelling of dust-caked sweat and animal blood to come before a panel such as ours and propose naming the most glorious mountain in our midst, The Big Tit? Or, for that matter, The Big Gut, a loose translation of "Gros Ventre"?

David McCullough told us about a time when he was researching Roosevelt's early life on the Dakota Plains. He could not get over the wind; harsh, howling, it was unrelenting.

"And it's a good thing," a farmer said, straight-faced, to McCullough. "Because if this wind ever stopped blowing, the chickens would all fall down."

Curly Bear Wagner, a Blackfoot from Montana, recalled a talk he had given recently about native culture. Afterward, a member of the audience approached him with an earnest question.

"How long have you been an Indian?" she asked.

George Horse Capture, of the Gros Ventre Nation, told a similar story. "A man and his wife, on vacation, were pointing in my direction," he said. "The man yelled out: 'Hey, Martha, come look at this.' I looked around. Then I realized they were pointing at me. 'Here's an Indian—look at this!' "

Of late, I had heard a lot of ranchers compare themselves to Indians, saying they were being pushed off the land. I was very troubled by this line of reasoning. In the eye blink of history it took to move Indians to the margins of their former homeland, the Federal government gave away as much of the West as it could, until there were no more takers. But first, the new inhabitants wiped out one of the great natural bounties of all time, the bison herds that had blotted the range. In the bison's place, they planted a European animal best suited to an English bog attended by sour-humored men in tweed. Today, that system is serviced by a handful of United States senators who hold it up as the high point of Western culture, a belief grounded in a one-dimensional version of a full-bodied history. Who owns the West? goes the perennial question. By the plundered-province view, it may be the last lobbyist to lunch with Senator Larry Craig of Idaho.

There were no whiners in Jackson that November evening. The ranchers had the mark of high-altitude western workers, with skin-cancer cheeks.

They did not complain about the government or the urbanites who sur-round them—86 percent of all Westerners live in a city, the highest propor-tion of any region in the country—or the Indians or the wild animals trying to regain a foothold in their old haunts. Just about weather, the curse of the rancher.

"The old earth which created us all is disappearing," said Drum Hadley, a rancher and poet from the Border Country. He seemed perplexed, and genuinely saddened. The Southwest was being sucked dry, red-earth calcify-ing and blowing away as the climate changed into something new and fear-ful. Cows were choking the timid streams, but nobody wanted to go the faux route, giving up the land to work as an ornament in a billionaire's fantasy.

Beyond our circle, all the troubles of the West were just outside the win-dow. In Jackson Hole, $5-million residences were being built on spec, and anything under a million was considered a starter castle. The terraces above the valley were stuffed with log mansions, some with a dozen fieldstone fireplaces. A home with twelve hearths is a home without a heart, deeply confused. There were trophy homes for movie stars, trophy homes for investment bankers, trophy homes for the idle rich, the hyperactive rich. But a cop, or a firefighter, or someone hired by the Teton County school district to teach the children of the trophy homes how to read, could not afford to live in the valley.

What happened to the old mountain towns of northern Italy, Ernest Hemingway wrote, was that the rich came in one season and never left. Money flows to beauty and then attracts more money, pushing out every-thing that does not fit. Aspen, Telluride, Park City, Taos, Sandpoint, Sedona, Jackson Hole, and the place where Hemingway fired a shotgun into his mouth, Sun Valley—the golden ghettos of the West might as well be sealed and gated, even if some of the streets are technically open. In Santa Fe, there is one real-estate agent for every one hundred people; closing costs are about as wild as it gets in some people's West.

What is left, what seems inviolate, is public land—turf without title attached to it, unique among the nations of the world. We sketch our dreams and project our desires on this American inheritance. And we fight over it with lawyers and guns and history. Nearly half of all Western land—better than 500 million acres—is public. I grew up in a big family with little money, but we had the outdoors: Rock Creek in Montana, Lake Crescent on the Olympic Peninsula, Upper Priest Lake in Idaho. We were rich. And only later did I realize why I never had a truly sad day in the outdoors: This was Wallace Stegner's Geography of Hope.

Not all Westerners appreciate what they are entrusted with, but much of the rest of the world certainly does. I saw a map of the West published in the German-language edition of the magazine *Geo*. It was a contemporary map, but what it highlighted was the invisible empire of the past: the native tribes and their homelands, the wild animal herds and their long-ago range, the silent cities of the Anasazi. The map also showed wildlife refuges, national parks, and the blank spots protected as formal wilderness. It was everything the old world of Europe does not have—sections of public land bigger than some countries, and a past yet to be fully deciphered.

Think of what should never be taken away:

The light that enchanted D. H. Lawrence, who said New Mexico's high country was "the greatest experience from the outside world that I ever had. It changed me forever."

The canyonland arches, showing the age lines of many geologic eras; they convey a random sense of mischief, something that could collapse at any moment, or in another thousand years.

Joshua trees in the Mojave Desert, looking like discards from the sketch-book of Dr. Seuss.

North Cascade Mountain alpenglow, in July, when it is the most perfect place on earth.

Bristlecone pines wrapped in centuries-old embrace with a patch of rock.

College football in Missoula, under the big "M" on the mountainside, the Clark Fork rushing by.

Fish that don't come from hatcheries, beasts that weren't hatched in theme parks, and full-throated thunderstorms.

The shadow of the Front Range at dusk, stretching to the horizon of the Great Plains.

Above all, the big empty, where humans are insignificant, or at least allowed to think so.

Thrill to the names—El Dorado, Searchlight, Medicine Bow, Mesa Verde, Tombstone, Durango, Hole in the Wall, Lost Trail Pass, Nez Perce National Forest. Active names, implying that something consequential is going on: the Wind River Range, the Magic Valley, the River of No Return, the Painted Desert, Wolf Point, Paradise, Death Valley, the Crazy Mountains.

WE WENT back and forth on the aches that divide Westerners, talking into the evening. Then Terry Tempest Williams said something that has stayed with me. She traces her family lineage back five generations to Brigham Young's day, when Mormons, like prickly pear cacti, were considered freaks of this land, something you could bring home to the geologic society in Boston and poke at under a harsh light. We sounded like her family at a recent reunion in Utah, she said. They fought, scrapped, and dodged. Her grandfather became upset at the bickering, finally brokering a temporary peace. He asked, What do we agree on? Two things: they all loved the land, but the old ways were not working anymore. Perhaps what the West needs, she said, is a grandfather—some grounding in a common story, not a mythic one, nor a plunderer's tidied-up view.

Statues are scarce in the West, for good reason: sometimes, it takes longer for concrete to dry than it does for today's consensus to become tomorrow's historical heresy. It may be easier to lasso the wind than to find a sustaining story for the American West. Still, as storytellers it is our obligation to keep trying.

So I have tried to find a true West at the start of the next hundred years, leaving the boundaries of the old metaphors in search of something closer to the way we live. This West needs very little adornment, but it does need a grandfather. This West is still one of the wildest places on the planet. It is home to buried cultures as intriguing as the imagined West of pulp fiction. It is the foundation of societies sprouting overnight in settings where it was said people could never live, and cities making disastrous errors because they are misreading the land. It is where Clint Eastwood finally arrived at in his best Western, *Unforgiven,* a pig farmer under a hard sky, pouring rotgut liquor down his throat while he laments how awful it is to kill a man. And one day this West may no longer be boastful about its worst qualities, or afraid of its best.

CHAPTER 1

Custom and Culture

Catron County, New Mexico

A nasty little side war is raging in the high mountains where the Gila River forms out of snowmelt and springwater near the Mexico border. Some of the old Anglo boys are threatening Forest Service rangers, burning the United Nations flag, cranking out demands on county stationery. And no sir, they are not militia wackos or the kind of people who call talk-radio stations to complain about the computer chip planted in their buttocks. You can find plenty of them on the staffs of some Western congressmen. These are county officials running this particular skirmish, helped by a United States senator or two, who in turn are backed by some of the largest landowners in the West. At the center of it all are a kid and his wife trying to run cattle on nearly 150,000 acres in the wildest country in all New Mexico—and trying to do it without a cellular telephone, at that. They don't own the land. But garrisoned on their own moral high ground, they swear that nobody is going to force them off.

I am in New Mexico less than a day, trying to track down the kid and the mythology that keeps him going. I feel underaccessorized—without boots, slab o' belt buckle, or other essentials of regional camouflage. I usually travel with a fly rod and running shoes. Call me New West, but three generations of older West in my family brought me to this point of evolution. I'm tempted just to put a pinch of chaw between my cheek and gum and start bitching about the goddamn guvmint. But that would be a reach; for the most part, I like the Forest Service.

In looking for the last real cowboy in America, I first have to make it past all the fake ones. In New Mexico there are thickets of them, swarming around the turquoise galleries in the Plaza at Santa Fe, pushing Petroglyph Vu homes at the edge of thousand-year-old rock art panels in Albuquerque, sweating under heavy hats at the Cadillac lot. They have long had these drive-through liquor huts in the Land of Enchantment, vice booths where you can pick up a pint of Jack Daniels and a *Penthouse* to go without getting out of first gear. Some of the aggressive peddlers of cowboy culture go them one better. They deliver. You want a slice of vaquero life, a Lincoln County War video, or a hoof-'n'-mane happy hour? Pick up the phone. Or wander into Albuquerque's Old Town on any Saturday afternoon and you'll see people shooting at each other and falling over dead, a group homicide staged by the New Mexico Gunfighters Association. "We do this to keep history alive," a heavily armed woman explains.

Finding the kid on horseback is a bit more difficult. I look up my friend Frank Zoretich. He has a flashlight of a mind that he has put to good use wandering around New Mexico for the last decade or so. Frank knows the best place to sit atop the Sandia Mountains and watch the sun bleed out of the sky. He can tell you what Truth or Consequences used to be called before the town sold out its name to a game show. He can explain what it is about those twenty-seven radio telescopes pointed at the heavens on the Plains of San Agustin, and why the light and air of New Mexico make you feel like your best days are still ahead of you.

I told Frank I was looking to find the cowboy, fellow by the name of Kit Laney, holed up in the deep canyons of the southern Rockies, where the mountains start to dogleg off to the west toward the Sonoran Desert. Frank invites me to go look at some maps and sip tequila. He drives a van with better than 200,000 miles on it—original engine—and his front seat is crowded with motor oil, windshield wiper fluid, water bottles, spare food, and antifreeze. The lessons of the Donner Party were not lost on Frank.

As we head out at dusk on a winter night, it seems like a fog has settled in. "No fog," Frank says. "It's a clear night."

"But I can't see anything."

"Windshield. I gotta clean that thing."

Frank is a ruminative road warrior, but instead of chewing while he thinks, he smokes. As a result, his windshield must hold a good eighth of an inch of nicotine from ten years of thinking-on-wheels. A long time ago, Frank left Seattle, where I first got to know him, and hit the road in his van. He was close to forty years old, despondent over a recent divorce, and had a little money saved. One day he steered himself out of the city and just kept going. His plan was to drive across the country, following whim, doing what most Americans ultimately feel they must do, which is to make some elemental connection to the big land. He sent back wonderful letters— funny and sharp and also personal. He didn't glorify the road so much as he talked about what it was like to be surprised by the little quirks of the country. As the months went on, Frank's money dwindled, and he became too familiar with the basement of loneliness. Still, he wanted to keep moving, and his friends wanted to keep receiving his letters. So he came up with the idea of publishing a newsletter, charging a nominal fee, that basically chronicled the life on the road of a forty-year-old guy, with submissions from his friends. His only compass was curiosity. He called his newsletter *Friends of Frank*, or *FOF.* The motto was: "Always Something About Somebody You Know." There were membership fees as well. Hundreds of people signed up. We received *FOF* quarterly, at best, but consumed it immediately. Alas, *FOF* kept Frank in gas-and-beer money but little else. After a few years, he pulled the van into Albuquerque and put *FOF* on a long hiatus.

He got hired at the *Albuquerque Journal.* After a stint doing the usual menial labor of covering car wrecks and incomprehensible public hearings, Frank convinced his editors to let him do what he does best—travel and write. He started a column, which later became a series of books and an organization—the Cheap Thrills Adventure Club—geared around the idea that there was a lot a person could do in New Mexico in a day without spending more than ten bucks or traveling further than 150 miles one-way.

Frank takes me to one of his favorite areas, a part of Albuquerque on old Route 66. On the outside, the strip looks as if it were frozen in the mid-1950s. There are Beaver Cleaver hardware stores, chili-dog and homemade-pie kind of cafes, and rows of little retail shops showing a face to the sidewalk of pre-espresso-age defiance. New Mexico has been a home to various people for at least eight thousand years; it has been nearly 500 years since the Spanish first planted a cross and flag on this land. And, yet, here is a little bit of 1950s America, unmarred, and it stands out like a medieval cathedral in a desert subdivision. This Route 66 strip, in fact, is on its way to historical preservation, protected by the U.S. government. My God, visitors may say in the future, there was a street in America without a warehouse store.

In the chill, we walk the strip and duck into a bar. It's a Tuesday night, and the place is packed. We order tequila, with beer chasers. He smokes, and talks about his adopted home, the place where his van is likely to die. We both come from a part of the West where green is the dominant color and chlorophyll is an uncontrolled substance. In the Wet West, that strip from the Pacific shore to the Cascade Mountain crest, no square inch of soot in a sidewalk crack or roof is safe from an invasion of some fast-growing transplant. After settling down in New Mexico, Frank needed several years to get over "brownshock," as he called it. I walk around as if in a planetarium, head spinning. The rusted tablelands, the baldness of the land, the mesas of potato-skin color. The wind announces itself in advance. My skin, used to the daily facial of Northwest drizzle, feels as if it's been next to a radiator.

Frank has been following Kit Laney in the news, somewhat. Consequential stuff, political swindles, fraud, and epic land deals that will affect every American—these kinds of things have never held much interest for Frank. But ask him about the definition of sand—"chunks of mineral smaller than 1/25 of an inch in diameter but bigger than 1/400 of an inch; anything smaller is dust"—and his motor starts to run.

From what Frank could gather from his colleagues on the *Journal*, Laney was holed up in the heart of the Gila National Forest. We unfold the map and order some mescal, a smooth cactus-kicker. A few guys who look like they wouldn't take to somebody who didn't have much of a belt buckle are sitting nearby, but I feel no discomfort. In addition to being funny and observant, Frank is about six feet four inches tall and extremely scary-looking when he's not laughing.

The Gila National Forest is in the deep southwest part of New Mexico, north of Deming, west of Truth or Consequences, south of Apache Creek. It's huge, more than 3.3 million acres, with peaks rising to eleven thousand feet. And it is the birthing ground for the river of the same name, the only reliable water that flows through much of the Southwest. The Continental Divide, the little black dotted line on any basic state map, splits the Gila forest.

Frank talks about all the cool stuff along the Rio Grande, east and west of the valley. Elephant Butte, which lives up to its name. The Bosque Del Apache, where snow geese and sandhill cranes crowd cornfields in the fall. The Ralph Edwards room in Truth or Consequences. But what about

Catron County? And the little rebel town of Reserve? And a place called Old Horse Springs?

"Can't tell you anything about that stuff."

"What?"

"Can't help you. Except, you should watch for snow."

"Frank? You're supposed to be the living map of New Mexico."

"Only part of New Mexico."

He shows me a little map from his Cheap Thrills book, with the 150-mile radius from Albuquerque.

"I don't know much outside the hundred-and-fifty-mile zone," he says.

The Gila was well outside the radius. It was, to Frank, essentially foreign ground. After all his travels, he had settled on writing about a small piece of a big land. We finish our drinks and head outside. The air feels good, so dry and cold it's like a chimney sweep on the lungs.

"Be curious," he says. "Carry extra antifreeze."

CLOUDS LIE atop the Plains of San Agustin, wet on dry, puffy on flat. There are no trees. No houses. The land feels uninsulated. I am the only person on the road at midday, just outside the border of Catron County. The Plains are a tilted table, pushed up close to a ragged sky. It starts to snow and I turn on my lights. I am a bit disoriented, traveling west and south, but it appears as if I'm heading into a distant galaxy, the stars of snow shooting by. Then something appears out of the oatmeal fog, distant rows of enormous blinking lights—the Very Large Array. They are metal blossoms, as Frank had described them, pointing skyward, each of them ninety-four feet high and eighty-four feet in diameter. It was the largest radio telescope in the world for a time, twenty-seven individual antennas probing the universe. Despite today's weather, the sky is almost always clear on the Plains of San Agustin; the flat, featureless land was chosen as the ideal place from which to listen to the heavens. It looks alien and even a bit spooky. I do not see any evidence that human beings are tending these sentinels.

The Wacko West finds its affirmation in whispered bits of ignorance about such things as the Very Large Array. Consider the evidence: a row of radio telescopes; stealth bombers swooping over the Mojave Desert, coming and going with the quickness of hummingbirds; Fish and Wildlife agents TALKING IN SOME KINDA CODE ON THE SAME RADIO FREQUENCY in Idaho; the hardy perennial about the coverup of a UFO landing in Roswell, New Mexico. It's a Wacko West feast. Dot-to-dot-to-dot.

Throw in a few grainy photographs of ordnance moving on train tracks. And hey, what about those German troops training on an old New Mexico army base? None of this would mean anything in a crowded space. But in open land it's another story. In truth, the Very Large Array is but a technical expression of human curiosity. Its unarmed appendages do nothing but blink and probe. Who's out there? Anybody home in the rest of the universe? Tell us something. It looks outward, trying to discern something among the stars, sixty sextillion miles away.

I chug up to the Continental Divide, leaving the fog behind on the Plains of San Agustin, in the drainage that flows to the Atlantic. I pause at a round-up site, one of the biggest of the West's old hoof highways. From 1885 to 1975, great crowds of mobile lamb chops, T-bone steaks, and future hamburgers passed through here, sometimes 150,000 cattle and twenty thousand sheep at a time. The livestock swarm made ten miles a day, mowing down every twig of life. It was the day of chuck wagons and butt calluses, frijoles, and a whiskey known as coffin varnish.

Downslope, in the Pacific drainage, where all the water is pulled into the San Francisco River, the land changes color. There are hints of green and pockets of bluish juniper trees in the mountain draws, and then a few big ponderosa pines—the fabled yellow-bellies. Some signs of human habitation appear, windmills pumping groundwater for cattle and cowboys, a few dying ranches, siding cracked by the dry air. Reserve, population 900, is the Catron County county seat; more than a mile high, it is a town under a siege of its own making. On many poles, the American flag is flying upside down. The last Catron County timber mill is deserted, its industrial carcass picked dry by thieves. There are two main streets in town, a bar, a handful of hunters' motels with dried blood on the carpets, a couple of restaurants, a county building. The whole thing has a haunt and stench to it.

In contrast to the Very Large Array, Catron County seems afraid of the rest of the world, the rest of the country, even the rest of the state of New Mexico. The county is bigger than half a dozen eastern states, and it holds barely three thousand people inside its boundaries. Big space, few people—sometimes that is an incentive for flights of daring that would be unheard of in a crowded city; more often in the human landscape of the West, it's a recipe for the worst kind of rural gossip. Talk radio, the great lubricant of lunacy theories right and left, recently aired the ramblings of a man who claimed that five thousand National Guardsmen had invaded Catron County. A call to arms went out, and some county leaders went into hiding in "safe" houses. Not long after that, a wildlife biologist, Tim Tibbitts, pulled into Reserve with an appointment to chat with a rancher about how to work with the many endangered species of the county. A red-faced man ripped open his car door and started barking at the biologist. "If you ever come back to Catron County," he said, "we'll blow your fucking head off." Imagine if someone wanted to talk about something other than a subspecies of the black-tailed prairie dog.

How did Smokey become the enemy? Fearing for their lives, Forest Service rangers have been ordered to travel in pairs, and never to be out of radio contact. Four pipe bombs and a large cache of plastic explosives have been found hidden in the forest. The rangers who work here have been seeing a trauma counselor sent by the government to help them cope with the stress of feeling hated. After spending some time here, Melinda Garcia, a psychologist with twenty-five years of experience in such urban battlegrounds as South Central Los Angeles, called Catron County "a war zone in an idyllic setting."

I stop for coffee and huevos rancheros. I pick up a copy of the local newspaper, *The Courier*—"The Most Cussedly Independent Weekly in the West, And Proud of It!!!"—published out of Hatch, which is eighty miles away. An upside-down American flag is pictured on the masthead, next to the words "In Distress." The front page is devoted to stories about conspiracies between the Forest Service and the United Nations, most every sentence ending in an exclamation point. My eggs arrive, and I smother them in Tabasco sauce.

The Courier goes to some lengths in this week's issue to explain how the forces of global tyranny are connected to the same people trying to bring El Lobo, the wolf, back to the Southwest. Wolf opponents in Washington, D.C., include Sam Donaldson, the broadcast pundit and dead-ringer for Mr. Spock of *Star Trek* (Wacko West Alert: Vulcan spotted in New Mexico high country!). Donaldson is an absentee rancher, grazing his cattle on public and private land in New Mexico at a per-animal fee that is a fraction of the cost of lunch on K Street. Beltway cowboys, like the real kind here, are lycophobes.

In a *Courier* column written by Jim Catron, a distant relative of the man for whom the county is named, Anglo landowners are presented as the rightful heirs to the culture of the rural West. While the Catrons and other Anglos did not arrive in New Mexico until the 1880s, they have, he says, left an imprint of culture and land use that defines the true West. That culture should be written into law. He envisages fifty American republics, each tailored to the local customs. So New York State, he writes, would be a society for gun-control proponents and homosexuals. New Mexico would be cowboy-centric.

After coffee, I ask the cafe owner where I might find Kit Laney. He looks at me suspiciously.

"You with the F.B.I.?"

"No, sir."

"Fish and Wildlife?"

"Nope . . . But how about that Very Large Array?" I ask.

"What about it?"

"Is there . . . a Medium Array somewhere in these parts?"

"You're with the Forest Service?"

"Nope."

"BLM?"

"I'm a writer . . ."

Sometimes in my story wanderings when I introduce myself people say something unprintable, even with my paper's lust for detail. Or, trying to be polite, they say, "You're a long way from home," to which I reply that, yes, eastern Washington State, where I grew up, is some distance from the high desert.

"Can't tell you about Laney. But whatever you say, you tell his story right. That kid's a hero."

WHAT THEY have tried to do in Catron County is freeze time. In the early part of this century, Catron was something of a boom county; plentiful grass, big forests, and rich veins of silver and gold drew money and immigrants. In the highest reaches of the land, Douglas fir, signature tree of the wet Northwest, prospered in microclimates of moisture. Large cattle companies funded by investors from London and New York, and logging outfits bankrolled by the railroads, soon controlled most of the public land in Catron. And by the 1940s they had such free rein of the place that the government was at their beck and call. The Forest Service, for example, spent the better part of the 1950s knocking down all the juniper trees on seventy thousand acres of national forest land. Trees drink water. The idea was that leveling the junipers would create more grazing land for cattle. At the peak, there were twenty-five sawmills chewing up pine and fir from the high meadows of the Gila National Forest, and a cattleman could run a herd of thirty thousand head over the land without paying a dime. It was the golden age of Catron County, a Western welfare state.

Today, not a single mine is left, the hoofed hybrids are but a shadow of what they used to be, the last of the sawmills closed in the early 1990s, and the population has shrunk by half in twenty years. Catron is a few ticks away from becoming a ghost county the size of Connecticut. The mill was heavily leveraged with junk bonds at a time when wood prices fell and supply dried up. What's more, the land was exhausted. The Gila, for the most part, was no longer a living forest. Trees died of diseases. Most of the native fish disappeared from the small streams. With the trees gone, there was nothing to hold the snow into spring; instead, runoff was quick and muddy, blowing out the river drainages. In the late 1980s, the Forest Service tried to bring some of the fish and wildlife back, limiting logging to protect birds and asking cattlemen to keep their livestock out of the streams. This did not go over well, to say the least. And it gave the people of Catron County a target for their anger against all the change in their midst. They were dying because of the Forest Service.

The county declared itself—formally and loudly—to be "under siege by outside forces that deny its democratic birthright." Elk were labeled a nuisance. Same with spreading stands of young pinyon-juniper trees. They demanded that the Forest Service again take up the practice of "chaining," as the process of scraping away trees is known. The county would fight any attempts to allow mountain lions, grizzly bears, or wolves to get back into the national forest.

The county leaders called on Karen Budd, a Wyoming lawyer who served her apprenticeship in James Watt's nature-phobic Interior Department, to help draft a new set of laws. In Catron County, Budd saw a way to revitalize the old Sagebrush Rebellion. The enemy was the same as before—the federal government, which owns most of the land in the West, including two-thirds of Catron County. Throughout the West, much of the public domain is just left over, the orphan acreage that wasn't worth taking. Now, time has given it value. On this land, the big operators are seldom seen; they lobby, deal, legislate, or steal, usually far from the source of the struggle. And then, months later, a forest is cut, or a rancher from an eastern corporation expands his lease another million acres, or a desert resort finds a sudden source of subsidized water. But in the forefront, where everybody can see the battle, image controls the debate. Kit Laney, the last cowboy, would become the symbol.

This time, the revolt would be centered in the counties, not the states. Budd seized on an obscure passage in federal land laws which requires that the "custom and culture" of a given area be taken into consideration whenever the government acts. That language was meant to safeguard Indian sacred grounds or archaeological sites that might otherwise be wiped out by, say, construction of a new road. Catron County residents took it as applying to *their* culture—that of Anglo ranchers and loggers. Trying to keep the forces of history at bay, they declared themselves victims, in need of federal protection—in their case, protection from the government itself. They were the endangered species.

Then they passed a resolution that encouraged every head of a household to own and carry a gun at all times and to keep plenty of ammunition stored. Locked and loaded, they were ready for war. All of this was to keep the Gila National Forest open for cheap grazing and unrestricted logging. And it came at a time when meat prices were tumbling, and nobody wanted to pay market prices for what scraggly timber was left in the Gila's played-out forests. But, as Karen Budd had hoped, Catron's defiance had a political domino effect; soon, more than thirty counties across the West had passed their own local-supremacy acts, and the press was in a sweat over county rebels in cowboy hats.

In the Catron County building I stop and look into the glass case on the ground floor. Inside are some stunning pieces of pottery, dust-covered from neglect. A series of yellowed typewritten labels explain that "paleo-Indians" lived in this part of the West about eight thousand years ago. Then, around 500 B.C. came the Mogollon culture (pronounced "Muggy-own"), the first of the pottery-makers of New Mexico. They lived all over the county—in pit houses and, later, in aboveground dwellings. The bounty of the forest provided more than enough food to give the Mogollon time to make pottery that went well beyond the utilitarian.

Walking around the edge of town, I notice cattle slopping in and out of coffee-colored creeks, grazing in front yards, or just lying in the middle of dirt roads. It is their place, obviously, under the custom-and-culture laws—and it shows. At dusk, I go for a hike, looking for a place to listen to Catron County at low volume.

I leave Reserve after a day. Nobody will tell me much about Kit Laney. They are protective, and he is revered. Just outside of town is the little Forest Service office. The rangers are scared to go outside. Bomb threats are phoned in on a regular basis. The shrink is due out again in a few days to try and smooth Smokey's nerves. The town of Reserve is named for the agency that came to take care of one of America's first forest reserves, the agency that now cowers in the shadows of its namesake. I learn that Laney is running cattle on one of the biggest public salad bars in this part of the state.

Almost all of his spread, the Diamond Bar Ranch, lies within the Gila National Forest. But Laney, taking the new laws of the county at their word, now calls it his own, according to his latest correspondence with the Forest Service. He will do what he wants to on the land, not paying grazing fees or following the rules of stewardship as outlined by wildlife managers. The Forest Service says he is trespassing, and he has an answer: Come and get me. "There will be a hundred people with guns waiting for them," Laney says.

FOR MOST of two days I travel over fresh snow on coiled roads in the moody Mogollon Mountains. It is a very lonely area in winter, a passing car every hour or so. The mountains, more than thirty different peaks reaching ten thousand feet, slough off clouds from the west, wringing a bit of snow from them as a toll for their passage. This is one of the few places in America where Rush Limbaugh does not penetrate the airwaves. I have been at the bottom of Death Valley, 282 feet below sea level, free of every artificial sound on the planet except one—Limbaugh's broadcast. But here, in the tangled fortress on the southwestern side of the Gila National Forest, it's a Limbaugh-free zone. The only radio stations I can get are Spanish-language. Across the dial, I pick up four Spanish stations at a point where the names of rivers and mountains are predominantly Latino, reflecting the families that have lived here for more than three centuries. The laws of old Spanish communities would make the Forest Service seem like libertarians. They had rules for everything—when and where cattle could graze, how much water could be used by which families, regulations on hunting a pig.

After the Treaty of Guadalupe Hidalgo was signed, the Latino ranchers and livestock herders of newly American New Mexico were assured that their land grants would be preserved. But it was a hazardous legal hike, going through unfamiliar and distant American courts to assure ownership of something handed down from a Spanish monarch or a Mexican general. For a lawyer with vision it was like being the sole attorney in late-twentieth-century Hollywood at a time when breast implants started to fail. Thomas B. Catron had that vision. He arrived in New Mexico in 1866 and quickly discovered that Spanish land grant litigation was far more profitable than dodging Apaches while running scrawny cattle on dry land. He settled cases for the Latinos, who were land-rich and money-poor, but for a steep price—a piece of their pie. Eventually, 80 percent of the old Spanish land grants ended up in the hands of Anglo lawyers and settlers. And the biggest landowner of all was Tom Catron—lawyer. The man for whom Catron County is named had a controlling interest in thirty-four land grants, covering more than three million acres. His biographer said he was the largest landowner in American history, owning an area bigger than the state of Delaware.

AT six thousand feet, on a steep side of the southern rim of the Gila forest, I bump into Silver City, a stone-fronted mining and ranching town with a peculiar-looking scar down its midsection—the Big Ditch, as they call it. More than a hundred years ago, Main Street, the polished product of a gold and silver boom that brought a commercial frenzy to this old Apache hot springs refuge, vanished. One day in late summer floodwaters stormed down from the mountains and buried the street under twelve feet of water. When the mud tantrum passed, Main Street was thirty-five feet below the ground floors of the commercial strip. A later flood scraped the ditch down to bone, fifty-five feet below the old street level. Town leaders blamed the cattle barons upstream, who had let their herds graze the mountain meadows down to bare nubs. But rather than fold, as so many dying Western resource towns had done, Silver City made a show of its open wound. Tourists could come to look at the freak canyon that sliced the town in half.

They still make a few dollars off Billy—"Don't Call Me Henry"—the Kid in Silver City. His mother, like many other tuberculosis sufferers of the nineteenth century, came to the desert Southwest seeking the breath of life. A single mother, Irish and new to the country, she died not long after she arrived, leaving Billy orphaned. The young sociopath, whose real name was Henry McCarty, spent his formative years here, as "The Ballad of Billy the Kid" makes clear:

> Now Billy the Kid was a very young lad,
> In old Silver City he went to the bad.
> Way out West with a knife in his hand,
> At the age of twelve he killed his first man.

Actually, the Kid, born in a New York City slum, likely did nothing worse than petty thievery in Silver City, but minor crimes while wearing a cowboy hat will not land you in a custom-and-culture preamble. The boy stole a tub of butter from a rancher, and then later robbed a Chinese laundry. Inside the adobe jail, he shinnied up a chimney and escaped. Everyone in Silver City had a big laugh over that, which may have contributed to Billy's mountainous insecurities. He had comically small, rounded shoulders, protruding front teeth, and a soft belly; he killed his first victim, a blacksmith, because the man made fun of his looks. Billy is said to have gunned down twenty-one people before he reached the age of twenty-one—Indians and Mexicans were not included in his count—but the more likely number was four. Most of his significant violence was confined to Lincoln County, east of the Rio Grande, where he was a hired gun in the war over who was going to profit most off supplying beef to army posts and Indian reservations. The Kid killed for cows. He joined the side of a British cattle broker, John Tunstall, and went to war against the House of Murphy, a rival consortium controlled by the local sheriff. Eventually, Pat Garrett tracked and killed the Kid, and then made a killing himself off his book about the young murderer, *The Authentic Life of Billy the Kid,* written in large part by a newspaperman, Ash Upson. It was the first real storytelling gold to be mined from the killer, but far from the last; more than forty movies have been made about his life. Billy's last words, a question in the dark that was answered by Garrett's pistol, were "Quien es?"

Every year thousands of people flock to the Lincoln County courthouse to finger bullet holes from Billy's days of terror. But the West may be maturing somewhat on the culture-of-psychotic-gunmen front. Before he moved to Florida and was ultimately executed, Ted Bundy, the late-twentieth-century serial killer from the West, committed far more murders than did Billy the Kid. But there is not a single curio shop, museum, or Chamber of Commerce tour devoted to Bundy's blood trail.

For Silver City, value-added Billy the Kid commerce consists of a few trinkets and a tour map. You can walk to a patch of bare ground on one side of the Big Ditch where Billy spent a few years in a shack (which has long since disappeared), or hike up to his mother's grave on a hillside east of town, or go see the hearse in which Pat Garrett was carried to his grave. Garrett is buried elsewhere.

"What you really should see," says the woman in the Forest Service office in Silver City, "are the Gila cliff dwellings—that's what everyone asks about." I had stopped off at the Forest Service office to get a Kit Laney update. In the comparative cosmopolitan comfort of Silver City, the rangers are less frightened of getting blown up or shot at, though they have not let their guard down. A bomb recently shattered a Forest Service office in Nevada. Laney, I'm told, has got his cattle up in Black Canyon, at the very time when early spring runoff is going to start muddying the upper valley.

The Diamond Bar Ranch, Laney's empire, is nearly 150,000 acres in the Gila National Forest—an area about as big as a midsized national park. He used to pay $22,000 a year to run cattle on public land. But now Laney is much more than just another guy getting a red-meat subsidy from American taxpayers. He's an outlaw.

Because Laney has stopped paying his grazing fees, the Forest Service has put him on notice that they consider him a trespasser. The question, asked from the Justice Department in Washington to bar stools in Silver City, is whether the feds will forcibly evict him.

"They better bring a gun," Laney tells a reporter. "I'm not going to go. They will have to plant me here."

I ask a ranger about this, and he says he is in no mood to take a bullet for Smokey. For that matter, he doesn't even know how to fire a gun. "Are you crazy?" he says. "I'm not a SWAT team cop. I studied forestry in school."

Forest rangers used to be pistol-packing protectors of the public domain. In 1919, when seventeen-year-old Norman Maclean spent a summer in uniform in the Bitterroots of Montana, every ranger wore a .45—including young Maclean. "They still picked rangers for the Forest Service by picking the toughest guy in town," Maclean wrote. One of his colleagues was said to have killed a sheepherder. "We were a little disappointed that he had been acquitted of the charges, but nobody held it against him, for we all knew that being acquitted of killing a sheepherder in Montana isn't the same as being innocent."

THE ROAD to the Diamond Bar goes north into the heart of the Gila. I take a detour to the west, following the slow, climbing way up a canyon along a fork of the river to a dead end near the base of the old Mogollon village. The country is wild and open, with thick stands of pine and cottonwood growing in the drainage. A wind from the north whistles through, and there's a dusting of snow from a few days ago left in the shadowed pockets. I walk toward the ruin, high above the canyon, where dwellings are sculpted into the cliffs. The light is catching it just right, so it looks sandblasted white. These Mogollon people disappeared around the year 1290, but you can almost see their fingerprints and smell their campfires. The original timbers between stacked rocks are polished, somewhat cracked, but solid. The walls are in place, built with stone quarried from the neighboring cliffs. There are about forty rooms. I hike up one of the ladders, find a comfortable sitting room in a Flintstone condo, and look back down to the canyon.

These cliff dwellings were perhaps the last homes of the Mogollon before they scattered. They had lived in the Gila region since 200 B.C., growing corn and hunting jackrabbits, pronghorn, gophers, deer, and mountain sheep. At first, their pottery was simple, the red-earth clay bowls and pitchers of day-to-day living. As time went on, they built bigger villages, aboveground pueblos, and figured out a way to store walnuts, cacti, squash, kidney beans, piñon nuts, and other foods for years. And then came an electric leap in creativity. About the year A.D. 900, the start of the Mimbres Classic period, the Mogollon began painting black-on-white geometrical designs on their pottery, an influence perhaps of the Anasazi, with whom they traded. One of their most striking works is a bowl that seems to represent Halley's Comet, which made an appearance in 1066. They sketched birds with human faces, scrolls and rectangles zigging and zagging into mathematical infinity, quails, turkeys, lizards, ducks, and rabbits painted in black from brushes made of yucca leaves. Fish and frogs—now mostly gone from the Gila—show up everywhere, riding on the backs of men, kissing women. There were mythic monsters and lusty humans. It all had a vitality to it, a sense of good times and exuberant spirituality—"an expression of the sheer ecstasy of living," as the archaeologist Paul S. Martin has written.

And it didn't stop there. Some of the best stuff was buried with the dead. Typically, a body was laid to rest with the knees up near the chest—as if preparing to spring out somewhere at a later date. A bowl in full Mimbres flourish was placed over the head of the deceased, with a "kill hole" no bigger than a quarter punched in the center to allow the spirit to escape to the other side. For more than a thousand years, the Mogollon prospered in these parched mountain valleys, growing crops in an area that received just nine to twenty inches of rain a year, with only about a hundred days between the last frost of spring and first subfreezing day of late summer. The Mogollon are never mentioned in Catron County's custom-and-culture laws. But Teddy Roosevelt, the asthmatic who got his second wind in the dry air of the West, set aside 533 acres here in the heart of the thousand-year-old ghost town, as the Gila Cliff Dwellings National Monument in 1907.

I MAKE it to the Diamond Bar Ranch without a shot being fired at me, but now I'm scared. A fly rod is no match for a shotgun. The road into

Kit Laney's territorial perch narrows and enters a country of mud, low clouds, and foreboding. The grass has not come up yet, but some meadows look matted over. The streams, the life-giving arteries of the Gila River, have eroded banks, tromped by cattle hoofprints. It's very cold. Willows and cottonwoods, which hold the streambanks together, are chewed to bits; their bare roots trail away, clinging to bits of soil around boulders. I don't see any cattle, though; they have been moved, possibly to avoid seizure by the Forest Service.

At last, I find Laney. Cowboys aren't my weakness, but Kit Laney and his wife, Sherri, are about as nice as any young Mormon couple you might find politely proselytizing the tourists in Temple Square—except that they are heavily armed. Laney tells me he's just trying to do what folks in his family have always done—scratch a living from the wild country of the Gila River drainage. He spends most of his time on a horse; the Laneys own two dozen of them. They live in a little place without electricity. He hauls water and cuts wood for the stove. They raise pigs, milk cows, and make their own butter and bacon. They have a big garden in the summer. Sherri makes horse saddles. Preferring to live like Jeremiah Johnson instead of Tim Allen, they shun the new Wal-Mart down in Silver City and weave their own clothes. They live off game, beef, and canned vegetables. Their grocery bill for an entire year, Laney says after warming up to me, is just over a thousand dollars.

"I'm fourth-generation Catron County, so's Sherri," he says. "We were both born here."

Laney's great-grandfather came to the county in 1883, a Mormon pioneer from Utah, pushing the southern frontier of the planned state of Deseret. Sherri is from a ranching family to the north. They bought the ranch—a small bit of private land and the permit allowing them to graze cattle on a huge swath of public land—in 1986, when beef prices were relatively good. At the time, the Laneys were a newlywed pair of twenty-three-year-olds, green but ready for saddle sores and palm blisters. Each of them had fantasized about owning a big ranch. Laney expected to run nearly twelve hundred head of cattle a year over the Gila National Forest. When he acquired the ranch, he says, the Forest Service assured him that grazing such a large herd would be okay, as long as he kept his beasts out of the streams that form the Gila. Laney made plans to build fifteen big water-holding tanks in the national forest, a place for his cattle to drink. And then he took out a bank loan, a half-million-dollar note on the Black Diamond allotment.

As it turns out, the world has plenty of cheap meat. Cattle feedlots are stuffed with steroid-pumped, ready-to-slaughter-and-wrap beef that can find its way into a hamburger bun much quicker and cheaper than anything a lone cowboy in southern New Mexico can do. The nineteenth-century wish of army general Phil Sheridan has come true. "Let them kill, skin and sell until the buffalo are exterminated," he said. "Then your prairies can be covered with speckled cattle and the festive cowboy." Laney's cows may be speckled, but he has nothing to be festive about. People are eating less meat, afraid of *E. coli* or high fat or, more recently, mad-cow disease. In the mid-1990s, beef prices tumbled. The price for a big steer went from nearly a dollar a pound to eighty cents, then down to sixty cents. Laney is not running a fantasy ranch. He needs cash to pay off the bank loan.

"Nobody's getting rich off this," says Laney. "But I'll tell you this: all the gold in Fort Knox would not get me to change my life."

He paused for a good long cowboy minute. "Yes, sir," he said. "I am the richest man in the world."

He works twelve hours a day, with some of the world's stupidest animals, placed in an environment that is foreign to their native ground. He might as well be raising chickens in Rockefeller Center. The problem, for Laney, is that the land he wants for cattle feed is owned by every American. Some of those shareholders don't like the mashed-out streams, the trails of cow turds, the bellowing Herefords in a place where they expect to hear bugling elk. They have been complaining to the Forest Service, which has done study after study about how cattle are ripping up the wilderness of the Gila. Eventually the Service asked Laney to reduce his cattle herd. He was furious. He sought help from the major cattle organizations, and Senator Pete Domenici, New Mexico's senior legislator. Then Catron County passed its custom-and-culture laws, giving Laney a legal justification for his defiance. But it couldn't bring beef prices up.

The way Laney figures it, he owns the right to use the water that runs through the section of the Gila where the cattle graze. If the government wants water to keep the public forest alive, they will have to pay him for it. "I'm saying to the Forest Service, 'You guys don't own this water.' And they may not even own the land. They never have been able to produce a title document."

And his cattle, he says, are part of the custom and culture of the region; thus, any attempt to reduce the numbers would violate the law. The Forest Service, after hearing from Senator Domenici, retreated. But then, not long before I hooked up with Laney, they reversed themselves. Too many other species of the forest were dying because of sloppy grazing practices. They told Laney to reduce his cattle herd by more than half in order to rest the land. They also decided he couldn't build the water-holding tanks, saying the big impoundments didn't belong in the wilderness of a national forest.

"That will bankrupt me," says Laney. "You can bet your life on it."

So he is free from bureaucratic entanglement, and he's also an outlaw. "Yes, sir, I guess some people might look at it that way," he says. "We have been told that we are in trespass. We have not paid grazing fees. So . . . will I have to shoot the next son of a bitch who tells me to move my cattle?"

I give him my own cowboy minute of silence.

"I can't tell you what's going to happen. But if they succeed in kicking us out of here, you will lose the custom and culture of three counties. Just like that, it'll disappear."

I HAVE no use for my fly rod in these arthritic woods in the Border Country. The Gila trout, a big fighter, weighing up to two pounds, the subject of many a fish tale among old-timers, is nearly extinct. You would think that one of the largest perennial streams in the American Southwest, brought to life by a wilderness holding deep snows in its higher reaches, would be full of life. But the Gila River is all but dead. And so is the forest. Much of it looks devastated. There used to be wolves, grizzly bears, Merriam's elk, beavers, black-footed ferrets, and river otters here. Most of them exist, now, only on the cracked pottery of the long-vanished Mogollon.

But there are plenty of cows. And a young couple, earnest and honest, backed by a local ordinance that proclaims them the end line of Western custom and culture, and supported by a United States senator with a strong grip on the entire federal budget, stand ready to die for those cattle that nobody wants. The great irony of this is that these cows, this sick forest, are all part of a land that was supposed to be a model for how the West could make peace with itself. The wilderness culture of the West started here. Most of Kit Laney's cows run through a part of the national forest called the Aldo Leopold Wilderness—America's first formal wilderness, a huge swath of land that was set aside for all time, designated as a place "where man himself is but a visitor."

Leopold came to Catron County in 1909, a pioneer Forest Ranger touched by the big, sweet-smelling ponderosa pines at eight thousand feet, the eagles snatching fish from the Gila River, the hardscrabble hunters who came to these mountains for meat and could spend more than two weeks looking to get off one shot at an elk that might feed the family. "Think like a mountain," Leopold used to tell his fellow rangers. He developed many of his ideas while living in Catron County, roaming on horseback in Smokey's uniform over the same country where Laney runs his cattle. Once, in a famous epiphany, he killed a wolf and watched as "the fierce green fire" drained from the animal's eyes. He was a Forest Service employee for fifteen years. During that time, the early age of the touring automobile, he saw many roads built into places that used to be the exclusive haunt of horse or human hoof. He saw all but three of the thirty mountain watersheds on public land in the Southwest nearly destroyed by overgrazing. "We abuse land because we regard it as a commodity belonging to us," Leopold wrote later. "When we see land as a community to which we belong, we may begin to use it with love and respect."

In the early 1920s, about ten years before he wrote *The Sand County Almanac*, a book that would make Leopold a household name around the world (his book has just been given its first printing in China), he came up with the idea of keeping some part of the Gila in its wild state, protected by law. He envisioned a place "big enough to absorb a two weeks' pack trip, and devoid of roads, artificial trails, cottages, and other works of man."

Congress approved. It was the first time that any country in the world set aside an area, not as a playground like Yellowstone, or a freak show of nature like Devil's Tower, but simply for the sake of its wildness. It is one of many reasons why Leopold belongs on the Mount Rushmore of American conservation, along with Teddy Roosevelt, John Muir, and Rachel Carson.

Leopold died in 1948. A few months before I saw Laney, one of Leopold's sons, Luna Leopold, came back to the wilderness named for his father. He was appalled by what he saw: the cow-mashed streams, the overgrazed meadows, the dying trees, a technicolor land fading to black and white.

"My father would be shocked if he were here today," said Leopold.

I ask Laney about Aldo Leopold and whether a bunch of cows descended from British stock should be able to run wild through what is supposed to be a slice of original America.

"No. Cows don't belong here."

I'm not sure I heard him right.

"That's what I said. I'll be honest with you: wilderness and cattle can never coexist. Wilderness areas are supposed to be, as the law says, untrammeled by man. There is no doubt that cattle have had a huge impact. Nine times of ten, backpackers run into our cattle. And that's not what a wilderness is supposed to be."

Still, Laney won't budge. He has cornered himself and can imagine no other life. The Mogollon lived for better than a thousand years in the slightly watered valleys here, but Kit and Sherri Laney cannot make a living on their nearly 150,000 acres.

"Cowboys are like bears and mountain lions," the Border Country poet Drum Hadley, a rancher himself, has said. "They need a certain range, a certain critical mass of land, on which to exist."

THERE IS another huge spread in south-central New Mexico, bigger than the Diamond Bar. The Armendaris Ranch is owned by Ted Turner, the man who founded CNN, and has become a land-rich padrone, with more than a million acres in New Mexico. He has replaced cattle with bison, brought in wolves, bighorn sheep, prairie dogs, and a few other animals that have long been missing. Turner might bring in rattlesnakes, he says, if he finds that they are endangered. To the people who make the rules in Catron County, Turner is the wacko. He sees himself as a modern-day Noah, after the landing, trying to restore the world. Turner doesn't get a dime in government subsidies. But his bison, when he sends them to market, are bringing in more than three times what cattle get, and they tend to stay out of the streams as well. He has more than two thousand of the big shaggy-headed ungulates on his ranch, defying the injunction of General Sheridan. In the few years since he decided to play Old Testament rancher, bison prices have tripled. The meat is sweeter than beef, with low cholesterol. Turner in a way may be to twenty-first-century New Mexico what James Catron was to the nineteenth century. He owns more than a thousand square miles of New Mexico—1.5 percent of the state. So how does a billionaire gentleman bison rancher cable television magnate fit into the custom and culture of the West?

THE CENSUS of 1870 reported that most of the women who worked in the West were classified as "domestic servants" and "hotel employees"—both euphemisms for prostitutes. The Civil War took the lives of 850,000 men, leaving an army of widows, many of them impoverished. For those who made their way West, and could not find a husband-farmer, there were jobs in brothels or saloons, or as "night workers" in hotels. It is likely, some historians argue, that for a decade or more the prostitute was the archetypal Western woman. But it is one thing to kill and become a legend, another to whore. Wyatt Earp, after shooting up a rival gang in Tombstone, went to Hollywood and lived off his creation. The woman he introduced around Tombstone as his wife, Mattie Blaylock, became a prostitute and later died of a drug overdose. But suppose she and others in the sex trade had taken the cowboy path to mythic elevation. Would prostitutes then have a claim on the custom-and-culture statutes? Would people be celebrating Wild Whore Days in Silver City?

The Indian chief Geronimo lived in Catron County for a while, in hiding, taking his restorative soaks in Gila Hot Springs. His "war" amounted to three dozen men trying to dodge five thousand soldiers. The last years of his life read like a cautionary tale against Indian assimilation policies of the time. He joined the Dutch Reformed Church, then got drunk one night, fell off a wagon, and died. Confederate deserters also found a refuge here. And so did Dave Foreman, the founder of Earth First!

This is a land of Latinos and Leopold, psychotic gunmen and radical vegetarians, beltway cowboys and billionaire environmentalists. Ranching is just one of the things people did to make a living.

Even so, running cattle on dry, broken public land in the arid West may still become a sacred right, protected from change itself. Some members of Congress have vowed to pass a bill that would essentially do the same thing to 300 million acres of public land as Catron County has tried to do in its backyard. Cattle-grazing would be preserved, by law, as the dominant use of land owned by every American. Outside of a few thousand people who hold leases to this land, nobody would have any real say over how the land would be utilized or managed. They could call their bill the Cowboy Preservation Act. But then prostitutes in Nevada, heirs to an old Western way, might ask for similar protection. Or 7-11 holdup artists harking back to Billy the Kid's ties to the land, backed by the folks who stage those Saturday morning gunfights in old-town Albuquerque, will seek a sanctuary for themselves. Or descendants of Spanish land-grant holders, legally robbed by the founding father of Catron County, could ask for congressional protection. Each has a claim on the West.

More than a century ago, when only a handful of bison were left on the open range, the Lakota Sioux broke into a Ghost Dance in winter, hoping that the power of their ritual would vanquish the soldiers, bring back the animals, raise Indian warriors from their graves. It ended in the last, awful spasm of violence in the conquest of the West, the rout at Wounded Knee. As cattle barons replaced people who lived off the natural bounty, so now the bison rancher with one foot in the new century is replacing the cowboy, and the once nearly extinct wild animals are being allowed to come home. Every cycle produces new victors and new victims. The constant is the government—always the target. They wrote and broke treaties with virtually every native group in the West. They dammed the great rivers, paid bounty hunters to kill much of the wildlife, and auctioned off the forests. Now, as they try to make amends, they wonder why nobody trusts them. In years to come, Leopold's legacy will be appreciated, and Smokey will have little to fear. But in the meantime, the last skirmishes of the old wars go on, in the hidden folds of the land. Laney's defiance is a kind of ghost dance. If only, he seems to think, he just ignores it all—the Forest Service, Ted Turner and his goddamn buffalo, the crash of beef prices—then the West of the 1880s can return. Even though nobody needs his beef, enough people seem to need the idea of Kit Laney, the Last Cowboy in America. So he stays put, boot heels in the ground, hiding in the woods of custom and culture.

CHAPTER 2

Plymouth Rock West

Acoma, New Mexico

Y ou stand at the lip of a cinnamon-colored ledge, four and a half centuries after the same ground rattled with Francisco Vásques de Coronado's column, and see nothing that could lure an army up the spine of the continent. From five miles out, you can see homes, terraced and weathered, facing south. It bears some resemblance to the pictures in yellowed books, pictures that go back a hundred years or more, labeling this view, these homes, as the ruins of Acoma. Some maps, sadly misled, contain the same caption. You rub your eyes at the spot where Spanish hearts sank and see a place pulsing with life. The ruins are alive. Nothing extraordinary appears to be going on, just the routine of a day. You are close enough to see that the pueblo is made of beige New Mexican mud, not gold, and so you can hear with minimal effort the sigh of the conquistadors, the empty wind blowing their Latin banners, which proclaimed Plus Ultra—More Beyond.

The way to counter the Western malaise of drift and rootlessness, says the poet Gary Snyder, is to find your place, dig in, and defend it. And so here is Acoma, possibly the oldest continuously inhabited city in the United

States, living by the poet's dictum. The Sky City is nearly seven thousand feet above sea level, burnished today by the low-angled sunlight of late winter. It is built on the crown of a sandstone butte that soars from a table four hundred feet below. In the usual tellings of the national story, Acoma is an asterisk. It deserves better, if for no other reason than because people have lived atop the same wind-scoured rock for perhaps a thousand years or more, and from that perch fought the first battle over religious freedom in what is now the United States.

The story of America usually starts in the East, with Pilgrims in New England and tobacco farmers in Virginia, finally making its way toward the sunset for barely a generation's worth of gunfighting and gold-digging, using a clock's tick of history, roughly 1849 to 1890, to define the West. The well-worn narrative, not unlike many modern Western politicians, is heavily influenced by the movement and slaughter of domestic cattle and grub-staking for off-colored rocks—a pitiful excuse for a history. The Spanish drove a herd of cattle across the Rio Grande 350 years before the streets of Laredo were knee-deep in cow shit. But nobody comes West today in search of ancient steak bones. They come to see why a place like Acoma is still standing.

Acoma is where one nation's motto of More Beyond met another's End of the Line. Plymouth Rock Pilgrims were yet to be born, nor had the first draft of the Jamestown narrative been sketched when a dust cloud carrying bearded men on horses arrived at the foot of Acoma in 1540. Loaded for gold and costumed for war, the Spanish were chasing an eight-hundred-year-old rumor: the gilded cities of Nuevo Mexico. Three hundred soldiers, trailed by Franciscan friars, long-conquered Aztecs, and brass cannons on wheels, had traveled north by foot and hoof more than a thousand miles, living largely on a diet of anticipation. They would gaze into the Grand Canyon, drink snowmelt from two-mile-high peaks rising from the whiskered face of the Sonoran Desert, chase bison on the Great Plains, and plod through city after city of people who knew how to live a reasonable life in a land without reliable rain. The vistas stretched to earthly infinity under a sky that made people feel insignificant. The Spanish understood north from south and east from west, but what they found most troubling were the two other dimensions of the Acoman compass—up and down, the directions in eternity.

The first residents of Acoma, descendants of the Anasazi, had also wandered, abandoning their hundred-unit apartments on the Colorado

Plateau. They buttoned up the carefully masoned homes, walked away from the maze of funnels and diversions used to channel water onto farm fields, and headed south. Over the years, they strayed down one withered wash or another, shouting into the sandstone walls, waiting for the echo that would tell them they had arrived at their long-prophesied new home. West of the Rio Grande, within view of the white-haired summit of an eleven-thousand-foot-high mountain, the shouts were returned. The echo epic was over. Here, atop the rock, on the flat, thin-soiled, unwatered high point, they founded Acoma, a Keresan word meaning the Place That Always Was. More Beyond? No, Señor Coronado. This is it.

YOU FEEL like a stranger here, not unwelcome, but uncertain. From the road heading west out of Albuquerque, you see nothing to entice you on a detour to the Sky City. There is a casino near the exit. The real payoff is ahead, down a winding road through modest homes, past a few vacant-eyed mules rubbing against barbed-wire fences, to the ledge that looks out to the initial views of Acoma. No pictures are allowed, even from afar, without permission. The Acomans want to control what they can of their image, their story. You think what a corporate cowboy publicist could do with this material, angling for subsidies in the name of tradition.

Down in the valley, closer to the pedestal of Acoma, is a flat plain sliced by an ancient road. At Christmastime it is lined with candles, a luminaria, all lights leading to the top. Now, at road's end, you either move up by foot or out by car. As in Coronado's day, an escort to the pueblo in the sky is required. You ascend.

In 1540, Coronado's men followed the same route, crawling up the rock, guided by handholds in the stone worn by the fingers of many generations. Pushed by the fading promise of Plus Ultra, the conquistadors scaled the flank with swords clanking at their sides. "The ascent was so difficult that we repented climbing to the top," Captain Hernando de Alvarado wrote. They would come to repent many things in the Land of Disenchantment.

THE PEOPLE who live at Acoma say their ancestors first came to the rock about A.D. 800, though most archaeologists date the point of habitation at about 1150. The more compelling fact is that they never left.

"From the beginning of time we have been told there was such a place," says Mary Tenorio, an Acoma native, who lives down below on the flat land. "So this is as far as we can ever go."

You mention the bones found on a bank in the Columbia River not long ago, the remains of a man about five feet nine inches tall, a man who by the reading of radiocarbon datings lived nine thousand years ago. You don't want to argue with Mary Tenorio, an artist, standing with you in the blood-slowing wind of a winter day, at the base of the Place That Always Was. The facial bones of the Columbia River man do not match the features of any other native people in the Americas. He appears to be of northern European stock, the anthropologists say. A white guy. You are not disputing the prophecy of Acoma, but simply wondering why some people stayed around and some did not, whether some people followed prophetic destinies and some did not. Maybe the Anglos from the Columbia Plateau simply died out before they could find a Place That Always Was. Maybe that will be the problem Phoenix will face.

Five hundred years ago, the entire Rio Grande pueblo community was more densely populated, in places, than it is today. The inhabitants lived in tight little communities, entirely surrounded, they believed then as now, by envy. There were about 60,000 people in the broad valley at the time of Coronado's arrival.

Along the ledge today, you can hear long-ago voices in Spanish and Keresan, dimming the fires of Coronado's imagination. You can imagine the look the conquistador gave his scout, as he checked his map, his eyesight. What the hell is this?

"The greatest stronghold ever seen in the world," one of Coronado's men wrote.

The curse of Coronado was what had come before him, the big shadow of expectations. He was thirty years old, an aristocrat, full of himself as only someone chosen for greatness by church and state can be. In the parlance of modern politics, he did worse than expected. His chief guides were pathological prevaricators. His financial supporters, the Spanish Crown and noblemen who had sold their homes to bankroll the next great treasure hunt, expected a tenfold return and enough adventure stories on which to dine into their dying years.

Barely twenty years earlier, Hernando Cortés had landed on the coast of Mexico and marched a path to the peak of Spanish glory. So confident was Cortés of Plus Ultra that his men burned their boats near Vera Cruz. Inland, after hacking through the Mexican rain forest and stumbling upon a golden valley, they found Tenochtitlán, the Aztec capital. With its floating gardens, canals, and massive pyramids, it was as grand as any city of sixteenth-century Europe, but also much larger—with a population of nearly a quarter million. Jewels were cheap, gold ubiquitous, food plentiful. The Aztec pact with the sun gods required a mere human heart—freshly cut and live—a day. Without this daily sacrifice, the sun would fall out of the sky forever.

Through dealmaking with native factions, superior weaponry, and the silent front flank of disease, Cortés gradually broke the Aztecs. Spain had its gravy train of gold to fortify its armies for another century of European wars.

"We have a strange disease of the heart," Cortés told the Aztec emperor Montezuma, "for which gold is the the only cure."

So what to make of Acoma, all mud walls and squawking turkeys, the people plain and squat, the ordinary lives of ordinary people a joke compared with Tenochtitlán? This Nuevo Mexico high country was supposed to be the heart of the Seven Cities of Cibola. The conquistadors went to bed every night on tales of the cities, said to have been founded by seven bishops who had fled the Moorish occupation of Spain hundreds of years before. And more recently, there had been all these encouraging reports, the advance word. After a disastrous landing in Florida, a little knot of lost Spaniards and a Moorish slave had straggled west across the continent, over eight years, through Texas and New Mexico, finally arriving in Mexico City, the headquarters of New Spain. They built a bonfire of lies, leaping details of the Seven Cities of Cibola, places where doors were trimmed in turquoise and stairways lined in gold. Somewhere in Nuevo Mexico. Somewhere in the Rio Grande Valley. Somewhere in El Norte. You had to squint, at first, but it was there. Once the Pueblo people saw how hungry the Spanish were for nuggets of Cibola information, they too started spreading rumors— basically as a way to send them on to the next village. Just over the rise, Señor Coronado.

Coronado traveled four thousand miles in all. He was a truly atrocious guest, arriving at one Pueblo village or another to consume most of their winter food supplies, trash their homes, mock their religion, and paw at their women. He burned at least one hundred warriors at the stake. Pinyon smoke never smelled so bitter. The Zuni pueblo of Hawikuh was described by one of the conquistadors as "a little crowded village that looks as if it had been all crumpled together." And Hawikuh was a Cibola highlight, one of the places where the streets were supposed to be cobbled in gold.

In truth, the villages were no better or worse than the basic western farm town of modern America. Each had anywhere from four hundred to two thousand people. They kept domesticated birds and raised corn, squash, and beans in irrigated fields. The food wasn't bad. "They make the best tortillas that I have seen anywhere," wrote Pedro de Castañeda, the first journalist of the West, who went along with Coronado, keeping a chronicle. Hired as a propagandist, he became disenchanted, ultimately siding with the natives. The Indians were good masons, good potters, and good clothiers, making colored outfits from the cotton they grew. They had never seen a horse. As for precious metals, the closest thing they had was turquoise, but certainly nothing to set a conquistador's pulse racing.

The first encounter between Europeans and natives in the West was violent. A battle with the Zunis knocked Coronado unconscious and made him thoroughly ill-tempered afterward. He was hit on the head by a rock thrown from a Zuni post. In all, he destroyed a dozen pueblos, breaking a promise he had made to the viceroy of New Spain that any conquest would be "Christian and apostolic, and not a butchery."

His low point may have been on the plains of Kansas, at the far eastern edge of the rumor-chase. When he found grass huts and animal-skin lean-tos instead of the gilded city of Quivera, Coronado garroted his guide, the latest in a string of artful liars. Quivera, the conquistadors had been told, was a city where the emperor took his afternoon nap under a tree bedecked with bells of gold, lulled to sleep by the wind against the ornaments. That story sustained them on the march to Kansas, but the way home had no similar motivating myth. Retreating back to the Rio Grande, Coronado said of the Great Plains and its bison herds, "It is nothing but cows and sky."

Nearing the top of Acoma, Coronado's men must have felt like a party that climbs Mount Everest only to find someone lounging on the summit with a bag of chips and a portable TV. They were shown kivas, the ceremonial cellars, and the elaborate village, windows facing the southern sun, cisterns filled with drinking water, pathways on the hard stone, hundreds of people going about their business atop the rock of Acoma. Women climbed up the ladders, water-filled pots balanced atop their heads, without spilling a drop. The villagers said their perch was impenetrable: nobody would ever take the fortress Acoma. And Coronado's men wondered, clambering back down the rock, Who would want it?

THE FIVE HUNDRED or so homes atop Acoma are still heated by wood, with mounded clay ovens outside that look like big beehives. The old timbered ladders, baked white by the sun, still rise to the top terraces, and there are deep footpaths along the tabletop of the rock. It is not a museum, but a living town, somewhat iced in time. The wind dominates all other sounds.

The Acoma people always had a cacique, the top religious head of the pueblo. His job was to watch the sun, keeping careful track of its movement so that the people would not miss the solstices. This did not impress the Spanish, who had their own fetishists but seemed well assured that the sun would rise every day, regardless of whether they paid any attention to it or not. Also, in this land where the dry air was full of illusion, Pedro de Castañeda had written, "What they worship most is water."

Signs of the ancient religion abound atop the pueblo, but the tallest, most dominant structure has nothing to do with sun worship or water shortages. As you move through the village, hearing half-stories of wars and miracles at Acoma, of the silver-crowned cane that was a personal gift from Abraham Lincoln for loyalty to the Union, of priests being thrown from the cliff, and defeat and redemption of the residents, you wonder about the church bell hanging above the Sky City, in San Esteban de Rey Mission. It seems so out of place. Coronado, the deflated conquistador, fled the rock, claiming no use for Acoma. The Spanish had come to New Mexico, one conquistador wrote, "to give light to those who were in darkness and to get rich as all men desire to do." The Acomans did not seem worth the effort of conversion, and they certainly had little that would fill the crown's coffers. Coronado went back to Mexico City in disgrace, later to be tried for mismanagement and cruelty to the Indians. But the Spanish were not done with Acoma.

OLD AGE was to the sixteenth century what drawn-out male adolescence is to the late twentieth century. You married as a teen, mourned the death of many of your children during the first few years of their lives, and counted yourself lucky if you lived past your thirty-fifth birthday—five years beyond life expectancy for European males. Don Juan de Oñate was nearly fifty years old, a fossil in armor and silk, when he finally pushed north out of Mexico City on a colonizing journey to the Kingdom of New Mexico in 1598. It was the same year that Cervantes started writing *Don Quixote,* so windmill-chasing was not yet ingrained into Spanish life as a national metaphor.

After years of delays and debate, Oñate had persuaded the Crown that it was worth taking another look at the cold, high mesas of the north. More than half a century had passed since Coronado's disaster. The soul-saving argument carried much sway, of course. But there were other incentives to prod the two-mile-long column that moved through the dust of El Camino Real—the two-thousand-mile trail from Mexico City that for centuries was the longest road in North America. The Spanish, like other Europeans, were still in ardent pursuit of a waterway across North America, the fabled short-cut to Asia. The ill-fated march of Coronado had not chilled the urge for chasing rumors; the Northwest Passage, known to the Spanish as the Strait of Anian, would be a wondrous trophy. Maps of the time also showed a dis-tant and vast island named California, somewhere off the coast of present-day Nevada.

Gold lust had not dissipated. The Spanish Crown was bankrupt, having frittered away its huge profits from New World mines on endless meddling in European wars. Maybe, some of Oñate's men told themselves, Coronado had missed something. A snowballing rumor had it that there were silver bars just lying around the ground of the Rio Grande pueblos. As a sweet-ener, Oñate offered prospective settlers prime New Mexican real estate, for the taking, and a low-level noble title. Essentially, it was the first American dream, conquistador version. Every man who lived in New Mexico for five years would receive a patent of hidalgo, the lowest rank of Spanish nobility.

As for the people already living there, that issue was in flux. There were an estimated twenty million natives in all of Mexico and Central America around the mid-sixteenth century. At one point, King Charles V suspended new expeditions into the Americas until the question of whether these peo-ple had souls or not was settled. A widespread view held that some races and groups were by nature set aside to be slaves to people of a higher order. This certainly was not a uniquely European concept. North American Indians, from the Haidas of the rain forests in southeast Alaska to the Apaches of the deserts of Mexico, raided and traded in human beings. The Spanish had their dark-skinned slaves, which they preferred to call servants, of Moorish and North African descent. Pope Julius II issued an encyclical in 1512 declar-ing that the native people of North America were more than muscle and fiber; in fact, he declared, they had souls. The bad news was, this meant that they were also burdened with Original Sin, thus putting them in urgent need of baptism, which would wipe the stain from their souls. So for many natives, the inaugural ritual of Christianity as practiced by sixteenth-century Spain came only after deciding it was better than the hellfire of eternal damnation or a torching from juniper twigs. Spain had forged a violent Catholicism. Its leaders, both spiritual and political, were tramping around the world forcing people to become Roman Catholics or die at the grill. This is still known, in some history books, as the golden age of Spain.

With a clean conscience, the Spanish Crown issued a *cedula* in 1583, authorizing the conquest, er, pacification, of New Mexico, for the purpose of saving the spiritually bereft. The stage was set for Acoma's tangle with the last of the conquistadors.

IT TOOK Oñate six months to move fifteen hundred miles up the trail to New Mexico, the old Plus Ultra banners fraying in the desert wind. He had the kind of family background where the word "destiny" likely followed the word "mama." He married a woman who was a descendant of both Montezuma and Cortés. His father, Cristóbal, had landed in those first Spanish boats to arrive in Mexico and had marched to the Aztec capital with Cortés. Oñate had done nothing of real substance in his entire life. He was desperate for the New Mexico *entrada,* and he brought along two of his adult nephews to share in the family triumph.

When he arrived, a few months shy of the last year of the sixteenth century, it marked the end of about five hundred years of relatively uninterrupted Pueblo life—a point that Oñate tried to make immediately. This time, the Spanish were not just visiting. They brought an army, cattle, building tools, and several walking levels of Roman Catholic Church hierarchy. Moving up the Rio Grande, Oñate set up the colony just north of modern Santa Fe, in a place he called San Juan de Caballeros. He then called together Indians from throughout the valley for what was known as the standard conquistador speech. The Pueblo people should consider their land occupied. There was much to learn from the Europeans. Most important, they could earn themselves a passage to heaven. But they had to submit. They had to give up the sun god talk and corn worship and kachina dances. They had to replace their sustaining myth—the southern exodus, shouting into sandstone walls waiting for an echo—with a new story, one of a predestined salvation at the hand of the One True Church. No one would be harmed, no women raped, no villages burned, if the people would take an oath of loyalty to the King of Spain.

Many of the Rio Grande villages, seeing an ally in their long fight with Apache and Ute raiders, took the pledge. One-by-one, the Indians came to kneel, kiss the hand of a priest, and then swear fealty to King Philip II. Acoma held back. They sent spies down to watch it, who then returned a hundred miles to the rock, reporting all they had seen. One bit of intelligence they brought back from the ceremony was that the Spanish fired off these massive metal weapons, the cannons and harquebuses, but they didn't seem to do much harm.

In the fall, Oñate became restless, and set out to find an ocean that was supposed to be just west of the big New Mexico mountains, between the mainland and the Isola di California. He went through Zuni and Hopi country, and they seemed agreeable enough, despite what happened to Coronado. Then he came upon Acoma. It was, one of his men wrote, "the best situated Indian stronghold in all Christendom." Though, of course, it was not Christian. Acoma was ancient, by New World terms; it had the settled rhythms, detailed oral history, the rigid religion, the too-familiar local powers, the cluttered byways, and the petty politics of a prosperous city that had been around for several hundred years. Consider the parallel to Avignon, in southern France. Avignon, another sky city, built atop a rock, was where popes lived for much of the fourteenth century. It had the same pretensions as Acoma, with, of course, much more of an army to back its conceits.

The people of Acoma believed in premarital sexual experimentation, war, and property rights, to a degree. They were generally monogamous, with family clans regulating marriage. Their main weapon was the big rock itself. Looking down at the high plains four hundred feet below, and across to Mount Taylor, then away west to the purple and blue horizon at day's end, they believed themselves invulnerable. Nobody in their known world lived higher up than the Acomans.

Oñate pranced around the base of the rock, looking for a strategic advantage, wondering what such a conquest would mean back in Seville. The Acomans fretted. They had spent the summer beefing up their defenses. It was only a matter of time, they felt, after watching what happened in the Rio Grande Valley, before the conquistadors would attack. At first, Oñate tried the old superstitious Indian trick, which had worked well elsewhere. He knew horses were something of an exotic presence in the north. A few of Coronado's mounts had gotten loose, but the Pueblos were still foot-bound. Oñate had his soldiers move their horses around, facing each other. He was trying to make it appear that horses could talk.

High above the chattering steeds, the Acomans considered their defensive strategy. They were going to roll boulders down from the perch, crushing the soldiers and their talking horses. But at the last minute, they decided to hold the stones. A delegation went down to see the Spanish, bearing gifts. Oñate and several men crawled up to the top. Once on the summit, the *adelantado,* or governor, of all the Kingdom of Nuevo Mexico, fired his big, unwieldy rifle. The harquebus made a great ka-boom, the sound bouncing off the walls of Enchanted Mesa, Acoma's twin to the northeast. But again, nobody suffered a consequence, so the firearm was deemed harmless. Oñate gave The Speech, demanding that the Acomans subscribe to the Act of Obedience and Homage. At the end of the day, he clambered down the rock and left.

Two months later, in early December, Oñate's nephew arrived at Acoma with thirty men on horseback. Captain Juan de Zaldivar wanted to trade for flour. This time, the Acomans seemed surly, telling Zaldivar it would be a few days' wait while they ground the flour. When Zaldivar took his men to the top to pick up the bags, they were attacked. Acoma could wait no more; these men in beards and armor, with their pledges and threats, their talking horses and booming metal sticks, must go. Stones and arrows were fired in one direction, steel balls and swords the other. An Acoma warrior crushed the skull of Zaldivar. Soldiers were tossed from the cliff; others jumped. In all, eleven Spaniards died in the first battle of Acoma.

When news of the fight arrived back down at the Rio Grande, Oñate went into a rage. Acoma would pay, and the punishment would send a message to all of New Mexico. By Spanish protocol, he needed church and state justification to declare war, which the friars granted him. Three days after Christmas, he dispatched nearly a hundred soldiers for a war "by blood and fire." His surviving nephew, Vincente de Zaldivar, would lead the attack.

When young Zaldivar arrived at the base of Acoma, he called on the Indians to surrender. Their response was a storm of stones, arrows, and ice chunks. Thereupon he issued a formal declaration of war. Trumpets blared, weapons fired, and the Spanish charged forth at the base of the impenetrable mesa. The large frontal attack drew the Acomans to the edge. At the same time, a small detachment led by Zaldivar sneaked around the rear, climbed up the backside, and mounted a surprise attack. For three days, they fought for the rock, a battle later celebrated in a Spanish narrative poem. Clubs pulverized skulls, and balls ripped apart chests. By the end of the first day, Zaldivar's men had managed to haul one of their cannons up by rope to the summit. From then on, it was no contest, as the boom was no hollow sound. By the third day, the natives were in desperate retreat. The Spanish burned their homes, throwing wounded Indians over the side.

Others committed suicide or killed their brothers and sisters, sons and daughters, in order to spare them death at the hands of the conquistadors.

In the smoke of the smoldering Sky City, the Spanish pronounced it a miracle. They had lost only one soldier. Acoma was nearly wiped out. The Place That Always Was lay in ruins. Nearly six hundred Indians had died. But the worst was yet to come.

The hands of the remaining men and the Acoma women and children were tied, and they were marched down the rock and east to the Rio Grande. It was freezing, in the dead of winter, the hard winds blowing from the north with snow squalls. At a village site on the river, the defeated Acomans met the victorious Oñate. They would now stand trial for the crime of breaking the Act of Obedience and Homage, though most of them had never taken any such oath. They were given a defense counsel who pleaded a sixteenth-century version of insanity: the Indians were uncivilized, he said, and therefore incapable of knowing what they had done. The outcome was never in doubt, and after a three-day trial, a guilty verdict was pronounced. Then Oñate issued his sentence.

Men over the age of twenty-five were to have one foot cut off and spend twenty years in personal servitude.

Males from age twelve to twenty-five were condemned to twenty years as slaves, as were women of the same age. This amounted to war booty for the soldiers who had found no silver bars in New Mexico. As Oñate said, "I order that all the Indian men and women who have been sentenced to personal servitude shall be distributed among my captains and soldiers in the manner which I will prescribe and who may hold and keep them as slaves for the said term of twenty years or more."

Two Hopis—then called Moquis—who had been captured on the rock were each sentenced to amputation of the right hand. They were ordered to return to their tribes with their bloody stumps as graphic warning.

Children under the age of twelve were given to the friars for Christian schooling. Sixty of them were later sent to convents in Mexico City.

And that was it. The book was closed. There would be no appeal, Oñate said, "this being a definite and final sentence I so decree and order."

Over a period of days, in front of crowds of Indians, men had their feet hacked off or their hands amputated. Slaves were given over to the soldiers. And the Kingdom of New Mexico, breached in blood and blessed by bishops a full generation before an Englishman tied up on the Massachusetts coast, was ready to enter its second year. Four hundred years later, the West has the lowest rate of church participation of any region in the country.

YOU HEAR the bells ringing at the old mission tower atop Acoma this morning, the sound drifting out of the rock-and-dirt tower and falling away in the winter air. Nobody bothers to look up from what they are doing in the pueblo. The bell was a gift from the King of Spain. Beyond that, there is barely a remnant scrap from the empire that won the battle at Sky City. As it was before 1540, the pueblo is still governed by a cacique, and Acomans still look to the snows of Mount Taylor for divine inspiration, and to the neighbor of Enchanted Mesa for spiritual sustenance. They talk about the sun and corn and water, as always, as parts of a world in which everything fits. And they talk about these things in English, but also in Keresan—the same language that was used while searching for the Place That Always Was. You hear very little Spanish spoken atop Acoma.

Even if Oñate had not made a second *entrada,* the river of Western history already had jumped channels, never to return to the old course. The Spanish brought horses, and the effect on North America was not unlike what happened after Henry Ford started mass-producing the Model T. From the Rio Grande, the tough desert mustangs, a Moorish breed, spread north. They ran wild, living on prairie grass and desert sage. With horses, the Plains Indians went from being part-time hunters to big nomadic tribes, chasing bison across far-away river drainages. The ripple spread to their social structure. It was men's work to hunt, women's to tan the hide. More women meant more hides. Monogamy faded; polygamy became tolerated, as did increased raiding and slaving to build up a harem of forced-work hide-tanners.

The Apaches, effective raiders on foot, became feared desert pirates on horseback, forcing Pueblo Indians to look south for allies. The Utes, Shoshone, and Arapaho roamed over an enormous area of the Great Basin with their hoofed mounts. Horses were glorified in rock art and ritual. By the early 1700s, horses had crossed the Continental Divide deep into the Pacific Northwest and were used by Yakamas and Nez Perce, who would later be known for their own hybrid, the Appaloosa. The Blackfeet moved out of the central Plains and started to set up camps across the raw country of northern Montana. All of this flowed from the few horses that had gotten loose from the Plus Ultra marches up the Rio Grande.

It took nearly four hundred years for the population of Acoma to reach what it had been when the Spanish first took a count; about a thousand people were recorded just before World War II, the same as in 1540. Barely a year after Acoma men had had their feet cut off and been ordered into bondage, the Sky City resumed many of its old rituals. Some Acomans had never left. But, more remarkably, the condemned ones, the men with a single foot and a severed stump, had also made it back. That part of the city that had been destroyed was rebuilt, this time of adobe brick—a technique learned from the friars.

Acoma lives up to its name. As for Oñate, he left his mark—a disputatious note in the desert. The only physical evidence remaining from the first governor's reign is the hieroglyphic scratching on a rock north of Acoma, called El Morro. It is still visible.

"Passed by here the Adelantado Don Juan de Oñate from the discovery of the South Sea on the 16th of April 1605," he wrote, in Spanish. He said he discovered the Gulf of California, having dipped his toe in the brackish waters. But the Spanish had already been there. In the end, desperate to achieve something other than a court-martial and ridicule, he was chasing another rumor—that men lived underwater at the far edge of the desert.

The "poor, isolated, cold and unlovely Kingdom of New Mexico," as Oñate's biographer Marc Simmons put it, went through drought, food shortages, and finally a mutiny. You can't eat a patent of hidalgo, the low-ranking noblemen-to-be concluded. After several years of grubbing and bitterness, the settlers fled south. Oñate sent Zaldivar after them, with orders to cut off their heads. But they made it safely back to New Spain, where they told of the tyrant Oñate, an *adelantado* out of control. He had, they said, thrown an Indian out of a second-story window in Santa Fe, among his recent fits of rage. Much later, back in Mexico City, Oñate was found guilty of numerous crimes, among them cruelty to the Indians at Acoma. He spent the remaining decade of his life trying to save his reputation. A man of nearly eighty, the last conquistador was reduced to a piteous figure in Madrid, begging the royals to grant him a pardon, or at least listen to his story one more time. Gradually, with great regret, the Cities of Gold were erased from the map of Nuevo Mexico. In their place, scrawled over a great area, the Spanish labeled most of what they had seen in the American Southwest as simply *despoblado,* an unpeopled howling wilderness.

OVER TIME, the forced weave of two cultures took hold. There was enough of the Old World that the New World liked. Horses would stay, as would some farming techniques, and orchards. To this day, an Acoma peach is a summer treat, distantly descended from a Spanish fruit. New

Mexico has most of the strands of the modern West, with a heavy Spanish and Pueblo texture. Its cities are full of urban exiles looking to the glow of nearby mountains to put an extra dimension in their lives. People run up and down mesas, trying to squeeze meaning from the land. New Agers come and go, sampling the rarified air but never letting it get into their bones.

Acoma goes on; it has no other way. A handful of people attend Mass at the mission built in 1629, while men in long black hair track the motion of the sun. The secret to old age in the West? Find your place, dig in, and defend it, just as Gary Snyder said. The Spanish thought this land, these views, this air, was foreign. Today, Europeans make up the bulk of visitors who marvel at the red rock, the wondrous light, the fact that in the American West, where trailer parks have historical designations, something shaped by human hands is still standing from a thousand years ago. In Avignon today, at the Palace of Popes, the walls are covered with graffiti; like French rock 'n' roll, it is a bad combination. Nothing of any real religious significance emanates from inside the stone fortress in Provence. Acoma never had the power of Avignon, but it still controls its small universe. It is not a reservation, a ruin, a ghost town, a toxic Superfund site, or a faux-Indian theme park. It is a city in the sky, looking out to the world as before, the Place That Always Was.

CHAPTER 3

A Colorado River Town I

Lake Havasu City, Arizona

Under the dancing summits of the Chemehuevi Mountains, the Colorado River is a pane of flat water providing a midday illusion. Heat, evaporation, white sky—and just like that, I'm watching a retro skit from Monty Python. Already, it is more than 100 degrees outside in the Arizona spring, and not yet noon. I have been in the Mojave Desert long enough that I wave back at Joshua trees. Now, here is Olde England rising from the sand at river's edge. Pink-faced people with silly walks are dashing to and fro among the paloverde. I see Sherwood Forest Nursery, go past inns named for the British Royal Crown and for Shakespeare. There is a Queen's Bay Golf Course, a King's Retreat, a London Arms Pub, and at the town center, the inspiration for the architectural alchemy, is London Bridge. Not a faux, Vegas-style re-creation, like those that have taken root up the river, in Laughlin. But a seven-hundred-foot span of granite that has been transplanted, stone by stone, from the Thames to the Colorado. If Acoma is the Place That Always Was, Lake Havasu is the Place That Doesn't Know What to Be. It is trying to be Europe in the West, perhaps, importing grandeur to a land without self-esteem.

English Village is built around the bridge. It's very green and Tudorish, with little establishments selling meat pies, savagely overcooked vegetables, and number 55 sunscreen. Away from the tourist center, the town—incorporated in 1978—has a half-finished, not-going-to-live-very-long, tax-revolt kind of feel to it. It seems childless and parkless and why-the-hell-not. I check into the Best Western Motel, a historic landmark without so much as crow's feet at the doors yet, the oldest establishment in town. At twilight, the sky turns a rose color and then turquoise, draped against the Chemehuevis. I order kung pao chicken and chop suey from London Bridge Chinese Food, opting for cultural dissonance as a way to blend in. Afterward, I light a cigar and stroll across the big span, five arches over a sluggish branch of the Colorado, my Nikes covering the same rock kings and commoners covered. The ritual for visitors is to touch the granite, to make a connection with something old and permanent from an ordered society on a damp island in the Atlantic, eight thousand miles away.

At Lake Havasu City, water seems cheap and abundant. Most important, it is transformative. It keeps houseboats afloat and provides a slick carpet for Jet Skis. It laps against the beach on land where only tarantulas and sidewinders once dared to crawl. It flows one way, to the west, in a canal that pumps excessive expectations into Southern California. And it goes the other way, east, in one of the biggest plumbing projects ever assembled, a 336-mile aqueduct that climbs more than a thousand vertical feet across the desert to Phoenix. In Europe, people scorn the "Chunnel" as a folly of debt and engineering overreach, trying to connect England to France underwater. In the West, it costs American taxpayers $5 billion to ship much of the Colorado River inland to a place without reliable water, and now—surprise—nobody wants it. Too alkaline, they say in Sun City and Leisure World. Too expensive, they say on the remaining cotton farms outside Mesa and Glenwood. The big canal scraped away Sonoran mesquite and saguaro cacti on land where Frank Lloyd Wright was going to show the world how people could weave into the desert ecology. Lake Havasupians shrug when I bring up the $5-billion canal—called CAP, for Central Arizona Project. So CAP didn't work out. But how about that London Bridge?

"Most people just like to touch it," says Norman Bear, who was the mason foreman when the bridge was reconstructed at Lake Havasu. Norman is American. His wife, Kathy, is from England. The message machine at their home answers with the clipped British accent of Mrs. Bear: "Hi, you've reached the Bears. We're not in our den at this time."

When Norman Bear came to the desert looking for work on the bridge project in 1969, he laughed at the astonishing incongruity of what Robert P. McCulloch had in mind. McCulloch was an industrialist and developer. One day he was flying low over the desert where the Colorado is plugged by Parker Dam, looking for a site to build an industrial park. McCulloch wanted a place where land was nearly free, water abundant, and electricity cheap. Lake Havasu, the reservoir created by Parker Dam, fit the bill. Pilots used to fly over this stretch of desert during World War II, training for bombing runs. And just to the south, on a nearly deserted Indian reservation, an internment camp housed Japanese-Americans for three years; most were American citizens. In other words, the desert here was disposable, contemptible, punishment land—the American Australia, in the eyes of the government. Like many Westerners who view their native ground as unfinished and imperfect, McCulloch thought his site needed something dramatic and regal; it needed a complete face-lift. It wasn't enough that the Colorado River does more on its own than any army of architects could sketch in a thousand years. McCulloch expanded on his vision in many a press interview, at which point people usually laughed and walked away. Norman Bear did not believe it himself until the mirage started to arrive at a place known as Site 6—a jumble of sun-blasted trailers tormented by an oven-breathed wind from the south. The containers were full of granite originally quarried in Dartmoor, about four thousand stones in all, each of them numbered. Norman Bear thought to himself: He's serious! In temperatures reaching 120 degrees, Bear and his men set out to reconstruct a European bridge of stone over sand in a place where nobody lived; there wasn't any water at the site either. After the bridge was in place, according to plan, would come a channel of freshwater, and then—presto—a city. The Pioneer West, circa 1970.

"Of course I thought they were nuts," says Norman Bear. "The London Bridge—here? It was crazy, crazy, crazy. Who would think of such a thing?"

THE Chemehuevi Indians were just starting to develop some familiarity with the mischief of the Colorado River when King Athelred the Unready, leader of the Saxons, sailed up the Thames in 1014. The premature royal was determined to take London back from the Danes; the key was the bridge. Under cover of darkness, the attackers sneaked under the wooden span over the river and pulled the pilings down, dragging London Bridge into the drink. Athelred thus set in motion a set of events that would ripple, ultimately, to a curious town created in America. A much stronger bridge, built of stone, was started in 1176 and took thirty-three years to construct. It lasted six hundred years and served at times as a place at which to impale the heads of people who had fallen out of favor with the British Crown. Over the centuries, freezes and fires took their toll on the span, but its celebrated sagginess gave rise to a nursery rhyme that every American schoolchild could sing. So the bridge had a link to the hearts of the former colony. By the 1820s, stone was laid for a new London Bridge, the one that would end up in the Arizona desert.

SOUTHERN ARIZONA, said Kit Carson, was "so desolate, deserted and God-forsaken that a wolf could not make a living upon it." Wolves, in fact, made a living, chasing jackrabbits, deer, and javelinas, the wild boars of the Southwest. A number of tribes, particularly the Hohokams, who lived in the valley where the Salt and Gila Rivers came together in wet years, did rather well for a time. When the water dried up, the Hohokams vanished. Later, dozens of smaller tribes took up residence, never living more than a few days' travel from the Colorado River. During the Civil War, a Union outpost was set up at Yuma, where the Gila joins the Colorado. The fear was that Confederate steamers might chug up the Colorado, establishing a base from which to go into California. Thirty years after the war, a town took shape in the Valley of the Sun, where scars of the old Hohokam canals were still visible. To live in Phoenix in summer required imagination. People draped wet bedsheets over themselves at night, or simply put themselves in a narcotic stupor in order to sleep.

"If our city wishes to keep pace with other towns on the coast," the *Gazette* of Phoenix editorialized in 1881, "then ordinances must be passed prohibiting the smoking of opium and making it a misdemeanor for any person to bathe in a ditch within the city limits."

To the rest of the country, the Southwest was a freakish land, populated by aliens. The Anglos living in Arizona weren't quite sure how to adjust to the place either. For a while, camels were imported. The color of the land was odd. The sky was a baked bowl. The people talked funny, looked a bit too colorful, acted different. Then, as now, there were more Indians in Arizona than in any other state. Utah was full of Mormons, long-bearded, polygamous, communal. New Mexico was seen as Old Mexico, a mistake some people still make, as when a Santa Fe resident called the headquarters for the 1996 Olympics in Atlanta to request tickets and was told she would have to go through the office of her own nation. As conditions of entry to the Union, the last states to join the rest of mainland United States had to change. Utah was forced to renounce polygamy. New Mexico promised to encourage more Anglo settlement. Arizona increased copper production and tried, also, to lure more of the kind of Americans who might be at home in old Kentucky.

Arizona, the forty-eighth state, entered the Union in 1912, and promptly sent Carl Hayden to Washington. He would stay in Congress, first as a representative then as senator, until 1968. One of his enduring obsessions was water. Arizona had plenty of it; one-fourth of all the freshwater in the West flows through the Colorado River. But it was in the wrong places, running through the big ditch up north and draining away to the Gulf of California in the southwest. To the east, the Salt River squeezed out of Apache hideouts in the Superstition Mountains but dried up by the time it reached Phoenix. In the year before statehood, Roosevelt Dam, then the largest ever built in America, was stapled to bedrock on the Salt River. It set a precedent: it cost $5.4 million, a true extravagance at the time, and benefited only about two thousand landowners, most of whom were supposed to pay for it but never did. It helped the cotton and alfalfa growers in the valley; but Phoenix wanted much more. It wanted to be green, to be wet, to be cool, to be watered year-round. And so Hayden made diversion of the Colorado River—the so-called Central Arizona Project—his life mission, spending five decades in Congress trying to reengineer his home state. Bruce Babbitt, the two-term Arizona governor and Interior Secretary under President Clinton, said political reporters in Phoenix used to have a single, all-important task.

"Once a year, somebody was sent from Arizona back to Washington, D.C.," Babbitt says. "Their job was to make sure that Senator Hayden—and the Central Arizona Project—were still alive. And so, once a year, there would be a banner in the paper: 'Hayden, Water Project on Track.' "

By temperament, the Colorado was sometimes a mustang in an open field, bucking, sprinting, unpredictable. Old-timers compared it to an Indian, calling it red and wild. From snowmelt in Rocky Mountain National Park to a saline marsh in the Gulf of California, the river scoots down the western slope of the continent, running fourteen hundred miles, usually in a hurry. It is vodka-clear, cold, and sweet in the mountains of Colorado; by the time it reaches Mexico, it is saltier than the sea it empties into. The river drops nearly thirteen thousand feet, coloring and carving parts of seven states in a basin that receives, on average, about four inches of rain a year. The river was red because it always carried sediment from one geologic era to another, building beaches, creating new wonders with hydraulic sandpaper. And in the Grand Canyon, a mile deep and ten miles wide, the river has exposed rocks dating to a time when the Earth was not yet fully formed. The Colorado Plateau, in essence, is a solid block of sandstone and shale, two miles thick; the river follows the demands of gravity through an easily carved crust. The key to the visual drama of the Colorado Plateau is simple: over several million years, water has sought the path of least resistance. The Colorado River has pushed a quadrillion tons of rock downriver in the last fifteen million years alone.

By the late 1860s, most of the blank spots on the map of America had been filled in, except in the Southwest and in Idaho. The Colorado, particularly from Glen Canyon through Grand Canyon, was a source of rumors, extravagant tales, and fear. In 1869, a one-armed, remarkably even-tempered Civil War veteran named John Wesley Powell mounted an expedition down the length of the river, attempting to clear away centuries of ignorance. Acting as nothing more official than the secretary of the Illinois Natural History Society, Powell descended Grand Canyon rapids in a wooden dory, strapped into an oaken armchair. When he launched his adventure, it was if he and his band of nine men had just stepped off the planet; most newspapers speculated that he would never be seen again. Throughout the journey, it was variously reported that Major Powell had plunged to his death over the steepest of waterfalls or been swallowed by white water.

Powell plodded on, never seeming to panic, even as some of his men deserted him. At times he turned poetic. In southeastern Utah, he wrote: "Wherever we look there is but a wilderness of rocks; deep gorges, where the rivers are lost below cliffs and towers and pinnacles; and ten thousand strangely carved forms in every direction; and beyond them, mountains blending with the clouds." Just before entering the mile-deep hole in the Colorado Plateau, he remained intensely curious. "We have an unknown distance yet to run, an unknown river yet to explore. What falls there are, we know not; what rocks beset the channel, we know not; what walls rise over the river, we know not. Ah, well! We may conjecture many things." When he scooted out the other end, the West was smaller, less fearsome, but ultimately more fantastic. There really *was* a mile-deep slit in the Earth, where sunlight, water, wind, and rock combined to form geologic art that no pen or brush would ever come close to duplicating. The West of discovery, the West of surprise, of awe, was gradually starting to replace the West of fear. At the same time, the wonders of Yellowstone were just being fully explored and explained.

As gripping as Powell's adventure had been, his more lasting service was in trying to shape a "dryland democracy," as his biographer, Wallace Stegner, put it. After running the canyons of the Colorado, Powell spent the next thirty years trying to convince Congress that America should try a different model for growing a civilization in the West, something more in keeping with the nature of the arid lands, the terra beyond the 100th meridian. A popular idea, accepted by most policymakers at the time, was that rain followed the plow. All that was needed to make the desert bloom, it was felt, was to dig up the earth and plant something of agricultural value; that in itself would form clouds, and bring rain. So a series of late-nineteenth-century homestead acts was passed, fostering the cruel notion that a sod-buster only needed a strong back and a year or two of patience before he could transform his personal 160 acres into a field of prosperity. Powell said it was nonsense. A quarter-section was one thing in Iowa, virtually worthless in most of the West. His idea was to encourage the growth of communities, even whole counties, united by a single watershed, working within the contours of the land and the limits of the sky to bring American life to the open space. It included dams and irrigation, but nothing like what later developed, Soviet-style, in the most Republican states of the Union. The prairie halves of Montana, Wyoming, Colorado, and New Mexico, depopulating for the last seventy years, are still paying for the crucial misconception by those who refused to listen to Powell.

In the early twentieth century, Powell's ideas faded away, and there was less official promotion of the notion that rain followed the plow as well. A Western water tradition known as "first in time, first in line" came about, a hydro-extension of gold-fever grubstaking. It means that whoever gets to the water first can use as much of it as they want, no matter what happens downstream. This philosophy, upheld in the 1920s by Supreme Court rulings, is not just the opposite of Powell's vision of shared water communities but it encourages developers, speculators, emerging cities, and entire states to grab as much water as they can, even if they might never use it. Once it is yours, nobody can take it away.

By law, reclamation was for small farmers and burgeoning communities or those threatened by killer floods; otherwise, there was no legitimate reason for the majority of American taxpayers to finance some of the biggest public works projects of all time. A farm taking water from federal irrigation was limited to 160 acres in size. In reality, water movement was about power, not Jeffersonian democracy, and the small acreage limit was no more followed than any treaty ever signed with American Indians. The axiom that water flows uphill to money became the guiding principle of the West. Big landowners wanted it but were not willing to pay for it, so they promoted a handful of senators who could tie up the upper chamber of Congress to bring it to them. In that sense, little has changed. A knot of Western senators recently held up the entire federal budget in a filibuster over the notion that reforming grazing laws on federal land might reduce first-in-line water for some well-connected landowners.

The first grand scheme of the water lords was to divert the Colorado near its end in order to enrich the Imperial Valley of California. At the turn of the century, a sixty-mile-long canal was built. But then the river reverted to character; it swelled with runoff and jumped around, seeking a faster way downhill. Eroding the canal, the Colorado broke through, then spilled onto hard ground in the most barren part of California, creating the Salton Sea, before it could be shoved back into its normal path. The hydro-engineers decided that the only way to gain control of the Colorado was to choke it higher up, after it flows out of the Grand Canyon. Calvin Coolidge signed the bill creating the first big dam. And as Commerce Secretary, Herbert Hoover, hero of many a tax-and-spend-phobic citizen, was the ultimate promoter of the biggest government project of its time. Hoover Dam backed up the Colorado River, powered the lights of Los Angeles, gave the Imperial Valley the predictable water flow it wanted, and convinced generations of politicians that there was nothing like a dam to keep them in office. Los Angeles, invigorated by Colorado River water and runoff taken by fraud from the Owens Valley to the north, went from a city of barely half a million people to a megalopolis with a population greater than half of Canada.

So was born the urban West—an "oasis civilization," in the words of historian Walter Prescott Webb. The swiftest rivers were shackled, and water was sent to places where cities could grow. The West was tamed, ultimately, by government—specifically, the Bureau of Reclamation, a jackhammer brigade known to some as the Bureau of Wreck. The Rio Grande, the Platte, the Missouri, the Sacramento, the Willamette, the Clark, the Snake, the Columbia—every major river in the West except the Yellowstone was dammed. At the start of the twentieth century, three-fourths of the people in the West lived in rural areas. By the end of the century, the West was the most urban area in the country. Utah is now more urban than New York

State. It all came about because water was brought to a select group of landowners and speculators.

As engineering practitioners, the architects of Hoover Dam deserve their place in the pantheon of pyramid builders and skyscraper creators. In the canyon, as you stand atop the dam, the impression is overpowering. To get under way, high-scalers dangled from cables while drilling holes for dynamite. Heat in the canyon killed dozens of men; others died when cables snapped or they fell into fast-setting concrete. In all, 112 workers lost their lives building the World's Biggest Dam. A day's wages averaged four dollars. The cement started flowing one day and it did not end for two years, until the dam was nearly eight hundred feet high. The river was lifted out of its channel, diverted, then moved back to its old course when the dam was in place, giving birth to Lake Mead. Just over 3.2 million cubic yards of concrete, weighing 6.9 million tons, was poured to create a sixty-story-high plug in the second biggest river in the West. In the course of a single person's lifetime, the Colorado had gone from mystery to machine.

Once the river was put to use, there was no end to what could be done to it. Parker Dam, built 150 miles downstream, followed Hoover in the mid-1930s, creating Lake Havasu. But it nearly caused the state of Arizona to go to war with California. The governor organized a makeshift navy, the Arizona militia, and had machine guns mounted on two boats to ensure that California would not get its way with the dam. Since the water was destined for Southern California, Arizona saw it as a resource-grab that would be to their ultimate loss in the first-in-line scramble for the Colorado. The Arizona side of the river was declared to be under martial law; no construction crew could set foot on it. But the Arizona navy, more like McHale's than MacArthur's, fell apart when the rudders of the two militia boats got tangled in weeds and cable. They had to be towed to shore by boats from the enemy—California. Parker Dam was built. Lake Havasu was created. Having nearly gone to war to stop the lake, Arizona had no use for it.

LONDON BRIDGE was falling down, and by the early 1960s, it was clear that no amount of shoring up would keep the granite span from sagging into the Thames. Gravity had presented Robert McCulloch with the centerpiece of his planned town. He couldn't build a cathedral or a casino, but perhaps he could transport the bridge, piece by piece, to the American West. He submitted a bid of $2,460,000; after authenticating the check, the British government said the bridge was his. It cost McCulloch another $500,000 to ship it, each stone marked with numbers indicating span, row, and position. The granite was sent eight thousand miles to the Mojave Desert at Lake Havasu, where McCulloch had been buying up most of the nearby property. He laid out a town—the main street being McCulloch Boulevard, leading up to and crossing the bridge. He then paid another $8 million to reassemble the bridge, hiring a civil engineer from Nottingham, England, to oversee the reconstruction. To give it the right gloss of empire and nobility, McCulloch had the then–Lord Mayor of London, Sir Gilbert Inglefield, lay the cornerstone.

The heat was intense. One day at Lake Havasu the temperature reached 128 degrees—the highest ever recorded in Arizona. Engineers worried that the Scottish granite would swell beyond their calculations; they knew that it would absorb a considerable amount of heat, so they had to build the bridge with eighteen inches of expansion. The hardest thing for Norman Bear was to imagine the bridge as anything but a span to nowhere, a laughingstock in the desert. The work crew mounded up and sealed sand, forming a mold over which the arches would go. But again, there was no water beneath it; they were building a bridge over nothing but real estate speculation. McCulloch flew planeloads of people to his imagined desert town, trying to convince them to take up residence in the next big Sun Belt retirement center.

"We called them lollipop flights," says Bear. "Full of suckers."

IN HIS last years in Congress, Senator Carl Hayden was a shrunken, balding, big-eared man peering out from oversized black glasses. As long as he had a pulse, his influence grew with every passing day. By the 1960s, he was chairman of the most powerful money-spending committee in Congress—Appropriations. Arizona boosters ran a two-pronged campaign for most of the twentieth century. One was to convince the world that the Sonoran Desert was paradise, a land of perpetual sunshine, with air that is the very elixir of life and a landscape that holds the most wonderful shapings of creation, from the Grand Canyon to the red rock dream world of Sedona to the saguaro cacti forests, with their long arms and spring flowers. In that respect they were right; Arizona in its birthday suit may be the most spectacular rectangle of land in all of North America. The other prong was a campaign of fear and pity designed to convince people that the cities of Arizona were on the verge of collapse if they did not get a massive diversion of the Colorado River. The state was portrayed as a man crawling across the desert, a day or two away from dying of thirst. Air conditioning had made Arizona livable year-round; now all it needed was enough water to make it look like everything that a desert is not.

At last in 1968, the year that McCulloch started shipping the London Bridge to the Mojave and Senator Hayden's final year in office, Congress approved funding for the Central Arizona Project. It was envisioned to cost no more than $1 billion. The government would pay the costs up front, on the condition that Arizona water users would repay the Treasury. The plan was to create an aqueduct that would siphon Colorado River water and send it across the Mojave Desert to the Sonoran Desert, where it would be channeled into a network of canals for delivery to Phoenix and Tucson. It would originate at Lake Havasu—a great bonus for McCulloch, for now his imagined city would have another reason to exist. Not only would Lake Havasu City be home to London Bridge, it would also be the start of the artery that would allow the biggest metropolitan areas of Arizona to expand without limit. Workers were needed to create the canal, and they would live in trailers and houses on twenty-six square miles of land that McCulloch had purchased and laid out as a private city.

Phoenix would have more canals than Venice once the Central Arizona Project was finally completed. And the city would be as green as Seattle. Mesquite and paloverde were scraped away, and golf course sod was tacked in place to the desert edges of the city. New subdivisions were created overnight. The model was Del Webb's Sun City, and later Leisure World (called "Seizure World" in a memorable gaffe by Senator John McCain). These were controlled-environment retirement cities, banning anyone under age fifty-five. They proved to be tremendously popular. McCulloch built his own planned community in Phoenix, using a gusher of subsidized water as the main attraction. He created the Phoenix subdivision of Fountain Hills, centered around what he called the world's tallest fountain. Soon, Phoenix was consuming the Sonoran Desert at the rate of an acre an hour. By the end of the twentieth century, its metropolitan area took up more land than Los Angeles; it was bigger, at two thousand square miles, than the state of Delaware.

Lake Havasu had its London Bridge in place by 1971; a few years later, the city had a population of fifteen thousand. Once the four thousand individual stones of the bridge were mortared to each other, the sand molds were removed from the arches. The ground was dredged, and then Lake Havasu spilled underneath the span. At last, it was a bridge to somewhere, even if it was just to the other side of an invented city. In 1978, one year after McCulloch died, the city was incorporated. The original, official purpose for backing up the Colorado and extending the lake was to create farmland for 160-acre plots. As it turns out, all eight thousand acres of arable land in the area are under water, at the bottom of Lake Havasu.

Up and down the Colorado, water dreams came true for the members of the engineer/speculator complex—the water kleptocracy, as the author Marc Reisner called it. It was clear, early on, that water users themselves could never pay for the enormous network of canals and diversions. So it was decided to build more dams on the Colorado River to generate electricty, which would then be sold all over the West as a way to help pay for the original water diversions. The biggest of these planned cash generators was Glen Canyon, a gorge of rainbow colors and old Anasazi sites just upriver from the Grand Canyon. It was buried under two hundred miles of water and named for John Wesley Powell—one of many ironies. The dam actually causes more water to disappear than it delivers to people; about 750,000 acre-feet of Lake Powell, baking in the desert sun, is lost each year through evaporation. That's enough water to supply all of San Francisco, which has been rationing water for much of the last twenty years. Lake Powell is "the most tragic act of federal vandalism to befall the American West," said the writer Bruce Berger. It also changed the character of the Grand Canyon, blocking the spring runoffs that once brought sediment loads downstream. Instead of red, warm water in the summer, what courses through the Grand Canyon now is sterile and ice-cold, piped from the bottom of Lake Powell.

Grand Canyon itself was considered for two dams. It was a waste, the Bureau of Reclamation Commissioner and chief dam builder Floyd Dominy felt, to have all that water going through that deep slit in the earth, without any of it being captured. Grand Canyon was a natural reservoir, needing only a few big plugs of concrete to complete its destiny, Dominy said in the 1960s. Many Westerners were appalled. Full-page ads ran in major newspapers showing the Sistine Chapel under the threat of a flood. What country, the opponents asked, would ever try to bury its greatest treasures? But that was precisely the point of those who brought London Bridge to Lake Havasu and smothered Glen Canyon under two hundred miles of muck and tacked a rug of bluegrass the size of an eastern state in the Sonoran Desert city of Phoenix: the arid West, its caves, chasms, and gorges, its mesas, sandstone walls, and slickrock frescoes, was in itself somehow unworthy without the veneer of old Europe or a plumbing system that tried to transplant a watershed to the driest part of the United States. The projects were driven by an Olympian inferiority complex over one of the best qualities of the native West.

IN THE shadows of the evening, a din of rhythmic sound bounces along the backed-up river. I walk along the shore of Lake Havasu and hear a song from the Artist Formerly Known as Prince. "And Tonight We're Going to Party Like It's 1999 . . ." Then a round of cheers. It's spring break at its beery and pot-smoking apex. Officially, Lake Havasu may be trying to become an outpost of Olde England. But in one respect, the society created in these arid lands by government water is little more than keggers on the Colorado. Every spring, with the eyes of MTV trained on the sunburned masses, thousands of students descend on Lake Havasu to eat fish-and-chips and flop around half-drunk in some of the most heavily subsidized water in the world. This emergence of spring-break Lake Havasu has not pleased Norman Bear or any of the other seniors who ultimately settled in the fake town built around the fake lake that laps under the imported bridge.

"That bridge will last a thousand years," says Norman Bear. "But we've got to do something about the partiers."

Water under the bridge is now a major concern of the state. The heat and all those human bodies have combined to make the channel under the London Bridge a cesspool of coliform bacteria. The governor has declared several public health emergencies. For a while, all the beaches were closed. As for the water leaving here for the big cities, the Central Arizona Project, it has proven to be a bust. It carries $5 billion worth of debt and enough water to take care of five cities the size of Cleveland. But it is far too expensive for most homeowners to use. Much of it is lost through evaporation on the way to the Valley of the Sun. So Phoenix went looking for cheaper water, and found it on the Indian reservations around the city. When the government divided up the river in 1922 among the seven states that signed the Colorado River Compact, they left out the Indian nations, which have both sovereign status and treaty rights to water. Now the Central Arizona Project funnels water to the tribes, out of obligation, and they sell it to Phoenix developers, happily consuming the Sonoran Desert at the rate of an acre an hour. Tucson has learned to live in the desert without the massive water diversions. Cacti, brittlebush, aloe, and other native plants were used for landscaping, and the city slowed down, looked at what it was doing to the desert and mountains on which its glow of life depended.

BRUCE BABBITT, descendant of an Arizona merchant family that first came to Flagstaff in the 1880s, stood atop the Glen Canyon dam not long ago, looking like a lucky lotto winner. A student of Western history, Babbitt has long revered the one-armed Civil War veteran who first floated the Grand Canyon. Growing up, he roamed the Colorado Plateau, his backyard playground, and then read Powell's journals. Now, as he straddled the last big dam ever to be constructed on the river, the dam built to provide electricity to pay for water that nobody wants or can afford, Babbitt was trying to re-create spring runoff on the Colorado. He would open the dam's floodgates to mimic something like a big seasonal flush. Water would carry sediment for beaches and sandbars of the kind favored by the thousands of people who float down the Colorado trying to feel a bit of what John Wesley Powell felt.

Babbitt proclaimed that the era of big dam building in the West was over. At the same time, the government announced a plan to spend $70 million to tear down a salmon-killing dam on the Olympic Peninsula, in the far northwest corner of the West. A little bit of character should be put back in the rivers, Babbitt said, somewhat meekly; the land should be given credit for what it is. What was this backpedaling and policy-shifting all about? Had the engineering wonders of the world, the technical triumphs that inspired song, led newsreel highlights, drew politicians to oratorical flourish, been a mistake?

In any event, the emperor of the outdoors was now trying to use a dam to heal a river. And it seemed possible that the government would spend the next hundred years in the West undoing what it had done in the previous century. Enough Westerners were comfortable with the new narrative: wild land, even dry and unwatered, was just as acceptable as the back nine of Olde England Heights in the Mojave. Actually, it was an old narrative, from Powell, who fought and lost the policy war in Washington. His words finally found an audience in the executive branch, a century later.

"We have only one Grand Canyon," said Babbitt. "This is a symbol of a new way to manage our rivers." He gave a signal, and then a big cheer went up, a boomerang echo of the hurrahs from dam-opening ceremonies from the previous sixty years. The first blast of a year's worth of stored water came roaring out of tubal prisons at the base of Glen Canyon dam, forty-five thousand cubic feet per second—about six times the controlled flow. Broadcast live on the "Today" show, it was, on one level, just a bit of river doing what it does, no more interesting than a tree growing. But some called it the hydraulic event of the century. The Colorado was big and red again. At the least, it provided the kind of youthful rush that the old landscape-carving river had not been through in more than a quarter-century. The initial burst was like fireworks, loud and dramatic, and then it tumbled away in a froth, pouring down the Grand Canyon, knocking boulders out of place, carrying snowmelt through walls older than most any other exposed rock on the continent, bringing life to long-dormant cubbies of soil, and down, draining away through Hoover Dam and then further, into Lake Havasu, under the glowing Chemehuevis to a city where people may one day feel they no longer need to be England, foreign and green in their grand beige setting.

CHAPTER 4

A Colorado River Town II

Supai, Arizona

The People of the Blue-Green Water have lived inside the Grand Canyon for at least 800 years, and they still get their mail by mule train. It takes longer for a rumor to reach the hamlet of Supai than it does to fly between three continents. Before there was Phoenix, Flagstaff, Denver, or Albuquerque, there was the town at the western end of the canyon. Yet, it is not on many maps of the West and cannot be seen from most air flights over the area. Nor are there any roads to the village. Sheltered by flanks of stone higher than anything ever built, Supai sits in a pocket of selective ignorance, neighbor to the Seventh Natural Wonder of the World.

On a weekday when the wind is cold and out of the north, and the sky still black, I am threading my way north up the Colorado River drainage, picking up Old Route 66 and a Navajo-language radio station at the same time. From Kingman, I angle through Hackberry, Valentine, Truxton, and Peach Springs, none of them taking more than a few seconds of road time to pass through, and then I'm in Indian Country, the Hualapai Reservation. I cannot make out much from the Navajo broadcast—a language the Japanese could never decipher during World War II—except that the Mariners beat Cleveland last night, 6 to 4; already, the Colorado Plateau seems a little brighter and a little warmer. The news goes on for fifteen minutes, and then comes an old George Jones song. "I work like a slave in the open-pit mine," is the refrain, the perfect pairing of music with landscape, the bluesy crooning, the lonely sky. Turning to the northeast, the last road to the canyon is a straight line, Indian Route 18, over ground that would be twenty-foot rolling swells if you were on a sailboat. I sometimes get a little too much lift off the rises, landing hard.

In the first light, I see livestock roaming over open pasture, clusters of pinyon-juniper, raptors at work overhead. Once, I stop the car to shoo away cattle blocking the road. I never see another soul, and there is no hint that anyone lives nearby. After sixty miles, the road ends somewhat suddenly at the lip of a high cliff, treeless and exposed to the wind. Horse trailers and rusted cars are parked at the edge. Low-angled morning sunlight reveals color in the canyon, purples and mauves, some limestone, in a wide crack in the earth. I walk to the edge, where there is a trailhead for a narrow spiral path deep into the chasm, dropping several thousand vertical feet to where the village of Supai is supposed to be, in a side canyon above the Colorado River. I am mostly curious about one basic thing: how have these people been able to live along the river for nearly a millenium without importing the London Bridge or requiring a nation to pay for a $5-billion water diversion system?

"HERE'S your horse," says Brian Chamberlain, a Havasupai Indian in cowboy hat and stiff leather chaps worn to a shine. "You been on a horse before?"

Of course. I mean, at the county fair as a kid, going around in circles, and in eastern Washington, trying once to impress a country girl with the unusual attributes of loving F. Scott Fitzgerald and Appaloosas. But no, not on a long ride down a canyon trail, where steering one way or giving the wrong command would mean a tumble into the rocky abyss and rehab in some place like Sun City, where a doctor probably wouldn't even treat somebody under the age of fifty-five without a waiver from the Del Webb corporation. But, then, no horse would be so stupid as to step off the trail. Right?

"Your horse is named Sophie. You think you can remember that?" Are you kidding, I say: "That's my daughter's name."

"You move the reins this way to turn right, that way to turn left. Pull it back to slow her down. Don't kick her too much. She'll start sweating after a while. She'll fart and shit along the way too. When we get to water, let her drink."

I had arranged to go to Supai with the mail, which leaves the hilltop three times a week. The postmaster from Peach Springs said this route was the last in the United States to be delivered by pack animals. Not because of some quaint tradition or bureaucratic ineptitude that would be absurd even by postal standards. It is simply the only way to get mail or anything else into the village of the Havasupai. People in the canyon do their grocery shopping through the Postal Service. "It may look like hamburger," said Leroy Hurst, the postmaster. "But once it comes through the door, it's U.S. Mail. I'm the only Post Office in America with a walk-in freezer."

Brian and his father are the only two people on the canyon rim in the morning. Everything I ask them, to me, sounds stupid as soon as it leaves my mouth. Sure, they are going down to Supai with the mail. What the hell else would they be doing here with these beasts of burden in temperatures barely above freezing at dawn? We feed the animals pellets from fifty-pound bags, my fingers cumbrous and cold, and then load up the mules with about two hundred pounds each. Strapped around their backs are twelve-packs of Coke, milk and bacon, potatoes, flour, two-by-fours, loaves of cheese, bags of nails, spackling paste, videos, canned vegetables, blankets, bread, chips, and official offerings from Ed McMahon holding out the chance that someone inside the most remote village in America will become a millionaire through the Publisher's Clearinghouse Sweepstakes.

Brian rides in front, on a surefooted mount. His father has left to visit friends on the south rim. I start out in the rear; at a place where the path briefly widens, I go to the front with Brian. Sophie moves deliberately, army troop style. She spares me any pranks and is responsive to my few directions. The first mile is very steep, downward over crushed pebbles and fist-size stones; soon the sky is little more than a sliver overhead. We descend a staircase of time. The canyon changes color with every turn, presenting a new world, a new geologic age; about two hundred million years separates the rim from the very bottom, a real challenge for creationists. It is just under nine miles to Supai, and another few miles beyond that to the Colorado River. Brian answers my lame questions in a monosyllabic monotone.

"You expecting it to heat up in the canyon today?"

"Nope."

"Get a lotta rockfall down here?"

"Yep."

"You prefer the winter or the summer?"

"Same, either way."

Brian lives in Supai, one of about three hundred residents of the only permanent village in the 280-mile length of the Grand Canyon. He speaks Yuman, the native dialect of the village, and English, the dialect of American television. There are VCRs in Supai.

The trail to Supai has not changed over the centuries; it is the only way to get through the canyon—down the water-worn slit in the rock walls. The Anasazi lived mostly upstream and across the chasm beyond the north rim. The ancients ventured into the canyon to harvest the fruit of prickly pear cacti, rice grass, and leaves from a bush later labeled Mormon tea (decaffeinated, of course). They used a compound that could reduce headaches and muscle pain, found in Grand Canyon willows. Yucca flowers were a decent side dish. Most ethnologists believe the Pai people, of which the Supai are only a small band, did not come directly from the Anasazi, but may have descended from people who lived on the south rim of the canyon. The Pai called themselves The Only True People on Earth, a not-unusual native designation, especially for a group as isolated as they were. Their language group extended from the canyon south to where Lake Havasu is today, onetime home of the Chemehuevi Indians, and beyond to the Mexican border. By the time that Father Garces—the first known white visitor—had wandered down this path in 1776, the Havasupai were already using ornaments and tools from Europeans and coastal Indians passed along through the extensive Western trade network. The priest found a village of farmers and orchardists, living well in homes of tightly woven straw over pine poles and surrounded by the perpetual sound from three waterfalls of Havasu Creek, the green stream that pours out of the canyon walls and is the source of the name Havasupai—People of the Blue-Green Water. They had a priest of their own, whose job was to keep track of the fetish bundle, a collection of sacred relics passed on from one generation to the next. Two priests from different worlds, talking fetish bundle secrets—that would have been an exchange worth hearing.

Hidden inside the glorious breach in the Colorado Plateau, the Havasupai were able to dodge conflicts on higher, more exposed ground. They did nothing particularly virtuous or diplomatic to avoid trouble; their survival was strictly a geographic fluke. The big brown land of the Southwest changed hands, wars were fought, railroads tracks were laid, mines dug, water diverted, droughts came and went; prospectors, gunslingers, dreamers, schemers, conservationists, and adventurers tramped through. By legal proclamation, the Havasupai became Mexican citizens after 1821, when all Indians living in the territory of the country newly independent from Spain were made part of the republic. Twenty-seven years later, after a war, the Mexicans handed the land over to America. All of this meant very little to the people living in what was, to the outside world, a deep hole of incomprehension on a blank space of the map. But the Havasupai were not socially reclusive, nor were they universal Indian brothers; they were never in hiding. The Hopis, a powerful, populous tribe to the east, were their main trading partners, and they acted at times as benevolent allies. The Hopi village of Oraibi claims to be as old as Supai. Other tribes, the Apache, the Utes, and the Yavapai among them, the Havasupai considered enemies.

The biggest tribe in the region, the Navajos, was crushed in the 1860s. Relatively new arrivals to the Colorado Plateau, the Navajos are Athabascans who call themselves the "Dine"—The People, or The Earth-Surface People. Their rivals the Hopis hated them; the Hopi word for Navajos translates to "head-bangers." From the Spanish, the Navajos learned to raise cattle, goats, and sheep, and became the preeminent weavers, shepherds, and silver-jewelry-makers of the West. They lived in conical hogans, some of which are still used today, and roamed over a large domain covering parts of four states, with Monument Valley and the Painted Desert as open-air living rooms. Like the Apache, they were slave traders and raiders. They also developed an unusual social custom: a married man was never supposed to look his mother-in-law in the face.

While the Havasupai lay low, a large force of volunteers from New Mexico led by Kit Carson went after the Navajos. Carson had already received a quarter of a century of iconographic press coverage when he was given the job of subduing the Navajos in 1863. A distant relative of Daniel Boone, on his own in the open land of the West since age fourteen, Carson had joined up with John Charles Frémont in the 1840s to map the Great American Desert and Terra Incognita, covering nearly four thousand miles in a cartographic foray second only to Lewis and Clark's expedition. The maps became bibles for overland travelers, making Carson and Frémont household names. Both are known, now, as names associated with casinos. Carson had married an Indian, was the father of Indian children, and was called Red Shirt by the Navajos. He knew all about the raiding hideouts, the guerrilla attack-and-withdraw methods, and the land which was the ultimate defense of The Earth-Surface People. The only way to defeat them, he calculated, was to starve them out. Carson marched north, burned Navajo farm fields, blankets, and homes, slaughtered their animal herds, cut down their peach orchards, and ripped apart their irrigation system. By early 1864, in the dead of a bare-boned Colorado Plateau winter, the Navajo were left hungry and shivering in the rock hideouts of Canyon de Chelly. More than two-thirds of the tribe, about eight thousand people, surrendered.

Just as many American Indians call themselves The People, most tribes have as part of their history a horror period known as the Long Walk. This was always a forced march from good land to bad, a parade of humiliation by conquered people. The Cherokee experienced it, so did the Creeks, the Nez Perce, the Modocs, the Arapaho, the Cheyenne, and many others. For the Navajo, the Long Walk was three hundred miles across the desert of New Mexico to a squalid, arid patch of ground near the Pecos River called Bosque Redondo. Their enemies, the Utes, Hopis, and Mexicans, preyed on them along the way. The Utes had already benefited from the bounty that Carson paid on Navajo livestock. In all, nearly a quarter of the Navajo died in the march or at Bosque Redondo. The wonder is that, today, the Navajo number nearly 200,000 people, and live on twelve million acres of sovereign land—the biggest reservation in America. At the time the tribal reserve was established, an Indian agent labeled it "the most worthless land that ever laid outdoors." There are no Kit Carson mementos sold at reservation trading posts, nor have they yet warmed to their neighbors the Hopi.

During the time of the Navajo exile, other Indians of the Colorado Plateau were also rounded up or gave up land to miners, cattle herders, and other armed trespassers. The Pai people who lived above the canyon and hunted in the pine forests of the south rim lost out to the Army and were marched south, to an internment camp at La Paz. That left only the Havasupai, small and isolated, living as always in the slit cut out of one side of the Grand Canyon. An American explorer, Frank H. Cushing, came in 1881 to the village of Supai, with its rows of corn, squash, beans, and cotton, its orchards of ripe fruit, and pronounced it "a veritable land of summer." They grew tobacco, aimed their prayers at certain rock walls and the sun, gambled, stored food in granite holes, took sweat baths, had no laws on divorce or marriage, and played a hoop game not unlike basketball. The government sent an agricultural specialist and a schoolteacher down the trail to Supai, but there was not much they could improve upon. The land of summer was made an official reservation, all of 518 acres, in 1883.

MIDWAY DOWN the trail, the canyon walls are so narrow I can lean over one way or the other and touch a slab of sandstone. It's clear from the water lines on the rock and the bare floor of the path that when thunderstorms come clattering through here in summer, the trail turns into a swift current of red water, no place for horses, mules, or people.

"Ever been in here during a thunderstorm?"

"Yep."

"What's it like?"

"Bad."

"How bad?"

"Real bad."

"No kidding?"

"Nope."

Brian's got a big wad of tobacco in his mouth. When we pause to give the horses a rest, Sophie lets out a long, breezy fart. It's a good thing he warned me. If not, we would be looking at each other funny. Or at least, I would think he would be looking at me funny.

"These horses fart a lot?"

"Sometimes."

We talk about hunting. He's killed deer and elk, birds and jackrabbits, but never had a shot at bighorn sheep, the rock-climbing phantoms of the Grand Canyon. I've bagged a few pheasant and some ducks in eastern Washington.

"And, you know, duck is very good in an orange sauce with garlic," I say. "Once you've cooked all the fat out."

"Chicken's better."

The red walls of the canyon narrow some more and then the funnel starts to widen. We pass the six-mile mark. By the eighth mile, it levels into more open country. All at once, it is expansive, with the sky broad, the valley flat and the walls of the canyon some distance away—an enormous natural amphitheater. We come upon Havasu Creek for the first time, running fast and clear. As we wade through the creek, Sophie stops in the middle of the stream, the water just below the saddle. She drinks for several minutes. I feel jazzed by the whole thing: the temperature twenty-five degrees warmer down in the valley than it is on the rim, the clear water, the range of rust colors and deep tans on the rock walls, the downshift from the rushed incrementalism of a typical American day to this languor. I start to blurt little spasms of superlatives.

"Yep. We got another mile to go."

As we near the village, there are peach trees and obese cottonwoods, up to six feet or more in diameter at the base. Stacks of cottonwood, which is fibrous, twisty, and hard to cut, are piled high for firewood. The village is in the middle of all the trees, like a big courtyard community. It is very basic and utilitarian. Every house has a horse or two tied up in front. There are no motor vehicles, except an occasional old tractor. Narrow red-dirt roads connect the homes. Basketball hoops hang from crooked, skinny cottonwood poles. Brian waves to a few people as we make our way through town. The arrival of the mail stirs the village, somewhat, although dogs dozing in the afternoon sun barely lift an eyelid.

Signs just outside the village warn that alcohol is prohibited anywhere in Supai or the canyon leading down to it. But the trail was littered with beer cans and bottles. At both Lake Havasu City, where alcohol rules, and here in Supai, where it is banned, Budweiser appears to be the king of beers.

"Ever been to Lake Havasu City?" I ask Brian, trolling for a comparative thought as the trail ends.

"Where's that?"

"Maybe two hundred miles down the river, south of Kingman. You've never been there?"

"Nope."

"Ever heard of it?"

"Nope."

"The London Bridge is there."

"The what?"

"London Bridge. They brought it to the desert from London and rebuilt it, piece by piece."

"Why?"

IN THE first century after the Havasupai were formally given their village land as a reservation, the river just below them went through changes greater than anything short of the reshaping brought by geologic tumult. From Lees Ferry to the Gulf of California, the river was throttled, rechanneled, backed up. After John Wesley Powell squirted through the Grand Canyon, press accounts of his adventure, complete with maps, etchings, and photographs, were published throughout the land. Americans were fascinated by this wonder in their midst. As always, one impulse was to tame it, control it, and remake it; another was to let it be. A survey crew studied the canyon in the 1890s, determined to run a railroad through the big ditch; when three surveyors lost their lives, the effort was abandoned. Miners poked holes in the canyon rim, the prospectors protected by a law from 1872 that allows anyone to make a claim on American public land for a mere five dollars, a law that Senators Larry Craig of Idaho and Conrad Burns of Montana continue to uphold as the epitome of Western culture. When President Teddy Roosevelt came to the Grand Canyon, he had a renewal of the religion he first experienced as a sickly boy on a ranch in the Dakotas. He came down this trail, met with Havasupai, and hiked along canyon paths, robust and snorting as usual.

"Leave it as it is," T.R. thundered from the canyon rim. "You cannot improve on it. The ages have been at work on it, and man can only mar it." He declared the Grand Canyon a national monument. Americans did not need castles or Renaissance churches for self-esteem, not with a natural history unrivaled by Europe. Western senators were outraged; the canyon, they said, was being "locked up" from commercial development, and speculative rights were being trampled on. But even though the land was protected, the river remained open for alteration. So, the dams pinched off both ends of the Grand Canyon, burying thousands of Anasazi sites, erasing beaches, changing the ecology of the canyon. A national park meant little to the Havasupai, except that it brought more people down the river. Barry Goldwater, when he rafted the Colorado as a teenager, was still something of a pioneer. Today, twenty thousand people a year ride the canyon rapids, dropping nearly eighteen hundred feet through the park.

At Supai, an ancient irrigation ditch, perhaps three feet wide and four feet deep, encircles the village, channeling some bit of water from Havasu Creek to the orchards and vegetable gardens. Other than that, there is not much that the Havasupai have done to alter their eight-hundred-year-old community. Supai is not dramatic or impressive in the way of Acoma or Canyon de Chelly. It is sluggish, a small farm town in no great hurry, with little overt ambition.

"What's it like to ride in a big jet airplane?" Brian asks, startling me with a multisyllabic burst. And now I really feel stupid, trying to explain something that is so integral to basic American life that nobody even describes it anymore.

"The food is bad. The seats are small. You get from one place to the other really fast. Sometimes, there's a lot of chop, and you bounce around and wonder if this thing that is half as big as your town is going to fall from the sky. I've never seen a view from a jet that matches what we saw this morning, dropping into the canyon."

"And what's it like in Las Vegas?"

The water of little Havasu Creek courses through the village of Supai, tumbles over three cataracts, and then flows to the Colorado. From there it goes on, through the turbines of Hoover Dam, providing the electricity that keeps the neon lights of Las Vegas aflame at all hours. Brian has never been more than about 150 miles from home. High school was up on the rim, and that's some distance.

"How about Alaska? I'd like to see that."

I tell him he would like Alaska, with salmon as big as first-grade kids, a still-forming landscape, wonderfully wacky residents. Not too many horses, though. I dismount Sophie, and say goodbye to Brian. I've got one more stupid question: I ask Brian if he would ever want to leave Supai, maybe live somewhere else for a while, somewhere out of the canyon or in a bigger town. He gives me a big tobacco-teeth-stained smile.

"Nope."

THE LANGUID pace of the village is contagious; what I feel like doing is taking a nap. Instead, I walk over to a little lunch counter and eat fry bread and a burrito, and down a cup of coffee. I lollygag my way around town, rousing a few dogs, but most of them don't bother. The homes are basic government-issue prefab. Some are masoned and timbered; most seem relatively new. Water is stored up on higher ground, in a big tank, and some of the sewage runs through a ditch, to a containment area. There is surprisingly little horse shit on the ground, given that the transit system is constantly creating waste. Most of it ends up in gardens. At the school, which goes to fifth grade, I hear the Yuman dialect and see Anglo teachers among the Indians. Kids in Chicago Bulls jerseys play baseball during the afternoon recess.

Some visitors, expecting a Native American Eden, have been disappointed by the village. "Upon closer inspection, Supai's charm wore painfully thin," wrote Colin Fletcher in his 1960s account of walking through the Grand Canyon. "Everything was dirty and scraggly; dogs, houses, clothing." Edward Abbey spent most of his time bathing nude in the pools below the village, coming close to death once when he was stranded between falls on a cliff; whiskey may have played a part. Wally Stegner was typically charitable. "There is something to be said for the policy that urges keeping barrier canyons around this tribe unbridged," he wrote in "Packhorse Paradise," an essay from the mid-1950s. "Inevitably there will be more and more intrusions on their isolation, and inevitably they must proceed through the phase of falling between two cultures, of being neither Indian nor white American."

In a little back office not far from the school, I find Wayne Sinyella, the tribal chairman. He's a Deadhead, as is obvious from the fetish objects in his office. On the wall are duplicates of two gold records by the Grateful Dead, one for the song "Sugar Magnolia," the other for "Trucking." Sinyella is still mourning the death of Jerry Garcia. "I love the Dead," he says. "What are we going to do without Jerry?"

The Havasupai tribe, he says, has had a couple of rough years. They have been fighting various mining conglomerates which, for their five-dollar claims, have been able to dig up the ground that is part of the watershed for Supai, ground that drains ultimately into Havasu Creek. They are extracting uranium for nuclear weapons and power plants. All told, there are ninety-four thousand sites on the south side of the Grand Canyon on which people have made mining claims. Since 1984, the tribe has been battling one company from Denver that has drilled a deep shaft above the village. What has saved the Havasupai, of late, is a crash in the uranium market. Former Soviet republics are nearly giving it away, making it less profitable to scrape it out of the south rim of the Grand Canyon.

Still, all those holes in the ground on the plateau above Supai mean living with a certain trepidation. Not only does Havasu Creek provide the blue and green to the People of the Blue-Green Water, but it ends in a series of waterfalls, just below the village, that are a big tourist destination. "Uranium-rich" would not be a helpful brochure description, though in New Mexico the humorist Tom Lehrer has coined one such ditty:

> Where the scenery's attractive,
> And the air is radioactive,
> Oh, the Wild West is where I want to be.

One of the falls is higher than Niagara. People swim nude in the lower falls, with its pools and bracing water at a place in the canyon where the walls can make it like a convection oven. En route to the pools, hikers camp in the village, for a fee, or buy native crafts, or stay in one of the twenty-four rooms of Havasupai Lodge, recently remodeled.

But Havasu Creek can be destructive as well. Supai is not a benign eco-paradise. In 1910, the creek rose beyond its banks and tore up the village in a flood that changed its entire face. Before the surge, most people still lived in thatch houses made of cottonwood poles, sod, and tightly woven brush. Afterward, the town was rebuilt of wood and canvas. A few years ago, another flood came through, again destroying much of Supai. Using helicopters, the Bureau of Indian Affairs lowered sections of prefab, three-bedroom houses into the village. At first, the Havasupai didn't know what to make of them; some were used for storage. Eventually, most of the village was rebuilt out of modular-home parts and common building material.

Stegner's prediction—the dilemma of choosing between two worlds—has come true. A group of investors from outside the tribe has been persistent with plans to construct a long electric tram down into the village, allowing people to be whisked into Supai with minimal exposure to the sun or the charms of a horse named Sophie. Other proposals call for bulldozing a road through rock to replace the ancient path. As it is, not even motorbikes can get through.

"I guess we'd probably have to put up with a traffic light then," says Sinyella. "And with a traffic light, you also get a traffic jam, don't you?" The Havasupai, he says, have considered these offerings from the world above the canyon, and have chosen to stay with what has kept them going all these years, lying low inside the earth. It is not that they couldn't use something better than a six-hundred-year-old irrigation ditch for watering crops, or a sewage system that backs up too often, or school walls that leak cold air in the winter and don't cool down in the summer, or even a new village on higher ground, living with the kind of security from the whims of nature that other communities on the Colorado River have insisted that they need, with the help of monumental subsidies.

"What has kept us together, all these years, is pretty simple," says Sinyella. "Isolation. And now that's the big reason why people want to come here."

ON MY WAY out of the village, hiking the slow, uphill miles back to the canyon rim, I pass about half a dozen parties, people giddy at the prospect of touring a place in America that seems to them somehow more authentic than anything above the canyon. I miss Sophie. And I pass Havasupai natives, speaking a hybrid dialect, carrying boxes of extra-large Domino's Pizza in from Kingman. Their ancestors started out here eight hundred years ago, thinking the universe was little more than the side trail and the broad canyon. While nearly everything else changed on the river, on the plateau, in the land above the canyon, they stayed hunkered down in the smallest of towns, tucked into a fold in the deepest of clefts in the earth. They are not, as it turns out, The Only True People On Earth. But enough people think they are something close to that, and so the world has worn the only path to their door.

CHAPTER 5

Stone Stories

Escalante, Utah

For a long time I was obsessed with rock art. Men with tails. Women holding the sun. Flying children. Animals that talk. A whole front page of twelfth-century exclamations and exhortations on sandstone. I blew out a tire looking for the kind of thousand-year-old petroglyphs that are kept off maps for their own protection. I cut a knee trying to get closer to a ten-foot anthropomorph, an armless spook of red paint floating above a slickrock canyon. I spent days looking for six-toed foot images in the Painted Desert, wondering about the power held by the Clan of the Polydactylics. I even went looking for the eight-hundred-year-old spaceship glyphs on Navajo land that keep so many people up at night; to my disappointment, they looked more like turtles. I was most interested in Kokopelli, the hunchbacked flute player with the gravity-defying hair and erect penis. He first showed up about A.D. 200, and for the next thirteen hundred years was scratched onto hoodoos, boulders, and cave walls from Monument Valley to the northern part of Mexico. He was full of lust, life, and music at a time when much of the world's great art was flat and Gothic.

Was he a god of good times, a field fertility shaman, or just a horny little bastard who knew how to blow a few notes on a wooden nose chime?

Nobody knows. And that is what's so stirring about the original art of the American West, and why a hike is never just a walk under open sky. There are no handy written summaries in five languages next to velvet rope, no self-serving notes from patrons corporate or Medici, no artists' explanations of any kind. No signatures or authorial symbols, even. It is first-hand information, without spin, revision, or self-evident ego. And it reveals itself in a gallery of oversized geologic wonders, mounted on walls of stone where it can look grand or goofy, pedestrian or brilliant depending on the light, the weather, the mood of the sky. The people who descended from the Anasazi, the great rock artists, have some signs and symbols in their cultural traditions that seem to connect to the work of the ancients. They recognize patterns of ritual and repetition in the chiseled representations. But even the most knowledgeable of Hopi, Zuni, or Pueblo priests cannot say with any certainty what those snakes that stretch to geometric infinity really mean, for example. Much of the religion, oral history, and fetish bundles around at the time of the paintings and etchings were left behind in the big move. Nobody even knows what the Anasazi called themselves; they suffered the ultimate historical indignity, being named by a band of people who neither knew them nor liked them. "Anasazi" is a Navajo term, meaning "Ancient Enemy." The Navajos, of course, arrived on the Colorado Plateau several hundred years after the Anasazi had disappeared. So you start with an initial mystery: who were these people with a peak population of perhaps a quarter-million throughout the Southwest, up to 100,000 of them in southern Utah alone?

The obvious explanation for most rock art is that it portrays hunting scenes. The artists drew or incised bison, sheep, coyotes, bears, antelopes, wolves, frogs, deer, or turkeys being chased by people shooting arrows or throwing spears. Hunting scenes. The modern equivalent would be an oil triptych of a family in the express checkout line at Safeway, on display at the Museum of Modern Art.

I want to believe that the best rock art of the eleventh- and twelfth-century Westerners is about something more than getting food or saying a prayer. In part, that has driven my obsession. When a row of people in a petroglyph are linked one to the other, as if in a line dance, and pointing skyward, is it a cultural highlight, a warning, or a diary entry from an intriguing night at the cliff dwelling? When frogs and fish appear in places where there are no amphibians today, does it mean that they screwed up, or we screwed up, or neither? Are the most animated of rock art panels narratives, prophecies, maps? Is there insight or knowledge, obvious to none of us, that we should know about? What of the glyphs in Chaco Canyon in northern New Mexico, where the ancients built a network of roads thirty feet wide, more than a hundred miles of them. For what? These people didn't even have horses. That kind of infrastructure is not easily abandoned. Surely, the Chaco Canyon art is not silent on the local improvements. Any lessons? Final thoughts? Kokopelli, talk to me!

This is a huge hole in the history of the West. A population density greater than that existing on the Colorado Plateau today drained away without leaving a decipherable reason for their exodus. A civilization that had evolved over a millennium—first living in pithouses, then in aboveground pueblos up to four stories high, finally scrambling skyward to the cliffside apartments—just closed up shop in the late thirteenth century, leaving much of what they had created, even the portable stuff, behind. The conventional explanation for the departure, that a prolonged drought drove the Anasazi south, has been under assault for the last few years. Climate governed everything, by the old reasoning. The yearly growth rings of trees tell stories of trauma and health, fire and frost. They are high-precision natural calendars. Radiocarbon dating can trace a pottery piece to an approximate date. The Colorado Plateau is fortunate to have witnesses in bristlecone pines, among the oldest living things on earth. Combine a pine-tree ring count with radiocarbon dating of an artifact, and you have the basis for educated speculation. What the latest round of studies indicate is that the most perplexing question of Western archaeology remains just that. The Great Drought, according to recent studies of tree rings, actually began after the Anasazi had already *started* their move. And it came at a time when some cities had mastered irrigation and construction of earthen dams, allowing them to control their flow of water—not to mention the highway system at Chaco Canyon.

So the why-did-they-leave debate is in play again, open to rock art interpreters who roam the washes and canyons, the cliffs and roadless mesas, looking for clues.

I was going about my rock art visits, not really sleuthing but certainly speculating, in the wrong way. Like a journey to the Uffizi in Florence, or a stroll among Etruscan tombs in Tuscany, I was doing the Grand Tour, well-prepared. I saw most of the exceptional finds: the Sinaguan riffs at the cliff ruins near Sedona; a flank of stone crowded with information called Newspaper Rock in southeast Utah; the seventeen miles of vertical rock etched with six hundred to a thousand years of Rio Grande life just west of Albuquerque (now threatened by development); the big sites at Canyon de Chelly National Monument and Mesa Verde National Park. In all those places, I was consciously seeking out a specific panel or site, hoping it would match what I had read or seen in books. I had reduced the rock art of the West to Michelin Guide precision, where things were rated in one of three categories: worth a journey, worth a detour, or the lone-star status of being merely interesting.

The better approach, I came to believe, was to avoid advance spin, to merely let it happen, to experience discovery—an endangered thrill. The first pictograph I ever saw was on volcanic rock just above the Little Spokane River, in an old-growth ponderosa pine forest. I was ten years old, maybe eleven, stumbling through the woods with a friend in search of a fishing hole. We detoured away from the river because it was muddy along the bank and hard to walk. Somewhat lost, scratched by brush, and hot, we were ready to turn back when we saw it. It was magic—a red-paint sketch of two guys shooting arrows at something four-legged. We knew they were guys because they had penises. The pictograph was under an overhang that protected it from the weather. It was faded but clear. We thought it was cooler than catching fish or throwing rocks at raccoons. It meant that Indians had walked before us, on the ground where we played. It meant the presence of time and community at the northern fringes of a city barely a hundred years old, where the suburbs were named for long-vanquished tribes. It was a puzzle, a treasure in rock. Our find. Years later, I went back to the river, only to see a well-worn trail, marked with a roadside historical marker, to a pictograph behind a wire-mesh fence. No longer wild, it was as if it had been put in a zoo. Worse, the art had been defaced, much of it chipped away, which was why it was behind a wire-mesh fence. Somebody had written: "North Central Rules, Fuck G-Prep."

Now, trying to duplicate the feelings of a ten-year-old in the woods, I set out on a primal rock-art expedition. The place to go, obviously, was somewhere on the Colorado Plateau, where glyphs and graphs are ubiquitous. (A pictograph is painted on rock; a petroglyph is chiseled or incised.) There is rock art all over America, but the best-preserved, the highest concentrations are in the arid lands where the ancients lived. Dinosaur fossils, some of them 145 million years old, are still around in Utah. With moisture rationed, things seem to last forever—a frightful thought when you ponder all the Wal-Marts covering Mesa Verde–sized pieces of real estate in Utah.

Much of the Anasazi work looks as if it were created yesterday. I narrowed my focus further to southern Utah, north of Grand Canyon and east of the tourist haunts of Zion and Bryce canyons. There, within a five hundred-square-mile area on largely roadless country run by the Bureau of Land Management, is more rock art than any place in the country. A quarter of a million archaeological sites lie within one day's drive of the Four Corners area, the only place in the country where the borders of four states intersect. Find a canyon, a wall of fine sandstone, a cave unmarred by uranium miners, and you're bound to bump into something intriguing.

But time was running out on the area I had chosen to visit. A Dutch-owned mining company had purchased claims to one of the biggest seams of coal anywhere in North America. It was planning to build paved roads and power lines, a mining complex twice the size of Manhattan, and then start trucking coal day and night for the next twenty-five years out of the heart of this wild country, west to Southern California for eventual shipment overseas. Every three minutes, a ninety-two-foot tractor trailer would rumble through a place whose main sound is the wind. The coal scheme had the blessing of the Utah congressional delegation, newly empowered by recent elections so that they ran the committees which oversee public land. At the same time, the state's leading politicians announced plans to open up most of the largely unvisited red rock country to further development—air strips, some golf courses, off-road-vehicle trails, oil and gas drilling, and other "improvements," as they call them.

"Nobody comes to Utah to see wilderness," said Jim Hansen, the Utah congressmen in charge of the public lands and parks committee in the House. "They come for the major tourist sites, the parks."

A realtor from Kane County echoed his representative. "I don't think anyone wants to see it. It's not even second-class scenery; it's third- or fourth-class."

The Utah senators and congressmen had their maps drawn up, dividing the red rock country into sections where power lines and pavement, bulldozers and truck blasts would replace open space and the native ground of hope. Yikes! Of course, none of this would harm any known archaeological sites, they assured critics; that would be against the law. And the industrial intrusions would be limited to a few small areas that nobody really cared about anyway, Senator Orrin Hatch argued. It was jobs for small towns, roads for the counties, revenue for the state of Utah, coal for Asia. With a sense of urgency, I lit out for the last section of the country to be fully mapped—ironically, the heart of the first major American civilization—the red rock land of southern Utah. I wanted to see a piece of the unscreened West before it was gone.

YOU CAN tell a lot about how people regard a certain area by what they call it. On the counter inside the lone federal government outpost in the town of Escalante, a uniformed BLM clerk is helping me with a map that unfolds to the size of an Amsterdam hotel room. Every square mile is colored by ownership—federal, state, Indian, private. Most of it is run by the BLM, landlord for one-eighth of the continental United States, an agency trying to shed an old tag as the Bureau of Livestock and Mining. In Utah alone, they manage twenty-two million acres. The place I am trying to get to must have been cursed and vilified; the names evoke eternal damnation or futility. There is a Devils Hob, a Devils Toys, a Devils Rock Garden (they have long dropped the possessive apostrophe), a Dirty Devil River, a Dirty Devil River Overlook, a Death Hollow, a Little Death Hollow, a Box Death Hollow, Carcass Canyon, Death Ridge, Last Chance Gulch. And then there are names that evoke Mormons unbound, or libidos powered by the desert sun: the Bishops Prick, Brighams Unit, Nipple Butte, Nipple Bench, Cads Crouch.

The broader area honors Father Silvestre Velez de Escalante, one of two friars who wandered northwest of the Spanish missions in New Mexico in 1776, trying to find a way around the Grand Canyon and the Apache country to get to California, where, in the same year that the Declaration of Independence was penned, the mission that would grow to become San Francisco was established above the Golden Gate. Father Velez de Escalante, the Curious George of Franciscan missionaries, never made it to California, but he certainly saw a lot of the country, going as far north as the place where Provo is today and west through Bryce Canyon, down the Virgin River near Zion, to the rim of the Grand Canyon, and back. When John Wesley Powell came through the region in 1871, on his second expedition to the Colorado Plateau, he named the last major range of peaks in the country. The Unknown Mountains became the Henry Mountains. He surveyed the Escalante River, which drains much of the canyon country of southeastern Utah to the Colorado River, putting it for the first time on Anglo maps of the West. Prospectors and Mormon colonists followed, and in their general disappointment, left behind the names printed on my BLM map.

Later came the National Geographic Society, heralding the red rock country as a place of wonder. The struggle between those who fear, exploit, or misunderstand the land and those who are open to its grandeur was evident in the descriptions of southern Utah by the exploring society from Washington, D.C. They were astonished at the ruins, the rock art, the desert clarity. A valley with monolithic chimneys, considered godforsaken by many in Utah, was named Kodachrome Basin. A dome was named for the Capitol. And on this place where heaven and hell, death and rejuvenation, sex and privation compete on the map, I want only to find a little space for discovery.

IN THE BLM office are blowups of petroglyphs from the area; it is like going into a small town to get a fishing license and seeing the trophy trout snapshots on the wall. My juices are flowing. I'm itching to get started.

"Most of these places I can't tell you about," says the BLM clerk. "They are Class Two or Class Three sites." Under the Archaeological Resource Protection Act, the government has designated three levels for rock art and ruins: Class 1 is open to viewing by anyone, Class 2 is open but usually remains off trail maps and a ranger does not have to describe its location, and Class 3 is off limits to anyone except by permit for scholarly or guided tours. The sketches, carvings, and shards of a civilization went untouched for a thousand years; but in the last hundred years they have been trashed.

The natives who followed the Anasazi, but were not descended from them, refused to touch the stuff. The Utes considered them haunted; making contact with an Anasazi relic was like opening an infection path to the soul. The Spanish called the stone etchings *piedras pintadas* (painted rocks) and generally left them alone. Don Juan de Oñate, however, in the last days of his tortured wanderings and ill-fated attempt at nation-building, was impelled to scratch his own marks at El Morro Rock in 1605—a boast of his explorations and a bitter editorial comment on how much the whole thing was costing him personally. In the late 1890s, a rancher named Dick Wetherill and his brother Al, a cowboy, unearthed stone tools, basketry, weavings, and funerary items in the dry caves of Grand Gulch, Utah. What soon became more interesting to the Wetherills than their cows was the emerging idea that there had been a big civilization in the very places that had been written off as worthless and uninhabitable. Cities, monuments, amphitheaters, roads, ball courts, and religious centers—a veritable Ancient Greece—lie just beneath the red dust. Dick Wetherill was one of the first to distinguish between the early basketmakers, who lived in the region until about A.D. 600, and the black-on-white pottery artists and cliff dwellers of several hundred years later. He was also one of the first to profit from the find. The Wetherills guided mule trains of artifacts out of the sites and back to their ranch. They sold to museums and collectors around the country, and were even hired by the states of Utah and Colorado to take treasures from the ruins back to the World's Fair in Chicago. An archaeological gold rush followed, the old city sites and open-air art walls were plundered in behalf of museums and schools, or by people who just wanted a thousand-year-old water jug for their fireplace mantel. By the mid-1950s, a group of scientists who went looking to study an undisturbed archaeological site in Utah could not find such a place. Virtually every known site had been looted.

The worst of the plunderers, a person who has taunted federal officials and scientists for years, is Earl K. Shumway, a convicted burglar who comes from a long line of Indian grave robbers. The elder Shumways and other pioneering Mormon families were hired in the 1920s by the University of Utah to furnish pots for the campus museum. They were given two dollars for every piece of Anasazi pottery. Lesser pieces, deemed inferior, were batted around and smashed up like spoiled tomatoes. A third-generation thief, Earl Shumway dug up his first grave at an early age, in the late 1950s. By then, cultural poaching was no longer sanctioned by universities or museums, but it was still an accepted way to make a living in small towns of southern Utah. Earl Shumway used bulldozers to scrape away some Indian sites, and hired helicopters to get him into other areas. When asked in 1988 how many Anasazi sites he had disturbed, he said he had lost count, but that it was probably in the thousands. He bragged that his chances of getting caught were one in a million. Shumway sold his artifacts to dealers, who peddled them in Europe, where a piece of art or a shank of an ancient civilization fetched its highest price.

In the American West, Shumway was long considered something of a nuisance, but little else. Despite the evidence against him, and his considerable bragging, prosecutors were reluctant to seek an indictment, saying it would be hard to get a conviction in rural Utah. He was a "pothunter," one of many, a term that makes its bearers sound no more harmful than a rancher or weekend hobbyist. To the Hopi, who have complained the most about the desecration of ancestral sites in Utah, Shumway was scum; they called him a "moki poacher"—someone who robs from the dead. Imagine if a thief were going through Arlington National Cemetery, they asked, digging up Civil War graves and selling off bits and pieces of the tombstones.

When Shumway was first convicted, in 1980, he was one of the first people ever fully prosecuted under the Archaeological Protection Act. He was fined $700 and put on probation. And, of course, he went right back to doing what he had always done, except that he became a full-time grave robber, instead of a mere hobbyist. Sometimes he earned $10,000 a day, he said. By the mid-1990s, the government went after him again, obtaining numerous indictments, and this time, putting him in jail for a sentence of more than twenty years. Among his final acts, he had stripped away funeral blankets from the bones of children and ripped open graves inside Canyonlands National Park.

"This is a devastating crime against our culture and our history," Wayne Dance, the United States Attorney for Utah, told me. The fact that he called it "our culture and our history" was telling, considering that much of the red rock country is named for the devil and that people like Shumway have long been paid to steal from it.

The poaching, chipping, and grave-robbing have gotten worse, the BLM agent in Escalante says. From Boy Scouts on organized camping trips to passers-through who don't know any better, everyone wants a piece of the past. But with every piece that is taken, every site that is touched, the chance to decipher the Anasazi mysteries slips further away. I feel a bit taken aback; all I want, I tell myself, is to feel the connection between artist and audience, to get the adrenaline rush of discovery.

"I shouldn't tell you this," says the BLM clerk. "But if you go in this general direction . . ."—she points to a place on a wall map—"you'll see some amazing things."

Car and Driver magazine did a recent survey to determine the most remote area in the United States outside of Alaska. The answer: the red rock country of southeastern Utah. It was the last place penetrated by the automobile, for obvious reasons. Putting a line of pavement over this stretch of rumpled rock would seem to be impossible. Much of the land is like the spiky spine of a dinosaur. In hues of rust and salmon are eroded benches, rib-caged cliffs, arches, bridges, plateaus, and canyons. The one paved road that was finally put in place, Highway 12, covers barely enough ground to fit a lane of traffic each way, in parts. I follow blinding hairpin turns, get swallowed by open chasms, and then rise again to ride the dinosaur's twisty spine. The town of Boulder is a few tumbledown ranches and not much else on one side of the highway. Population: 112. Next to Boulder are the ruins of another town, an Anasazi village abandoned about the year 1200. It had had perhaps two hundred people, judging by the foundation. I walk around the old village with Larry Davis, a state archaeologist; for twenty-five years he has been trying to understand this place.

"Reach your hand down on the ground and take a scoop of that dirt," he says.

I do so, bringing up a handful of dry sand and pebble pieces.

"Now, look at this . . ." He sorts through the scoop and finds a few small pieces, not pebbles at all, but bits of clay. When he blows on them, a small paint design is evident. The effect is electric, a touch with the ancients. "Those are pottery shards."

Every day he walks this ghost village, finding pieces of the larger puzzle. Some of them fit; most do not. He has the community outlined to a point where he can imagine what went on virtually every hour of the day.

"I'm not sure the locals see the beauty or the point of any of this," he says. "I've had people say to me, 'How much can you learn from the Anasazi?'"

A chilling wind has started to blow through the ruins. We are at nearly seven thousand feet, and I feel the slap of cold. "What can you learn? How to live. Mistakes to avoid. These people had quite a culture, and then they left in the thirteenth century. This area is not real fertile, but they made it work. And with good times, population increased. It got crowded, and then things went bad. They couldn't support themselves. The whole civilization crashed." Skeletal remains suggest that some Anasazi children died of malnutrition and pneumonia. The woods around some of the village are still denuded, all the timber cleared for firewood and building.

The exodus was supposed to be temporary, Davis believes. "A few years ago I went down into one of the canyons, where there was a real find. There was a doorway into a room full of stuff. Not a burial site. The doorway was sealed. It was obvious—these folks planned on coming back."

AT A high point on the road, I stop and look, because a sign says this is a place where you can see everything and nothing. The everything is a view of all the red rock country and beyond—the distant Henry Mountains, the Aquarius Plateau, and the Kaiparowits Plateau, where the Dutch-owned mining company wants to start trucking out coal night and day over the next quarter of a century. The nothing is just that, no signs of industrial intrusion, no roads or power lines, none of the brown air that gathers well to the north in the Salt Lake Valley. The plateau is atop a wall nearly fifty miles long, rising six hundred feet from below. In her essays Terry Tempest Williams is always talking about places in the West where you can "listen to the silence." The silence is loud at this promontory. The sign says the best view is at night, with Orion overhead and utter blackness everywhere else.

When Robert Leroy Parker and Harry Longabaugh—Butch Cassidy and the Sundance Kid—needed a place to hide after a string of bank robberies, down below is where they went, to Robbers Roost. And the point at which Robert Redford, the actor who played Sundance in the film, realized he loved Utah more than any state was when Robbers Roost was imperiled. The plan in 1970 was to run a string of coal-fired power plants across the red rock country, all the way to Montana. It would look like parts of the former Soviet Union, black and steely, clanking with noise, the purple soot obscuring the canyon views so that people could run air conditioners in Salt Lake City and Las Vegas. Redford stopped making movies for a while and devoted his time to keeping the coal-fired power plants out of the arid West. He was tarred, feathered, and burned in effigy in Kanab, a town that could be the future headquarters for the Dutch-owned mining company. After that plan failed, Senator Hatch introduced a bill to give most of the five hundred million acres of public land in the West to the states, counties, and private owners. Americans, apparently, were not to be trusted with their public land.

I drive an hour or so from the high vistas, away from the places the National Geographic Society visited, and go deeper into the canyons named for hell and the devil. I find a gulch where green water about ten feet wide and no more than three feet deep is loping downward, inevitably toward the Colorado. It seems perfect. The rare ribbons of water in the red rock country were major travel corridors, campsites, and playgrounds for the Anasazi. They loved to mark the walls of the life-giving arteries coursing through their land. I park and set out along a dirt and pebbled path bordering the creek. There are no campsites or picnic tables; somebody has removed the trailhead sign. The canyon bottom is stuffed with cottonwoods, willows, and cacti and is much warmer than the high ground above. I don't know where I'm going except to the next bend in the river. Light fills the ravine, sun reflecting off the water to the high sandstone walls. Growth-stunted pinyon pines have latched on to small sandholds of the rock. I'm looking for gold, my stake. And since Orrin Hatch's bill went nowhere, this land remains open and free to the wandering soul. The eye starts to see things: Is that a sketch of a hunt, or just another place where the rust bleeds out of the rock? Where is that little flute-playing hunchback with the hard-on?

The ancients would typically find a high, smooth surface of vertical stone covered with the dark brown patina known as desert varnish, a color that develops over centuries of oxidation of the rock's minerals. To create a typical petroglyph, a tool was used to scrape a lighter image into the varnish, which looks white in poor light. For pictographs, black from charcoal, red from hematite, and white from kaolin were ground into dust and mixed with oil from animals, plants, or urine. It binds and holds as well as the paint plaster of a frescoed church wall.

In the late afternoon, I'm sunburned and running low on water, but I feel like Humphrey Bogart in *Treasure of Sierra Madre*, wanting to push on, obsessed. Two women approach from the opposite direction. They, too, look pink and parched, but they have a postdiscovery glow about them.

"Keep going, another mile or so, and then start to look up," one of them says.

I don't really want this bit of intelligence; I'm trying to keep my discovery journey pure. But I drain them of details. Exactly how far up the canyon? Which rocks? How high up?

"There are some smaller glyphs at first. Just look at eye level along the rocks as you go," she says. "That's when you know you're getting closer. It's going to be a little hard to get up to the bigger ones."

"You might have to wade," her friend says.

"It's worth it."

Now my feet are wet, and my skin is raw from bug bites and sun. Blister my feet and let the deerflies have at me, the carnivorous little bastards. This is not cheap scenery. I don't care if I run out of water or have to live for days off the remains of a microwave enchilada from the Escalante mini-mart. By late afternoon, with perhaps an hour of light left in the canyon, I am starting to despair. I have seen some small, intriguing petroglyphs, as the hikers had said. But nothing else. I have struck out. I go into the river and dunk my head; it's a brisk, cleansing douse. My lightweight hiking shoes, which I treat like sandals, are a nag. The water squirts out of them as I walk; it's neither rhythmic nor comfortable.

The canyon gets wider and deeper, and there are more trees, older and thicker in the basin. Plenty of oaks, some very solid pines, and junipers. It's an oasis, green and blue. And above it, the rock could not be more polished if it had been quarried for Michelangelo, rising hundreds of feet straight up. The geologic lines, the colors from epochs of violence and fire, are clearly drawn, as are the horizontal markers from a time when the stream was much deeper. I gaze up a side canyon, and there I see something red, tall, and asymmetrical. But it looks as if it belongs.

Heart racing, I gallop across the stream and stumble toward the rock wall in the side canyon. I hurdle the seven-foot width of the smaller spring channel. I see it now, a wonderful, three-figured pictograph, as wide as a movie screen. It is enormous, multidimensional, and high above the canyon floor, fifty feet or more. The artist must have labored from a tall ladder for days in order to sketch the panel, for the river line is well below the picture. I take dozens of pictures, from myriad angles, moving as close as I can get to the very base of the wall. The pictograph is of three people, perhaps holding hands, but they are so tightly linked that they look welded to one another, as if forming a single living unit. They have somewhat triangular upper bodies—a common feature of the late Anasazi basketmaker period, around A.D. 600—and their shoulders are padded, well above the arm muscles. I cannot tell if they are men or women; they are without legs, their bodies cut off just above the knees, which makes them appear to be floating. Atop their heads are horns, or antennae, or some sort of headdress. The picture says Welcome, or if I were in a bad mood, Go away. Then I see something I'd missed up to this point: a suspended figure, many legs, no real chest, a head, just below the three humans. A shaman? A guard? A guide to another world? The entire pictograph leaves me without a clear sense of whether the artist was saying goodbye after five hundred years, with the humans following the suspended multilegged traveler, or signaling a new era.

All I know is what everyone else knows: these people flourished in a land that does not give up its resources easily. They may have been gluttons, overconsuming food, water, and wood, or they may been petty and warlike, the hungry bands raiding rival clans, which may explain the sudden move to protected cliff sites. But in the end, what they left behind were pictures such as this, and the possibility of chance encounters. They are magnificent, the native color of canyon red, and I stare at them until all the light is gone from the canyon.

MONTHS LATER, the President of the United States, Bill Clinton, declared the Escalante Canyons and Kaiparowits Plateau a national monument, setting aside 1.7 million acres for the ages. He tried to evoke Teddy Roosevelt, who protected the Grand Canyon as a national monument in 1908. T.R. had opened the twentieth century with a law to protect the past, the Antiquities Act, which he applied most effectively to America's natural heritage. For Roosevelt, the West was a salvation, not only for his body, as when it made a sickly boy strong, but for his heart, after he had just lost his wife and mother in a single day, a time when he said the light went out of his life. Clinton had no such touchstones to evoke at the ceremony, except the traditional argument of doing something for the future.

As in Roosevelt's time, when miners had plans to dig up both rims of the Grand Canyon, there were howls of outrage. The mining company said sixty-two billion tons of coal will now have to go untapped, locked up under the unvisited emptiness of the red rock country. Kanab lost the two hundred coal-mining jobs. Utah's leading politicians were incensed. "This is the mother of all land grabs," said Orrin Hatch, the senator who had once tried to take five hundred million acres out of the American public domain. Congressman James Hansen vowed to cripple the monument by depriving it of all funds.

There was one curious aspect of Clinton's speech. He had gone to the south rim of the Grand Canyon in Arizona to declare a national monument in Utah, several hundred miles to the north. It was as if he had gone to Boston to declare Broadway a Manhattan cultural treasure. T.R. went right into the pit of the battle and dared his critics to challenge his view that the canyon needed protection. Clinton chose the safety of a beloved national park, the place where most of the five million annual canyon visitors come for drive-by views of the great cataract.

Later, Hansen had a change of heart. He was still furious that the red rock country had been set aside as a national monument. But he had a new strategy on how to spite those who tried to protect it. Visits to Capitol Reef and Arches national parks, to the east of the Escalante wilderness, have quadrupled in the last decade. They, too, started out as national monuments. The "industrial tourism" that Edward Abbey feared has arrived, with waves of mountain-bikers competing with motorized three-wheelers to clamber over slickrock trails. In Moab, once a near-ghost-town after the uranium mining bust of the 1960s, a new hotel rose every month. And all over the Southwest, in restaurants and on T-shirts and iron grillwork, there appeared the likeness of Kokopelli, reborn in the commercial boom. Hansen now said he would try to fully fund the new monument and make damn sure that roads, trails, and visitor centers were planted throughout the open lands. In essence, he would try to ensure that the place was overrun— that the price of setting aside the red rock country was industrial tourism.

I knew then that if I were ever to return to the Escalante Canyons it would not be the same. I had had my random encounter, my rock art trophy. I felt like a hunter who had killed the last buffalo.

CHAPTER 6

Chaos or Cancer

Las Vegas, Nevada

Following the signs—"At Least Our Rain Forest Isn't Disappearing"—I found the Mirage. Traffic was backed up all the way to Utah. Parked in the lot a quarter of a mile away and schlepped a single bag to the heart of the most-visited place in the West: the Las Vegas Strip. On the escalator, a woman, coatless and deeply concerned, said it might rain—a felony in this city, yes? Behind a glass wall, a white lion was sleeping. I crossed through the rain forest, mist all around, an arboreal version of Muzak. Heard tropical birds, the sound of water breaking against stone, slot machines. Without compass, I navigated my way to the lobby. Behind the check-in counter was a two-story-high wall full of live fish, blinking back at the perpetual daylight of windowless and clockless Vegas. Guy in a purple jacket, from Roswell, New Mexico, called up my name on the computer. One of the fish was huge, the size of a car windshield, but sluggish, giving me the eye.

"A hundred and nine dollars a night. How did you get this rate, sir?"

"Why?"

"Just an hour ago these rooms were going for two-hundred-eighty-five a night."

"What happens if I wait another fifteen minutes?"

"I can't control the market, sir. You want to take a chance?"

"I'll take the rate. What kind of fish is that?"

"The big one?"

"Yeah."

"Something tropical."

The town is a mess, streets torn up, dust in the air so thick that the TV weatherbabe is advising small children and people with respiratory problems to stay indoors. And this is before the demolition crews have their way with the Sands Hotel. The latest Vegas thrill, blowing up big hotels that have outlived their theme, is the main-card draw for later in the week.

"You've got a view of The Strip, sir."

I had asked for a mountain view.

"When they blow up the Sands, you can see it from your window. We're expecting a quarter of a million people to watch it go down. Oh, and the fish . . ."

"Yes?"

"It's a grouper."

Found a ten-dollar blackjack table. Lost eighty bucks. Won back forty of it. Felt like Mark Twain when he arrived in Nevada. "We were stark mad with excitement—drunk with happiness—smothered under mountains of prospective wealth." Heard a factoid from a card dealer: a million dollars in twenty-dollar bills weighs 102 pounds. Decided to stay at fifteen when the dealer had a six and a two showing. He pulled a queen. Passed the white lion again, still asleep. Tried to visit the desert dolphins—closed. Went outside just in time to see the volcano explode, water the color of Dennis Rodman's hair spilling down the tiers of the faux mountain. A bigger tourist draw than the Grand Canyon. Walked up the Strip to New York, New York, the tugboats floating in the Hudson River out front, the Statue of Liberty half as tall as the one France gave America. Had a sidewalk bagel. Thought it strange that nobody told me to go fuck myself. Waited seven minutes for the light to change at Tropicana and Las Vegas Boulevard, the world's most congested corner. Walked inside the Golden Lion's mouth at the M-G-M Grand. Lost sixty bucks in a hotel with 5,005 rooms. Found the pool, with fake waves and sand. It seemed to have its own tide, not answering to gravitational pull. They don't have surfing, which is promised in the next fantasy hotel down the Strip.

Went to the world's fourth-largest pyramid and stared down the young sphinx out front, the Luxor Kid. Wondered if he would make it past the millennium, or suffer the fate of a slumping Vegas theme. Inside, saw the Nile River flowing through an atrium that could hold nine Boeing 747s stacked one atop the other. Lost twenty bucks. Had two drinks—Jack-on-the-rocks. Free. Wandered back to the Mirage, thirsty. In the lobby store, I paid four dollars for a liter of water.

THE Mojave Desert is the hottest place on Earth. Once, the National Park Service recorded a ground-level temperature of 201 degrees; the air can reach 134 degrees, though 120 is more typical in summer. People still die of stupidity while walking around cracked ground that looks like the Earth turned inside out, feeling their skin start to sting, the brain swell, unable to sweat. A dog left in a car parked at Circus Circus in July would last maybe fifteen minutes. A desert tortoise can go longer, living off a cup of water in its bladder for days without a drink. Since air conditioning, dogs have proliferated; the tortoises are nearly gone.

When it rains in the Mojave, it sometimes kills people. They get stuck in a wash that looks no more dangerous than a jogging path at Desert View Heights in the morning, but turns into a river strong enough to move boulders during an afternoon thunderstorm. Or they drown in the casino parking lots, as happened to several people during a rainstorm in 1992.

From the basement of Death Valley, at 282 feet below sea level, to the ice roof of Mount Charleston, 11,918 feet above, the Mojave is fifty thousand square miles of the quirkiest land on the planet. This is creation with a hangover and cottonmouth. The entire object of a roadrunner's life is to try to catch bugs in a thermal furnace without breaking a sweat. A kangaroo rat needs no water; it produces it metabolically through digestion of seeds. One of the Indian names for the desert was Tomesha—Ground Afire. General Patton's soldiers, training here to fight Germans in North Africa, had their own name for the Mojave—God Forgot. Joshua trees grow in the Mojave and nowhere else. They need at least six inches of annual rain to survive, so they hug the higher slopes of the desert, waving those signature arms like referees at a Raiders game. The Mormons, confused but at their allusive best, named the trees for the Prophet Joshua, who was pointing the way. To what, though?

Until a few decades ago, only a handful of people lived in the Mojave, trying to coexist with the various curiosities of dry-country evolution.

There was an inland sea here, then a tropical forest, then a lot of tumult and violence. The plates rubbed and scraped, the crust broke, and from the gastric core of the Earth came the mountains of the southern Sierra. Westerly moisture from the Pacific stopped dead in its tracks at the new wall, and on the other side, life without rain—the Mojave. In some places, zero inches a year; rain is a rumor. And when it does fall, it evaporates before it lands. In Las Vegas Valley, in a good year, four inches of rain. Other years, a single inch. The mountains always held some snow, and that which didn't evaporate trickled through the crushed rock and ran deep, to an underground river. Some of this water came to the surface, reliable and clean, in a small oasis in the middle of Las Vegas Valley. Las Vegas, in Spanish, means "The Meadows."

The Paiutes knew about it. In the summer, they lived in the mountains, seeking the natural air conditioning of high elevation. In the winter, they came down to the valley, to the dash of willows and greasewoods thriving around three large artesian springs. The Paiutes collected mesquite beans and ground them into a pulpy flour for bread. Willows made perfect baskets. And the floor of the desert was full of jackrabbits, grouse, snakes, and other forms of portable protein. Their rock art was not quite neon, but it was lively, with a lot of eternity spirals and animated clan figures, particularly in the western Mojave. An American army lieutenant, floating down the Colorado River in 1855, paused not far from the Las Vegas Valley to offer a snub for posterity. "Ours was the first and will doubtless be the last party of whites to visit this profitless locale," wrote Joseph Christmas Ives.

But profit was the founding idea of Las Vegas. Even as Lieutenant Ives wrote, the Mormons were trying to plant a flag of the sovereign empire of Deseret in the Mojave. They viewed the valley springs as a place where they could gouge travelers moving along the Spanish Trail from the Rockies to Southern California—something that the Saints had perfected in Salt Lake. In 1855, Brigham Young sent thirty colonists to the artesian springs in the middle of the desert, ordering them to build a fort, control the water, and try to extract lead from the mountains. They constructed a shack outpost on a perch overlooking the valley, cutting mesquite trees for fences, and diverting water for irrigation. But the soil was hard and alkaline, and no amount of mountain water could bring a sufficient amount of crops to life in Las Vegas. What's more, a monopoly on the springs proved difficult. The Paiutes still used it. And the flow was strong enough out of the ground that it could not be easily contained in one place.

Young was told that Vegas was no place for human habitation, that a biosphere of Saints would not take root in the hottest place in the land. A day trip was like an expedition outside a spacecraft; life-support systems had to be in tow. And the Mormons suffered from the same thing that people at the scientific base at Antarctica go through today—the malady brought on by lack of green. So after three years, the colonists folded their sun-cracked settlement, a rare failure for Brigham Young, and Las Vegas returned to a few bands of Paiutes.

What brought the place back to life was a melding of technology and sleaze. First came the railroads, inspired by the same idea that had led Young to think some profit could be made from a desert oasis in the middle of a well-traveled trail. The tracks of the San Pedro, Los Angeles and Salt Lake Railroad went right through the Mojave. But the railroad still needed a place for the steam trains to be restocked with water. The three artesian springs of Las Vegas proved ideal. This came about by design, and some graft, courtesy of William A. Clark, the Copper King and one-term senator from Montana. He was a Las Vegas founding father no less worthy than the first mobster, Bugsy Siegel, but far more corrupt. The senator purchased eighteen hundred acres in the valley for himself, arranged for the train depot that would boost land prices, and then bought water rights to the three artesian springs. Shortly after the twentieth century began, Lombardy poplars, alfalfa, and fruit trees were growing in the old Paiute winter home. Clark had proved Lieutenant Ives and Brigham Young wrong: you can bend the desert to your will. The West, after all, is about possibility.

Clark County, the most populous in Nevada, is named for a man who tried for twelve years to buy a Senate seat. He finally succeeded only after handing out bribes to legislators; the money was pressed, in W.A.C.-monogrammed envelopes stuffed with thousand-dollar bills, into the palms of citizen legislators empowered to elect a senator. "I never bought a man who wasn't for sale," Clark said. Today, one shudders to see the oxymoron etched in stone outside official county buildings: Clark and Justice in the same line.

The first well, going more than five hundred feet deep, was dug in 1907. And not long after that, a two-mile-long redwood tunnel was built to channel water from the artesian springs to a dusty town-site. Just to demonstrate how rich they were in the very thing that was said to be denied them, early Vegas inhabitants let the water run all day, gushing out of the ground and trickling away into the desert. Pictures show bearded, sun-hardened men standing next to open spigots, laughing. Can't live in the middle of the

Mojave—hah! From its very start, Las Vegas used more water per person than any other town in America.

The mass sleaze came about by design as well. When the little grid of Las Vegas was sketched near the train depot, the idea was anything but the classic Jeffersonian town model, which called for parcels to be set aside for a college and parks. Vegas was drawn, in 1905, as a shakedown train stop where different kinds of thirsts could be slaked. One section of town, Block 16, was given to whores and saloons—a pioneering resource that has left its mark. Today, prostitution is legal in the Pahrump Valley, north of Vegas, and nearly 5 percent of the women who work in America's fastest-growing city are employed in the sex trade. Block 16 was an instant hit, with many a multiple-story building, while the rest of the town withered.

By the 1930s, the entire state of Nevada had only ninety thousand people, most living around Lake Tahoe in the north. Las Vegas did not have a paved road until 1925, when barely three thousand people lived there. Then Nevada decided, as a Depression-era gamble, to attract moral outcasts, drifters, and losers—at least those who weren't already in the state trying to scratch something from the played-out gold and silver mines. Before the drive-by method was perfected, getting a divorce took some effort. Nevada made it easy. Anybody willing to spend six weeks in the Silver State could be declared a legal resident for the purpose of separating from a spouse. But during those six weeks stuck in Nevada, a moral outcast needed something to do. And why not spend the time giving up what money would be left over from the divorce? So the state legalized casino gambling as well. The Mormons were on to something with their vision of Vegas as a place to soak travelers; they simply didn't have the right plan.

Bugsy Siegel is said to be the great modern pioneer of Vegas, seeing the desert pit stop as a place that could be glossed up and made classy, a town where every lunch-bucket lug could be a Monte Carlo cad for a night. His Las Vegas took hold in 1946, at the fabulous Flamingo, away from the honky-tonk dives around Fremont Street and Block 16. His Las Vegas was women in sequined gowns and blackjack dealers who called you sir. But it was Howard Hughes who took it corporate, showing the way for future junk-bond financiers, theme-park tycoons, and insta-home fantasists. Hughes arrived in 1966, via a midnight ambulance to the Desert Inn. He stayed for just short of a decade, buying hotel properties from the Mob. It was a great spot for a wacked-out billionaire, a state with no corporate or personal income tax, and a local government that needed mere spill from a table to see the way to civic enlightenment. The Strip grew from Mojave dust. The Sands, the Aladdin, the Dunes, the Desert Inn, the Frontier, Caesars Palace, followed by a new airport, a convention center—all of it just west of the old town by the train depot. And, more important for the new powers in town, all of it was outside the city limits. They were free to build the ultimate Western city, the boomtown that never went bust, the something-for-nothing metropolis that blew itself up every few years, the land that welcomed people without a past because it would never have a past.

The other Vegas legacy of Howard Hughes was Summerlin, a walled enclave of pumped-up homes northwest of the Strip, twenty-six thousand acres, all of it sealed from the world of random encounters. Summerlin will approach 200,000 people soon, a development where everything from climate to house colors is strictly regulated. When Hughes finally left, he departed Las Vegas as he had arrived, under cover of darkness. In nine years, the drapes of his suite were never opened.

The town had its first serious water shortage in the late 1940s. For a time, no water flowed from faucets at Las Vegas Hospital. People panicked. Even lawn-watering was banned. But this could not stand. "Whiskey is for drinking," Mark Twain said about the West. "Water is for fighting over." Las Vegas dipped a straw into Lake Mead, the reservoir created by Hoover Dam, the water that buried Paiute ruins and a stone-walled Mormon fort, and the good times rolled again. Water use shot up to eight hundred gallons a person per day—four times as much as Los Angeles. Some elite architects, Robert Venturi among them, pronounced the city fabulous. It was anything goes, alive, electric, original, American! It was the frontier of urbanism. Forget those prune-faced Puritans and their miserable City on a Hill. Forget Wallace Stegner's civilization to match the setting. Forget Edward Abbey's apocalyptic fear of a bloated urban monster rising in the desert, a cancer of melanomas. Here was the new century city dream. Lakes were created on alkaline flats. Rivers ran through neighborhoods built on sand. The rain forest grew in the Mirage. By the early 1990s, a new home—red-roof tiled, with white stucco coat and a rug of Kentucky bluegrass out back—was rising every hour.

The population doubled in ten years, until more than a million people lived in the valley. They pushed out toward the Spring Mountains one way and Lake Mead the other, with inflatable neighborhoods named Mariners Cove, Harbour Vista, Green Valley, Desert Creek, Shoreline Estates. The lords of such estates swam in artificial lakes and lounged on artificial lawns. The murder rate rose to the highest in the West—increasing while the rest of the country's violent crime statistics were going down—but most newcomers were safely ensconced in communities that were "gated and guarded," as the signs said. And a brown cloud took up residence over the valley, giving Las Vegas the worst air in America outside Los Angeles and Phoenix. But in the desert who wants to go outside anyway? They laughed at Howard Hughes in his hermetically sealed room, growing his nails until they curled over his hands like wax from a dripping candle, living in a home devoid of daylight or contact with any human other than a heavily screened sycophant. But they flocked to the neighborhoods built to match his neuroses.

Could this, the West's gift to city-building, be the height of American urban evolution? the Stegner vision unfettered by anything but market forces, a million and a half people living in a place not unlike a poorly planned lunar colony? It was not a city to match the setting, but a city to defy the setting.

As long as the Colorado River poured through turbines at Hoover Dam, there would be enough electricity to keep Vegas at seventy-two degrees, year-round. And as long as the pumps drew from the deepest cellar of the Mojave and the tub behind sixty stories of concrete at Hoover Dam, there would be enough water to create the rain forest in Nevada. So, why worry? Unlike Arizona, which requires developers to show proof of a hundred-year water supply before they can go ahead with a project, Nevada has no such restrictions. You want water? Promise it to people fleeing the exurbs of Southern California, and the city will deliver, somehow. Anything to keep the one-house-per-hour construction train moving on time, to keep the Hudson River knockoff in front of the Statue of Liberty knockoff flowing, to keep the Nile inside the Luxor moving, to keep Mariners Cove from looking like the desert. The underground reservoir that gave birth to the artesian oasis was pumped for every precious drop, and any gallon that could legally be taken from the Colorado River was used. Steve Wynn built his boiling waterfall in front of the Mirage and then went one better next door, at Treasure Island, creating a Caribbean moat. Then he blew up the Dunes for Bellagio, named for the most beautiful small town in all of Europe, on the shores of Lake Como. "If you want to make money in a casino," Wynn said, "own one." Down the Strip, Paris started to rise, the City of Light without rude waiters or bidets in every room. And in place of the Sands would be the biggest hydro-dream, a $2-billion knockoff of Venice—the city of canals.

As a fantasy, it is all wonderful, a great escape. What's not to like? A virtual world within a few square miles. Like me, more than thirty million people a year are following the signs—At Least Our Rainforest Isn't Disappearing. But in order to build Venice and Paris, more of the Colorado needs to be brought to Vegas. Or the Virgin River needs to be dammed, drying up part of Zion National Park. Or the basins of northern Nevada, watering holes for elk, cattle, and people, need to be siphoned to Clark County. Otherwise, Las Vegas is approaching something that nobody in this town ever wants to face: an adult saying no.

BACK AT the Mirage, the dolphins are still under lock. Tank trouble, I'm told. The rainforest hasn't disappeared. Saw a guy in hip-waders trying to prune a philodendron. The Fever has started to take hold. Not gambling. I'm trying to keep that at a low simmer, dropping no more than fifty bucks a pop during the long, forced stroll through the casino to the elevator. The heat is over the impending collapse of the Sands. In a few days, it will be gone, imploded, 1950s gin-and-tonic America at its leisure height, reduced to dust. There's a buzz on the streets and inside the gambling pits. When they pulverize that great block of Vegas antiquity—a hotel not quite fifty years old—it will be the largest non-nuclear explosion in Nevada history, I'm told.

PATRICIA MULROY may be the most powerful person in Las Vegas, a public servant at that. The mayor, Jan Laverty Jones, a former TV pitchwoman for a car dealership, has no power; but she looks really good on television. Mulroy, on the other hand, is head of the Southern Nevada Water Authority. She can move rivers, keep cities alive, make other states tremble, destroy farms, eliminate entire species. The power is almost biblical, that sense of controlling creation. Los Angeles had William Mulholland, the Irish immigrant in top hat, watch fob, and three-piece suit, for the job of creating a modern city out of a semidesert. Vegas has a woman in purple lipstick, who talks tough, can charm when she wants to, but remains as focused as a raven on roadkill.

By deliberate contrivance, Las Vegas today is doing exactly what Los Angeles did a century ago, when it grew from 50,000 people in 1890 to 200,000 in 1904. Its orange blossom allure, neo-Spanish romanticism, and freewheeling moral climate, stoked by railroad migration pamphleteers, were in peril by the turn of the century. Los Angeles, the city that might have taken shape within the natural constraints of the basin, would have topped out at perhaps 100,000 people, Mulholland warned. At his urging, voters in the Southland passed the largest bond issue in the history of the United States at the time—$23 million—to create an aqueduct from the Owens Valley, through the Mojave desert, uphill through the Tehachapi Mountains, and then downhill to the San Fernando Valley and soon-to-be-spreading mass of L.A. "The Owens River is ours," the *Los Angeles Times* editorialized, not long after a group of investors had conned a small group of alfalfa farmers and fruit orchardists into selling their water rights for a song. "Our business now is to hustle and bring it here and make Los Angeles the garden spot of the earth and home of millions of contented people."

Contented no more, Angelenos have been pouring into Las Vegas, into Mariners Cove and Harbour Vista and The Lakes (with its ten miles of artificial shoreline), to try to make another Garden Spot amidst the cracked earth. Mulholland's engineering miracle was so bravura—fifty-three tunnels bored into the mountains, five hundred miles of roads, a construction crew of six thousand men—that the aqueduct that drained the Owens Valley to make Eden in Los Angeles should have lasted more than a century. But water brought subdivisions in place of orange groves, and that brought rivers of backed-up cars over plains of asphalt, which brought wretched air that killed people who came to Southern California for their health. So, they are repeating the entire cycle all over again, only the arc from birth to boom to urban suffocation is much quicker this time. By the end of the twentieth century, Los Angeles was not only the metaphor for a Western city gone bad, but its residents were forced to lose the bluegrass lawns, and accept a civic routine of dodging the low-flow shower police. It is Pat Mulroy's job to make sure that Vegas will at least have no limits on lawn-watering as it slips into decline.

I find her in a backlot of her agency, where water is bursting out of open hydrants, a virtual hydro-show on the pavement of the parking lot in the midday heat. Muscled, shirtless utility men are wrestling with hoses. The water czar has been supervising water games with the crews; they say it's a drill to learn how to turn a gusher off fast. In the time I watch her, a good-size Vegas lake trickles off the pavement and into the sand.

"It's nothing," says Mulroy. "More water evaporates on the way to Phoenix in their canal than we need to keep growing."

"Growing" is the key word. Seven states share the Colorado, but only one is on steroids. And only one has reached the legal limit of how much water it can take from the river. And only one has virtually no restrictions on future use. And only one gives you the Nile and the Hudson (and soon, Venice) in a state with but a single year-round river, the Humboldt, up north, that originates inside its borders. Even Arizona, where the developers have long run wild, uses water at only half the rate of most people in Nevada, which is to say, the Las Vegas metro area.

"These casinos with their water attractions, they use recycled shower water," she says. "They're good conservers of water. It's lawn-watering that's our problem. People like green grass in the desert."

In the other Colorado River states, Mulroy is sometimes referred to as "The Water Witch of the West." They don't call her that in Vegas, of course. I would not be surprised if some casino put her image on an ornamental gate. Essentially, she is holding a great swath of the Southwest hostage until Las Vegas gets what it wants. One bit of leverage is the Virgin River, architect of some of the most stunning canyon country in the West, bringing bits of green and pools of clear water as it snakes through Zion National Park in Utah. But as it makes its way to the Colorado, the Virgin takes a little bend into the state of Nevada. As soon as the river slips into Nevada, it is at risk. Mulroy reasons that the water authority should be able to dam the Virgin—their river—and take from it what it will. But without the hurried flow of the Virgin, Zion National Park would be left to feed on broth. Its color and character and muscularity would change. There would be no sandy beaches from spring floods, no polished sandstone in the lower valleys, no aspens. Mulroy knows that this option horrifies many people—choking off one of the world's premier national parks to keep faux lakes going up in gated subdivisions of Vegas. And she would face ecoterrorists rising from their yeast farms if she ever tried such a thing. But it's a good card that she holds tight, keeping everyone guessing.

Another option lies to the north, in the basins where real pine trees grow in real Nevada national forests. One range of mountains after the other—the Snakes, the Egans, the Pancakes, the Hot Creeks, the Monitors, the Toquimas, the Toiyabes, the Shoshones, the Desatoyas, the Clan Alpines, the Stillwaters—marches from Utah to the California border. These are big peaks, scraping the sky at better than ten thousand feet in most places. They gather a good knitting of snow, which trickles down into the valleys, then melts into the aquifers. Some of it comes back up as springs—seeps of clear water—which is why there are so many elk, bighorn sheep, deer, and mountain lions prancing around central Nevada, even though there is not a single decent river. Las Vegas has filed plans to do to the basin and range country of the central part of the state what it did to the old Paiute watering holes. They want to drain the groundwater that brings life to a huge part of the state and, through a series of pipes and aquifers, channel it all down to a place that epitomizes what most of the world would be doing on Saturday night if the Nazis had won the war, to paraphrase Hunter Thompson.

Up north, in the dying little towns in the Great Basin, they have no idea how to fight Las Vegas. Nye County, the biggest in the area, is a hothouse of cranks waging a tired sagebrush rebellion by fax and talk radio. Dick Carver, a county commissioner, is their leader. He took a bulldozer out, with a pistol strapped to his leg and a copy of the Constitution stuffed in his shirt pocket, and told the Forest Service to let him plow open a road into a wilderness, or else face the consequences. That act landed him on the cover of *Time* ("The Angry West!"). He got a bad sunburn posing for the picture, seven hours of staring into the sun. It made him look even angrier. He lives in the Big Smoky Valley, a basin that would become the Big Worthless Cracked Desert Floor if Las Vegas gets hold of its groundwater. The largest town in Nye County is Tonopah, which was *the* boomtown at the start of the twentieth century, gold dust on the streets. Now it is sandpaper-beige and listing to one side. Tonopah looks about a half step short of the grave, huddled against the wind, buildings shuttered and haunting. It resembles the little town that Clint Eastwood toyed with in *High Plains Drifter,* finally torching the place after proving the moral hypocrisy of its citizens. What chance does Tonopah, preoccupied with its media war with Washington, have against Pat Mulroy?

As Edward Abbey said, there is no lack of water in the Mojave Desert unless you try to establish a city where no city should be. Tonopah, in its final days, is what Las Vegas might look like if it hadn't tapped into the great vein of the Colorado. There is no overwhelming need for whatever minerals can still be forced from deep under Tonopah's ripped-up hide. But everybody wants what Vegas has—lights, fantasy, the Fever, and all you can eat for $8.95.

Las Vegas will not put the bullet in Tonopah's head or dam the Virgin River, if it gets the third option. That is to redo the Colorado River Compact—the Law of the River, a pact that governs how every drop of the river will be used. To be fair, Nevada got shortchanged in the 1920s, when the law was drawn up, because nobody then lived there. Now, Nevada is home to America's fastest-growing city, doing for vice what Detroit did for automobiles; and it is desperately thirsty. All it wants is another fifty years of water.

The plan: Take some of that Colorado River flow from California (which has got too much as it is!). And borrow a little from Arizona (they're not using it all). And then, the canals of Venice can be filled on land where the Sands used to stand. And there will be bluegrass—which needs about forty inches of rain annually—for all. Without a change in how the Colorado is divvied up, Vegas will brown, wilt, and blow away, Mulroy says. A big Tonopah. But, couldn't Las Vegas learn to love the desert, as Tucson has done, using a third as much water as Vegas does, losing the lawns in favor of cactus and paloverde? Or couldn't it say no to a housing subdivision or two?

"If you tried to slow growth around here, you'd have chaos," says Mulroy. "You can't expect that this community, all these new people and all these *babies* and all these *families,* are going to just go away."

So if Vegas is in fact the living embodiment of Abbey's memorable crack—"Growth for the sake of growth is the ideology of the cancer cell"—then the choice is clear. Chaos or cancer.

"A resort community like ours, we don't have any choice but to keep growing," says Richard Bunker. He is head of the Nevada Resort Association, and, donning his civic hat, is vice chairman of the Colorado River Commission of Nevada. Bunker is a rare person in the Mojave Desert: a native. As a kid, he went on camping trips to the very spot where the Sahara now stands on the Strip. At sixty-three, he has seen Vegas morph from a sand-lashed train depot to the Arnold Schwarzenegger of cities. He works out of a new office off Howard Hughes Parkway. Inside, a perpetual mist keeps a little bit of the rain forest growing on the ground floor.

He refers to Vegas as "a product," never as a city. "You have to continuously reinvent the product, or people will stop coming here," he says. "But right now, we're quite healthy. There's no corporate income tax, no inventory tax, no state income tax—people love to come here."

He mentions the brown cloud, a recent arrival. On this day, it looks purple. "You just gotta stay indoors on some days," he says. "But look, water is the key to everything. If we don't have water, we suffocate. So we go to the courts and present our dilemma as water for people versus water just being wasted downstream."

While the other states balk and watch in horror, Vegas is leaving nothing to chance. About twenty-five miles from the city, a mechanical mole is at work, digging a fifteen-foot-wide tunnel from Lake Mead to the city, a $2-billion dare. Mulroy says this underground Suez is just an upgrade, for the time being. But that is like building a domed stadium to fix a leaky cabin roof. Nobody in any of the neighbor states is fooled. If Vegas builds it, water will follow, one way or the other.

"**TEN**! Nine! Eight! Seven! Six! . . ."

Got a few slugs of tequila inside of me and a full Vegas buffet festering. The Mirage is quite culturally sensitive, in addition to being a home for orphaned dolphins, white tigers, and rainforest plants that wouldn't survive without recycled shower water. Its breakfast buffet has a Jewish section, whole mountains of gefilte fish and lox next to the usual heart-stopping fare. I passed, waiting for the dinner, a Sands-implosion special buffet—and then I ate too much prime rib. Outside, the streets are jammed, though people are kept a proper lawsuit-avoidance distance from the big event. We are witnessing the execution of a great institution in the predawn darkness; it is enough, for now, to shake many of us out of the catatonia that comes from being in a city with 115,000 slot machines. The Rat Pack nested there at the Sands, Dino, Frank, Sammy, and broads who could hold their liquor and knew how to dance in stiletto heels. "Tell me quick. Ain't love a kick in the head," Dean Martin sang. Showbiz royalty packed the place. It was Monte Carlo without forced theme. Its day is gone. In another ten years, perhaps, there will be a faux Sands Hotel, built on a 1950s Rat Pack theme, rising somewhere on the edge of the Mojave.

"Five! Four! Three! . . ."

Dynamite has been strategically placed up and down the sides of the Sands, along its burnt-red-and-white exterior, and inside the main support beams. The old neon cursive—The Sands—has but a few seconds left. An army of video cameras is aimed at the hotel. For Vegas residents, these executions are wearing thin. The noise, the dust, the muscle-popping din of the City on Steroids trying to remake itself at all hours is too much. People may be trying to sleep in Mariners Cove, but there is little they can do, because The Strip, by design, is outside the city limits. And by its very nature, it has to shoot its old and infirm, and constantly cannibalize the past to stay alive. They sutured New York, New York, ancient Egypt, Caesar's Rome, and medieval Europe to a hardtack of clay, and all around them, in the cloisters where people go to sleep at 10 P.M., and school and work in the morning, they are creating the Los Angeles of *Blade Runner.* The lament most often heard from old-timers in Vegas is this: the streets were safer when the Mob ran the town.

"Two! One! Bring it down, baby!"

A symmetrical blast. Smoke plumes on the side. The Sands lets out a whimper and crumbles in a wheeze. The crowd roars. Yes-s-s! A ripple of high fives. Awesome! A cloud of white dust rises and disappears into the darkness, spreading to Harbour Vista and The Lakes and beyond to ground not yet turned to bluegrass because the water has yet to arrive. Back at the Mirage, I'm dropping quarters into a slot. The lights atop the machine go off. A woman comes around and peels off three hundred-dollar bills. I'm delirious. You *can* get something for nothing, and Venice can rise in a land without water. Put a $2-billion straw in the Colorado and Vegas will respond like a man at the all-you-can-eat buffet; you consume until you're sick. The dismembered corpse of the Sands is visible across the street: a thirty-foot pile of rubble. Clean it up and bring in the canals. From The Strip, the lights of the tallest building west of the Mississippi, the Stratosphere, are straining for attention. It is one of the newest skyscrapers in America, 1,149 feet above the desert floor, but already it seems doomed. Nobody goes there, perhaps because it is in the old funky Western part of town, the place that gave birth to Block 16 and the big neon cowboy and the Golden Nugget. Vegas started as a cowboy fantasy retreat. You roll into town, lose a week's pay, get drunk, get laid, and get out with a few stories to tell the boys back at the ranch. Now, it's the American Vatican for Vice, requiring grand ritual and show for pilgrims dressed like six-year-olds. So how long does the Stratosphere have until it too will be shot in the darkness before dawn?

FROM THE Kelso Dunes, I can see much better. This is the desert without illusion. Or I should say, the desert with clarity, which brings with it its own illusions. Dry air, following a wind, late in the day—the windows are clean. Done with Vegas, I wanted to make contact with the Mojave. So I went west, past Stateline, into California and then took a left at a 134-foot-high thermometer outside Bun Boy in the town of Baker. From there, south into the Mojave National Preserve, the world grew silent and open. I turned off the radio, because it seemed a trivial distraction. Using an old BLM map, I found a washboard road and followed it to the Kelso Dunes. I went as far as I could go. Then I walked across dry grass and sand, and hiked up the dunes, seven hundred feet to the top. With each step, my feet sank, as if I were walking through fresh snow, and with each step, a little bit of Vegas excess, of free drinks and three-thousand-calorie buffets, was forced out of me. The winds constantly rearranged the sand, sifting and cleaning it.

At the top, I watched the evening light bring to life the highest flanks of the vertical desert; in some places, the exposed layers formed a near-complete record of Earth's past, all the melting and molding, the spill of iron and hardening of granite, the earthquake cracks and sun-colored sides. Then it was gone, and there was a twilight of mystery and strange sounds, the Mojave freaks coming out at night. In the darkness, I thought of Twain's remarks at the end of his adventure in Nevada. He went bust in the mines, gagged on the water—"like drinking lye, bitter and in every way execrable"—laughed at his own greed, got drunk and silly with people he had nearly killed a few days earlier, and then cozied up to the desert just before he left. Sitting around a campfire at night, naked to the outdoors, was for Twain, "the very summit and culmination of earthly luxury."

The purity of night in the Mojave Preserve is marred only by the throbbing light well off to the east—the pulse of Vegas, growing by the hour. Las Vegas needs more water not just to stay alive but to preserve its life-sustaining illusion. They seek it for the same reason Ponce de Leon went after the Fountain of Youth in Florida. The city will likely gets its water, and then will continue to spread and fatten for another twenty years, maybe even fifty, but then Vegas will consume itself. It will need to be bailed out by the federal government and protected by the National Guard. Give it another hundred years and it may well join Crackerjack, Skidoo, Calico, and other ghost towns of the Mojave. Another five hundred years and some archaeologists will be puzzling over the site of the Sands, a ruin no less intriguing than Mesa Verde.

Abbey's cancer is already happening. And, in a sign that the end may truly be near, the casino magnate Steve Wynn has started to warn that something terribly wrong is happening in the fantasy city he helped to create. He says it is time to "slow down and think about what we're doing." These words—slow down, think—usually get checked at the Vegas airport. At Lake Mead, just a few miles from where the city draws its water, there are fish with twisted spines and mutated genes. The males have female egg protein in their blood plasma, making them unable to reproduce. If human embryos followed a similiar pattern, extinction could be around the corner. Biologists theorize that the fish took in too much of the liquid waste of Las Vegas. In all their plumbing and engineering, the water czars made one monumental error. As it turns out, the people of this most daring of American cities draw their drinking water just six miles from the same spot where they dump their waste, a stream of barely treated effluents that are particularly heavy with pesticides from hotels trying to make sure that not a single mosquito visits the Strip. The Paiutes never drank from the same place where they buried their poisons. Nor did the Mormons. But of course, they never thought you could put a million and a half people in the middle of an unwatered desert.

CHAPTER 7

The Empire of Clean

St. George, Utah

> This was a fairyland to us, for all intents and purposes—a
> land of enchantment and awful mystery.
>
> —Mark Twain,
> *Roughing It*

In the Beehive State of Utah, nearly every town, church, and family of any standing keeps a record, a daily diary of the Mormon Dream. Typically, it is a ledger of life on two levels—one long on struggle and triumph, the story of the creation of Zion in the American West, the other more spiritual but no less detailed. They know in Orderville exactly who was hungry in 1912 and who committed adultery in 1956, but they also know whether somebody's ancestor from the fifteenth century has been given a valid passport to eternal life. Every wagon train drama, every horrific entry from the epic, killing mistake of the handcart migration, every basketball championship over the Italian kids in Carbon County, is written down, somewhere. No state has more keepers of history, or better archives, honeycombed in climate-controlled vaults, than Utah.

Some may see this as vanity, the written ornaments for what was to have been a great sovereign nation, the divinely inspired dictatorship of Deseret, taking up nearly a third of the West. Buffing for posterity, with perhaps only a slight bit more self-indulgence than other people, is certainly part of it. But the greater purpose transcends group chauvinism. For most of these histories will serve ultimately as a guide to the guest list of the hereafter. Life deeds count. Having good descendants is even better. Postmortem sealing in the Temple has brought more dead people into the circle of the eternally redeemed than living. Because there is so much at stake, Mormons have made a workaday craftsmanship of keeping the past alive. There is a record, the Saints like to say, of everything.

But while this system may work fine for heaven, it could still prompt a crisis in this world. Mormonism, the onetime cult, the founding idea of a radical state, is now the fastest-growing religion in America. The church sends out forty thousand missionaries a year. Utah, host of the 2002 Winter Olympics, has stepped onto the world stage. Come see what we have created in the Great Basin, they say with pride. Look at the industry, the cities, the model communities. Utah is American life lite, without cynicism or corruption, producing more babies per capita and healthier adults than any other state. Smoke-free and nonalcoholic were part of the Mormon canon long before they became the stuff of presidential initiatives. The Empire of Clean presents itself as the polar opposite of the other desert dynasty, Las Vegas. This is never more clear than at the Utah/Nevada border at Wendover, where half the town is given over to neon smiles, gambling warehouses, and homes with curtains shut for midday sleepers, and the other half is buzzing with industry and commerce the old-fashioned way, the tallest building in town being the Latter Day Saints' church. The two town councils, sharing the only road through town, despise each other so much they often refuse to meet.

What keeps so many Saints whistling through the years is a group narrative that goes like this: persecuted religion flees to the West, establishes a sanctuary in the desert, blooms and prospers to become the envy of the world. All true, in a broad sense. But what is typically forgotten is the stories about how Mormonism, the most homegrown of American religions, was for a long time at odds with the most basic of American ideals. So for all the surface cheer and the overt displays of history, no state may be more afraid of its past than Utah.

Throughout the West, other communities have come to terms with things their Rotary clubs may never discuss. Pancho Villa's guerrilla war in

1916—the last invasion of the United States—and the illegal expedition by General Pershing to try to capture him in Mexico, keep dozens of people on payrolls from El Paso to Tombstone. The mass murders of striking miners by Pinkerton mercenaries under cover of martial law is museum, trinket, and tour fodder in Idaho's Silver Valley. And San Francisco long ago turned much of its waterfront over to a theme built around syphilitic old salts, profiteering gold-rush merchants, and whores with soft hearts—the Barbary Coast, possibly the most unhealthy time ever to live in the City by the Bay. Utah is going in the opposite direction, cleaning out the unwanted parts of its history. In Temple Square, octogenarian leaders of the church worry that a letter or note may still turn up, making Brigham Young look more like Charles Manson than Charlton Heston. And above town, the old abandoned fort on a bench overlooking Salt Lake, a favorite spot for sunset strolls, remains as a squat, intractable reminder of a war that very few Americans have ever heard of, the war against the man whose statue is everywhere in this state, the leader of the only true American theocracy ever to get beyond the fledgling state. In a clear-eyed view of the West, the Mormons are one of the main reasons why this part of the world is so full of wonder, and shame.

THE Mountain Meadows had yet to green up on the spring day when I went up to Dan Sill Hill to look out over the most blood-soaked piece of ground in Utah. The valley is farmed for hay, grazed by cattle and horses during certain months, and is well-watered during the runoff, when snow from the northern reaches of Dixie National Forest joins up with springs to bring life to the lower elevations. A few shade trees and windbreaks have been planted. Otherwise, it is bare and empty. The people in St. George, less than an hour to the south, are friendly to a fault about most anything a traveler needs; they feed on questions from the curious. The climate in Utah's Dixie, as they call the area around St. George in the southwest corner of the state, is sweet and infectious. It is only when you start to ask about Mountain Meadows that people treat you like a stranger.

"Go north, I guess," a church guide at Brigham Young's winter home told me.

"There's nothing up there," another said.

And quite likely, some could call what I saw up on Dan Sill Hill nothing. You turn off on a little side road—cough and you miss the sign—wind your way to the vista, and then get on with the task of deciphering the most cryptic historical marker in the West. A new slab of Vermont granite is mounted on the site. No stone commemoration was more fought-over. Not even at Little Bighorn—where the name of the site itself has changed, and the official explanation of what happened has gone back and forth with the shifting sentiments toward Custer and Crazy Horse—has there been so much Sturm und Drang over what to say about a deed long gone. At least at Little Bighorn, early on, there was postmortem evidence that *something* grave and maybe even historic had taken place. At Mountain Meadows, the valley held all the secrets. Or as Juanita Brooks, a good Mormon from St. George who spent more than fifty years trying to find the truth of what happened below, has said, the valley "is so sterile and barren that it would actually seem to bear the curse of God upon it." Now there is this:

IN MEMORIAM

IN THE VALLEY BELOW
BETWEEN SEPTEMBER 7 AND 11, 1857
A COMPANY OF MORE THAN 120 ARKANSAS EMIGRANTS
LED BY CAPT. JOHN BAKER AND CAPT. ALEXANDER FANCHER
WAS ATTACKED WHILE EN ROUTE TO CALIFORNIA.
THIS EVENT IS KNOWN IN HISTORY AS THE
MOUNTAIN MEADOWS MASSACRE.

Who were the attackers? And why did they attack? How did the victims die? What did they die for? Was it war, robbery, an *E. coli* virus planted in the food? The most pedestrian of roadside historical markers in Utah is crammed with numbing detail about a simple crossing of a river, a first planting of a peach orchard, a pioneer recalled. Throughout the West, there are national monuments, fully staffed museums, whole symposiums built around the many massacres. The Whitman Massacre of missionaries at Walla Walla, the Meeker Massacre of Ute Indians, and the Sand Creek Massacre of Cheyenne, to name just a few. But here, site of what was the worst carnage ever inflicted on a single band of overland emigrants in the entire nineteenth century expansion of the West, the stone has nothing to satisfy these questions. Next to the one declaratory paragraph is a list of the dead. At the top, by alphabet, is William Allen Aiden, age nineteen—the young man who was shot off his horse as he rode into a place where he thought he would be protected. And there is William Cameron, his wife, Martha, and seven of their children. Another family, Jesse and Mary Dunlap, and their seven children. A second family of Dunlaps, Lorenzo and Nancy, the entire clan killed, down to the four young girls, Mary Ann, thirteen, Talitha Emaline, eleven, Nancy, nine, and America Jane, age seven.

They died, these "Arkansas Emigrants," in a round of executions that took less than five minutes, by the written accounts of several participants. Believing that they were walking into the hands of rescuers in the midst of hostile Paiute country, the emigrants had disarmed themselves and formed a single file away from their wagons. And then the rescuers, followers of Brigham Young, more than fifty white men, many of them elders and bishops, and Indians under their control, turned around and opened fire. Most of the emigrants were shot in the head, from point-blank range. Some were hacked to death, throats cut. The meadows were full of wailing, screeching, horror. Those too sick or feeble to walk were found trembling inside the wagons; they were shot in the face or chest. The bodies were hastily buried, many later dug up by wolves. A few of the smallest, most helpless children were spared; no one else was let out of the valley alive. The toddlers were hurried away, adoptions into the night, to join broods of polygamous families, too young to be witnesses. But some from those family lines, descendants of both the keepers of the secret and the victims, did not forget. Or their hearts would not allow them to.

IT WAS a subversive territory, a rebel stronghold before there ever was rebellion in the South. Though settled by Americans, the State of Deseret was for a long time a place where the Constitution of the United States meant little. Brigham Young had barely crossed through a forested canyon of the Wasatch range in 1847, pronouncing "This is the place," in the Great Salt Lake Valley, when he made clear his vision of the Empire. The boundary lines went well into Idaho and part of Oregon to the north, to the Mexican border in the south, California in the west, with a seaport near San Diego. Find me a place, Young had said, that nobody else wants. The Great Basin, too high and curved for any water to drain the salt and mineral deposits out of it, was such a place, he reasoned. The chalky bottom of an old rock tub, bigger than Texas, would be home. Paiutes and Utes, Shoshone and Navajo lived at the edges, but had no armies to speak of. Three hundred years after Coronado had come through, the Spanish were long gone, leaving lyrical names on sierras and at river junctions. The mountain men had trapped it and mapped it but could never see making homes in it. The Mexicans, taking over after their republic was established in 1821, issued broad decrees of citizenship, and were very generous with land grants, but still could not get people to build cities in the brown acreage where the largest body of water was saltier than the ocean itself.

The Mormons were tired of fleeing, worn down by the intolerant, the leers, stares, and cheats. The death in 1844 of the ever-dexterous prophet and founder, Joseph Smith, at the hands of a mob in Carthage, Missouri, and the burning of what had been the Mormons' finest creation, the second-largest city in Illinois, Nauvoo, had pushed the Saints to the edge. To get an idea of how American politics has changed, recall what Smith's titles were when he was executed by the mob: he was the mayor of Nauvoo, commander-in-chief of his own uniformed militia, and prophet, seer, and revelator of his own religion. He also was a candidate for president of the United States, running on a platform of bringing "the dominion of the Kingdom of God" over the American states. As mayor, he had ordered his private police force to destroy a printing press that had been churning out unfavorable journalism about the religion he had founded. A better civics lesson in why the Constitution separates church from state and press from government, and dictates due process of the law, has seldom been found in one place at one time.

With Smith now a martyr, it was war or flight for the Mormons, perhaps both. Enough of the United States, declared Brigham Young, who succeeded Smith. Enough of the raw, sixty-year-old democracy. A New England carpenter by trade, he was called the American Moses by George Bernard Shaw. And like Moses, he needed a miracle or two to keep his people moving. Miracles had come easy to Joseph Smith, who kicked around as a water-diviner, itinerant treasure hunter, and loquacious con man before discovering the gold tablets—on his property in New York State—that form the basis for the Book of Mormon. They have disappeared, of course, as all founding religious documents are prone to do. Professing to tell the story of two lost tribes of Israel—one of which became white American Indians, while the other was condemned with the curse of dark skin—the tablets were an anthropological fairy tale, by any fair judgment. But the bottom line of this new American religion provided some powerful incentives to potential converts. It had an easy-to-follow map to heaven. The practice of the faith itself was fun, with much dancing and optimism. And for a young man of reasonable appetites, the prospect of a lifetime of sex with multiple partners fully sanctioned by the church was a terrific side bonus. God himself, said Joseph, had told him through a "call" that he could bed innumerable women as his brides. His bodyguard was among the first to follow the Prophet's path, taking five wives.

Brigham Young was a detail man, a superb colonizer. During his long tenure as leader of the church, he had but one divine revelation. It was a logistical vision: the Saints should move west in orderly companies of ten, fifty, and a hundred people, each group having a captain. The first miracle of his reign came in 1846, when the Mississippi River froze solid enough to allow the Saints to escape west on an ice bridge. The practical God had spoken. Very soon after arriving in Utah, the Saints spread from the Salt Lake Valley out into the canyonlands of the south, into the Lake Tahoe Basin of Nevada, up along the Snake River, into San Francisco and the Sacramento Valley, throughout Arizona. But just a year after Brigham led his followers into the Great Basin, the federal government undercut him. President Polk, ever the expansionist, had routed Mexico and purchased what became the American Southwest for $15 million. Brigham had planned to carve his empire from Mexico, but there was that demon federal government pre-empting him. He was furious.

"God almighty will give the United States a pill that will puke them to death," Young thundered. "I am prophet enough to prophesy the downfall of the government that has driven us out. . . . Woe to the United States!"

The Empire went ahead anyway. The new territory may have been offi-cially named Utah, after the Ute Indians, but it was still Deseret (meaning "honeybee") on Mormon maps. In two years' time, twelve thousand people followed Brother Brigham into the Salt Lake Valley. In a land short of water, roads, and government help, Young put down more than 350 towns in his time. They were built along the lines of the same master plan for a livable city that is on display in the center of Salt Lake City today, with broad streets, ample sidewalks, the houses set back a considerable distance and zoned to keep them apart from commerce and the slop of agriculture. Orchards of cherries, peaches, apples went up in the desert valleys, watered by streams that were held back in reservoirs near the foot of the mountains. Lombardy poplars shaded homes. The Saints, wrote Stegner, "were the most systematic, organized, disciplined and successful pioneers in our history." Stegner, a non-Mormon, was an admirer. What he liked was the bond of community in a land of harsh individualism. One year alone, 101 people were murdered in the secular mining town of Alta, while the Saints went on building a virtually crime-free society. By some views, Smith was something of a Marxist, and the Mormons were early communists. He created an eco-nomic system, called the United Order of Enoch, in which property was given over to community use, and any surplus grain or produce was used for the good of all. In addition, the church leaders tithed 10 percent of everything earned. The Order of Enoch broke down when the worker bees saw that the bishops and high council members were keeping surplus houses and goods. Still, Stegner was impressed. "Their record in the intermountain region is a record of group living completely at variance with the normal history of the West," he wrote.

Gold strikes brought a surge of overland caravans through Utah, Gentiles not Saints, following the old Spanish Trail to California. And it brought a surfeit of cash to the church's merchants, who had a monopoly on stores. It was said by wagon-train veterans that it cost nothing to get into Utah, but a hell of a lot to get out. When non-Mormons tried to open rival businesses, Young crushed them with boycotts. There was no real free enterprise in Brigham Young's Utah. He drove out Jim Bridger, a tough-nutted mountain man, who said, "I was robbed and threatened with death by the Mormons, by the direction of Brigham Young, of all my merchandise, livestock, in fact everything I possessed. I barely escaped with my life." But then, Bridger was one of the people who had believed that nothing could ever come of the colony in the Great Basin.

Brigham Young's word was absolute. Like the prophet Smith, he was not only the leader of his church, the seer and revelator, but held all political power as well. And he was commander in chief of the Nauvoo Legion. Many of his followers were peasants from Europe, fleeing feudal states and futures of misery and landlessness. They were given free Atlantic passage by a Mormon emigration fund, later outlawed by the federal government. In the desert Zion, they had security and hope but had to follow orders from priests, bishops, and ultimately Young himself. When he told a group of people to head out to, say, Las Vegas and found a colony, it was a command not subject to debate. Some converts, feeling the religious imperative to move to Salt Lake at any costs, simply starting walking the fourteen hundred miles from the Mississippi River to Salt Lake. Thus were born the handcart brigades, people who were without horses, oxen, or common sense.

"The Lord through his prophet says of the poor, 'Let them come on foot, with handcarts or wheel barrows, let them gird up their loins and walk through and nothing shall hinder them!' " Young said in an edict from the church office.

Today, in the glow of modern Utah, the handcart brigades are held up as an example of profound perseverance. Gird up their loins they did, these followers of Brigham dragging all their belongings in rickety little two-wheeled contraptions across the Great Plains and over row after row of mountain ranges. But it became the first great Mormon crisis in the West, an act of groupthink slow suicide that the historian Richard White calls "the greatest single disaster in the overland migrations." The fatal party set out late in 1856, in mid-July. Early on, they ran short of food, burning far more calories pushing three-hundred-pound wheelbarrows uphill than they could replace on a daily ration of half a pound of flour. By late August, they were dying, literally dropping along the trail, or collapsing at night while staring at the fire. The stragglers pushed on to the Rockies, where they were crippled by fall snowstorms. Many, especially children, froze to death. By the time a rescue party reached them in late November in Wyoming, three hundred miles short of Utah, more than two hundred people had perished.

The next year, 1857, brought an even bigger disaster. Newspaper accounts out of Utah told of a militant, clannish state run by an iron-willed theocrat, forming in a broad area of the West. At the same time, of course, the South was stirring for a fight and a break with the Union. At the first national convention of the Republican Party in 1856, its platform labeled slavery and polygamy "the twin relics of barbarism." Utah had become a national issue. Young did nothing to appease Washington. He despised "the Americans," as he called non-Mormons in his sermons; he wanted nothing to do with them. "We want to live free and independent, untrammeled by any of their destestable customs and practices," he said. By the middle of 1857, he was stripped of his title of territorial governor, and a series of outsiders were sent to rule Utah. But Young still held power. As church president, he established an invisible government, issuing decrees, planting colonies, mustering his militia. He set up a Mormon court system, staffed by religious sycophants, who ran the legal system of the territory, rendering the federal courts useless.

Young stoked hatred of the Gentiles. They had killed the Prophet, driven the Mormons from New York, Ohio, Missouri, and Illinois. If they had their chance, they would drive them into the ground, he preached. But they would not have their chance, not in the State of Deseret. In 1847, Young boasted that he needed just ten years and he would have enough of an army of his own to take on the United States government. Ten years later, Young had not only a well-drilled, fully mustered private army but a secret police force known as the Sons of Dan. The Danites, much feared by non-Mormons, viewed themselves as avenging angels, killing people as payback for the murder of Joseph Smith. Back in Washington, President Buchanan had heard enough. He sent an army detachment of twenty-five hundred soldiers west, led by Colonel Albert Sydney Johnston, to control Young and make sure the flag of America was flying over the theocracy of Deseret. It was, for the time, an astonishing commitment of manpower against a domestic force—nearly one-sixth of the entire United States Army. Young could match him with a force of equal size, one that had the advantage of being motivated to die for God. His second in command, Heber Kimball, who had married forty-three women, even boasted that "I have wives enough to whip out the United States."

The Saints were never more ready for war. But if they were to lose Utah, they would destroy it in the process. Young ordered his men to burn the fields and crops on the way to Salt Lake, so that the approaching army could not get any food supplies. An alliance was shored up with the Paiutes to the south, the Mormons promising spoils to the natives if they would help them fight the Americans. Young also told his followers to get ready to torch their own homes, reducing to ashes the carefully constructed villages of the colony. People were called in from outlying towns, abandoning their houses. It was the moment when Brigham Young might have done something that would have ultimately linked his name in history to a person like Jim Jones, the cult leader from 1970s San Francisco who had his followers commit mass suicide by drinking cyanide-laced Kool Aid rather than face an inquiry from outsiders.

"We must waylay our enemies, attack them from ambushes, stampede their animals," Young said. "We must lay waste to everything that will burn, houses, fences, grass, trees, and fields, that they cannot find a particle of anything of use."

Just as the Saints were preparing their scorched-earth plan in midsummer of 1857, the Arkansas emigrants passed through Salt Lake, on their way to California. Bad timing was only part of their problem. The wagon trains had come to rely on their stopover in Salt Lake to replenish supplies, even at horrendously inflated prices. Now Young ordered that no grain or staples be sold to the Americans passing through. He deprived the travelers of the only source of food from merchants, he said in an affidavit twenty years later, because his own people needed it. Insults were exchanged. The Saints accused the emigrants of poisoning Mormon water and throwing around blasphemies about the Prophet Joseph; the overland travelers said that the Mormons were hostile and threatening. By the time the wagon train reached southern Utah, it had taken on demon status. Among those aboard were said to be some men from Missouri, a state where the Saints had faced a particularly hard time in the courts and from which they had been run out by a vicious state militia and a fanatical governor. In the slow, rumor-filled heat of summer, the overland Missourians came to embody everyone who had persecuted the Mormons. All sermons were directed at war, and the only information most Mormons received came from the church-run press, the *Deseret News*, which was running a series on how the saintly Prophet had been murdered. Killing the Americans, it was said, would avenge the blood of Joseph and others.

Paiute leaders met with both Young and his subordinates. They had been told, according to a number of people who attended the meetings, that they were free to attack the wagon train. Who exactly told them that is unclear. But Young himself wrote, in a letter to the church president in southern Utah, "The Indians we expect will do as they please, but you should try and preserve good feelings with them."

The southern Utah church president, Elder Isaac C. Haight, had written the commander-in-chief in Salt Lake, asking what he should do with the wagon train passing through. This followed a Sunday service and an emotional meeting in Cedar City, where the Mormons first discussed the idea of killing the travelers from Arkansas—group premeditation. The militia head was called on, and he said he could bring fifty-four men to the task. Some Mormons wanted only to harass the American travelers, or perhaps steal their livestock. But a majority of voices favored "doing away with them," as several witnesses recounted. They set up the Paiutes to do the killing, holding out the promise of loot and stock. Their justification was one familiar to groups that kill on behalf of God: they were doing the Lord's work.

That was Sunday, September 6. The letter from Haight was sent to Brigham Young that day, supposedly asking for his advice on the plan. But Brigham did not give advice. He signaled yes or no, and that was that. On a decision as monumental as slaughtering an entire company of American civilians, down to the children, at a time when the eyes of the nation were on a dawning war in the Great Basin, Young later claimed he was never informed of any such plan. Virtually every letter sent from church regional presidents to Brigham Young is archived in Utah. But the letter from Isaac Haight to Brigham, raising the possibility of an ambush that could lead to a war that could crush the church, has disappeared.

By Friday of that week, the emigrants had been under attack by the Paiutes for several days but had held up fairly well. They were running low on food and ammunition, however, and they had suffered a number of casualties. Several were badly wounded and in need of immediate help. The Mormons decided to call in the Iron County Militia, headed by Colonel William Dame, to finish the job. At the same time, the emigrants sent a boy,

Bill Aiden, out to get help from the whites. He was shot off his horse by a Mormon sniper. His death may have pushed the Saints over the edge, for now they may have felt they had to kill everyone to cover the murder of Aiden. Indians could always be blamed for going after wagon trains, but an assassination of one white by another—witnessed by two people who escaped—was something else. It would only aid the American cause for battle against the traitor Brigham Young.

The ultimate plan—hatched by a Mormon bishop, the church's regional president and one of the original followers of Joseph Smith, and possibly others—was chilling. The Mormons would approach the besieged train with a white flag. They would tell them that they were saved from the Paiutes if they put down their arms and marched out single file. At a signal, the killing would begin. Each Mormon was assigned to shoot one man in the head, and the Indians were given the task of killing women and children. They could plunder any goods from the wagon trains as well. The plan worked just as outlined. A church leader, John D. Lee, remembered how welcome he felt as he came to the rescue of the wagon train, the families sobbing with relief at their deliverance from the siege. Trusting blindly, the emigrants left all their guns behind and walked slowly into the open grave of the Mountain Meadows—men first, women and children herded off into a separate area.

Major John M. Higbee then called out a signal: "Halt! Do your duty!" At that, the Mormons turned to face their fellow Americans, and from only a few feet away, shot them dead. All the witnesses—the shooters—say it was over in a few minutes. The tough choice must have been deciding which children were so young as to be spared, for kids barely old enough to be in first grade were murdered. The order from above was: "None who are old enough to talk are to be spared," wrote John Lee. After the slaughter, the Saints praised the heavens. "Thanks be to the Lord God of Israel, who has this day delivered our enemies into our hands," said Lee. A trusted Saint since his days with Smith, John Lee was Brigham's right-hand man in southern Utah. His bond to the prophet had been sealed in church; what's more, Lee was an adopted son of Brigham Young. After the killing, he rode to Salt Lake to give Young the details.

The militia men, the Mormon bishops and priests, all agreed to a vow of silence. They would blame the Paiutes for everything. Word spread to San Francisco of a terrible massacre, the worst yet in the fifteen years since the Oregon Trail had opened the way to cross-country emigration to the West. It was said to be purely an Indian attack, though given the fact that Utah was in a state of war, many people doubted the official story. Brigham Young's formal report implied that the Arkansas emigrants had asked for trouble by their behavior toward the Indians and the Saints. This version, on file in the *Journal History of the Church,* reports that the militia went to the rescue of the emigrants but arrived too late to be of any help. "The Indians had killed the entire company, with the exception of a few small children," Mormon officials wrote. By Young's edict, the case was closed. He refused to cooperate with federal prosecutors. "The more you stir a manure pile," he said, "the more it stinks."

YOUNG NEVER had to use his army. He razed the largely empty forts of Bridger and Supply, and raided some supply trains. The troops sent West by Buchanan were stalled well east of the Wasatch Range, forced to spend the winter some distance from Utah. In the meantime, the Mountain Meadows coverup became more elaborate. A government investigator heard plenty of rumors but could find no one to talk, nor written evidence of Mormon complicity. The Utah War was effectively over. Buchanan's attention was drawn to the South and slavery. The Nauvoo Legion, the Sons of Dan, the Indian allies dubbed the "battle axe of the lord"—all had been marshaled, as it turned out, for a single mass murder of a group of unarmed civilians. Young's reputation was intact. When Horace Greeley visited him in 1859, he found him pleasant and direct, "with no air of sanctimony or fanaticism." Wrote Greeley, the most influential journalist of his day: "He is a portly, frank, good-natured, rather thick-set man, seeming to enjoy life, and to be in no particular hurry to get to heaven."

A few years later, Young let out, in so many words, that he had kicked a little Gentile butt. Though the federal government had sent numerous officials and another battalion of soldiers to keep watch over the Mormons, Young's invisible government held. Mark Twain found Young in complete control of Utah in 1861. "They maintain the semblance of a republican form of government," wrote Twain. "But the truth is that Utah is an absolute monarchy and Brigham Young is king." The king stopped in the Mountain Meadows on a tour of the southern towns, pausing to read a makeshift monument that federal troops had erected in the brown grass. "Vengeance is mine saith the Lord, and I will repay," were the words on a little wooden cross planted in a rockpile above the massacre site. "Vengeance is *mine,*" Young said aloud. "And I have taken a little." He ordered the monument removed. It was.

THE HOUSE in St. George, with its white picket fence, red-tiled porch, and chorus of flowers responding to the baton of spring, is everything the Mountain Meadows is not. Full of life and well-tended, it is that best of all monuments, the kind that allows you to sit and walk and share the same views as that of the Great Man. The clapboard sign out front identifies it as the winter home of Brigham Young. The carpenter from Vermont was definitely not following the Order of Enoch when he built this two-story sandstone and adobe manse, trimmed in white and stuffed with fine period pieces. So be it; he was the empire-builder and deserved his southern palace. For the ten million members of the Mormon church, this is something like Jefferson's Monticello. Selected thoughts are on display near rocking chairs or in reading rooms.

"And here . . . here is the master bedroom where Brigham and his wife slept," says the church elder who is leading a dozen of us through the house. Our guide is a pleasant older man with reddish hair and a thick three-piece suit, heavy for a warm day in Utah's Dixie. I am on my best behavior, listening with due respect. No quips, jokes, or inappropriate questions. In the garden, I had spent about half an hour asking how cotton is grown and picked, receiving a detailed lecture on the ways in which the Saints made their clothes from the fur-balled fiber sprouting in the backyard. Not a bad red wine was made from the grapes of southern Utah as well, though the Saints, of course, never partook. Inside, I was fascinated by the wood trim; blond and aged, with fine grain lines.

"It's oak, isn't it?" I asked the elder. "Where did they get oak trim in southern Utah?" His face lit up.

"Look closer. It's not really oak. It's pine. They used a quill to paint grain lines on the wood, so that it just looks like oak." He was beaming now, after we had been led upstairs. Out the window, I could see the St. George Temple, selected by Brigham as the first to be completed in Utah. It is unbelievably white—bleached and polished like a beauty queen's smile. It glows amidst the sprawl of St. George, a town pushing itself out among the red dirt and mesas at a pace that will soon make it as unrecognizable as any other strip-mall town given over to Target and Wal-Mart. The temple, not open to Gentiles, is where Mormons are sealed to each other for eternity and where the dead are given the proper anointment to get into heaven. I could have spent an hour in one of Brigham's favorite chairs staring out the window, but then we were in the master bedroom, and my curiosity ran wild. As homey and settled as the room appeared to be, I could not help but think about the sexual acrobatics, the variety and jealousies, the passions and explanations, that must have gone on in that bed. Was it crowded at times? Or did Brigham mostly brood alone in his later years, as some records indicate?

"Where did the other wives stay?" I ask.

"Excuse me?" says the elder.

"Yeah. While he was sleeping with one, were the other babes . . . on deck, in another room?" a kid, about eighteen, asks by way of follow-up. I am glad it is him, not me. The elder blushes.

"Brigham had only his dear wife in this house most of the time."

"But he was married to dozens of women," I say.

"Most of those marriages, they were symbolic more than anything else," says the elder. "Marriage was a way for women to be sealed. It was a ceremonial procedure."

Historical face-lifts are common at the shrines of any religion or nation. But Brigham had sex and plenty of it, with a different woman every night of the month, sometimes. He had a row of houses in Salt Lake where he kept his harem. He complained about the demands of servicing them. He was short and stout, as Greeley has described him, about 250 pounds or more in his later years, but he preferred thin-waisted brides. The man fathered fifty-six children, according to church records. His descendants could fill a football stadium, and one of them, Steve Young, the NFL quarterback, would give them something to cheer about. All of this did not happen through symbolic sealing alone. But the Mormons, because they have been embarrassed about polygamy for so long, because it is something that Joseph Smith, and Brigham himself, had said came from a direct "call" from God, now treat this extraordinary diversion from the mainstream of Western society as some sort of minor symbolic ritual. Rosy-cheeked nineteen-year-old girls hand out pamphlets in Temple Square, beneath the big statue of kindly Brigham, wherein it is explained in a virtual footnote that, "As did many prophets and patriarchs of Old Testament times, Brigham Young had more than one wife."

Yes, twenty-seven wives, to be exact. And Brigham, unlike his modern followers, did not keep this a secret. He preached of its virtues. He defied Washington and polite society every time he reminded an audience about his "duties," as he called his bedmates. It was not to learn about desert irrigation that the great sex pioneer of the nineteenth century, Sir Richard Burton, came all the way across the Atlantic and trudged the length of America to see firsthand this society of sanctioned promiscuity. The West of possibility, the West of shaking off the old, was taking root in the Great Basin. Burton had explored unknown reaches of Africa, had endured countless adventures, had seen communities that no other European had ever laid eyes on, but he was fascinated by this new civilization where a man could sleep with many women and not go to jail or hell for it. He saw polygamy as something that sprang naturally from the Western landscape.

"In Paris or London, the institution would, like slavery, die a natural death," wrote Burton. "In Arabia and in the wilds of the Rocky Mountains it maintains a strong hold upon the affections of mankind." But he noticed, also, that it was a one-way street. Women did not take multiple husbands. Men had the stamp of ownership on these wives. "Servants are rare and costly," said Burton. "It is cheaper and more comfortable to marry them."

We are ushered out of Brigham's bedroom quickly. I pause at the living room, sealed by velvet rope. I cannot take my eyes off a formal portrait of the patriarch. It hangs above an ornate coal stove, with crystal and alabaster vases on the mantel. Brigham had put on a lot more weight by this time; he is in his late seventies, and he does not look happy. He still keeps the Mennonite beard, with clean-shaven lip. He has a black suit on, white shirt, with bow tie. He is holding a cane in his left hand. His right hand is resting on a table, next to a top hat. The expression stern. He seems to be saying, "Get on with it."

Outside, in the desert air of St. George, I am still in search of a double-shot of espresso, but I also want to find a woman who may one day have a memorial of her own. Juanita Brooks lived in St. George all her life. She was a wife and mother, doing her duty for family, but she was also, like so many Mormons, a citizen-historian. As a girl, she lived in a one-room adobe house just across the Nevada border, a life of subsistence agriculture. She loved the outdoors and her church; in both sanctuaries, it was the mystic aspects that attracted her. She had once participated in an exorcism of spirits from the body of her dead cousin. Early on, Brooks became interested in the piece of history that happened just to the north of St. George, in the Mountain Meadows. At the time, the last witnesses to the massacre had not yet died and some of them had a conscience. Hearing of her interest, an old man approached Brooks in 1919. She was a schoolteacher, small, with crooked teeth, barely twenty-one years old. Nephie Johnson was one of the first settlers in southern Utah, a well-known pioneer living out his last days in a glow of reverence. But he had a story that he had wanted to tell for sixty-odd years. He had never opened up to the prosecutors and historians who had tried to get at the truth of Mountain Meadows. But with Brooks, he felt comfortable. "My eyes have witnessed things that my tongue has never uttered," he said to her. "Before I die I want it written down." She listened. And what he revealed was stunning. He told part of the story. Then he fell ill, and on his deathbed yelled out, "Blood! Blood! Blood!"

Juanita Brooks was a student of pioneer diaries. She became known as such a methodical collector of these narratives that she was named to the federal Historical Records Survey in the 1930s and was put in charge of diaries at several major libraries. Through it all, she patched together a story quite at odds with what her church had been saying over the years. She found military records, notes, and letters, revealing precisely who had been at Mountain Meadows that week in September 1857, who had given orders, who had been told to lie. It was Brooks who found the remark by Brigham Young about getting his vengeance at the site of the massacre; it was in the diary of the man who would succeed Young as church president and prophet. But the comment—so damning it could change the consensus view of Young—was later deleted in the official *Journal History of the Church*.

The Mountain Meadows story, as told by the Mormon hierarchy, largely blamed the killings on the Indians, part of a pattern of letting Utah natives bear the brunt of the blame for the crimes of the Saints. When three of John Wesley Powell's men crawled out of the Grand Canyon in 1869, saying they preferred the comparative safety of Mormon settlers to the unknown danger of Colorado River rapids, they were killed while searching for whites. The church said Indians had done it, blaming the local Shivewits, and the claim went unchallenged by many historians, Wallace Stegner among them. But in the 1980s, a century-old unpublished note surfaced. It was written by William Leamey, a Mormon in good standing. The only people to die during the American exploration of the Grand Canyon, Leamey wrote, had been murdered by Saints. He had witnessed the execution of the three men at a church ward house. It had deeply troubled him ever since.

Twenty years after the Mountain Meadows massacre, when blaming the Indians proved inadequate, one man was sacrificed by Brigham Young to the Gentile press and prosecutors. Young gave up his adopted son, John Lee.

The Indian nickname for Lee was Nah-gaats—"crybaby." He had a thick head of swept-back blond hair for most of his life, and had married eleven women. He had been with the Saints almost from the very start, when Joseph took his followers from Missouri to Illinois. From the mobs in the Midwest to the burgeoning empire in the Great Basin, he had seen it all, and been through it all. Never had his faith wavered. He agonized before the slaughter in Mountain Meadows. At the time, he was a major in the Nauvoo Legion. But once the deed was done, Brigham took care of him. Over the years, a number of federal investigators had kept on the case, and Lee's name always surfaced. The story of the direct involvement of Mormon officials would not die. Lee was even offered bribes to tell the story of full church involvement in the massacre. He was too much of a Saint, he said, to ever say a bad word against his church. For a time, Lee and several other church leaders in the south had to flee, keeping a lookout on their homes from atop nearby hills. By 1870, national pressure had grown for some sort of accounting by the Saints. Young told Lee that he had to disappear, and that he would be excommunicated.

"I am willing to bear mine, but I will not submit to carry all the blame for those who committed the massacre," said Lee. Brigham assured him he would be taken care of. He fled south, leaving his palatial stone mansion in southern Utah to live in a shack of twigs and sod in a barren notch on the Colorado River. He opened a ferry service—Lee's Ferry, still the jumping-off point for river trips leading to the Grand Canyon. John Wesley Powell met Lee when he came down the Colorado River in 1869. The territorial governor of Arizona, upon seeing Lee's "Lonely Dell," as it was nicknamed, said he too would take up polygamy if he had to live in such a place.

But Lee remained steadfast in his belief that Young, despite his public statements, would always protect his adopted son. Federal prosecutors caught up with him in 1875. For a man said to be a mass murderer, he remained remarkably calm, at first. He had good reason to be: his trial was determined from the start. Tried for his role in the killings at Mountain Meadows in 1875, Lee faced a jury of eight Mormons, three Gentiles, and a fallen-away Saint. A church bishop had turned state's evidence, detailing the plan and Lee's part in it. At the trial's end, the four non-Mormons all voted to convict, but the eight Saints voted not guilty. Hung jury, no verdict.

Cries of outrage rang throughout the nation. Once again, it looked as if the Saints were in for a long period of persecution. The federal government was ordered to take control of the courts, an attempt to knock out Brigham's invisible judicial system. As the pressure mounted, Young decided to sacrifice Lee. At the second trial, a parade of witnesses who had lost their tongues in the first proceeding suddenly were full of detail. Yes, it wasn't all the Indians' doing, they said. Yes, the Saints had been involved. But it was not anything the church or its leaders had participated in. It was all the fault of that hotheaded man over there in the box, John D. Lee. The accused himself remained confident that no court in Utah would find him guilty, despite the evidence. His jury for the second trial was all Mormons.

But a guilty verdict was indeed what they came back with, and Lee was sentenced to die. As his execution date neared, he wrote an autobiography; it reeks of bitterness. "I have been treacherously betrayed and sacrificed in the most cowardly manner by those who should have been my friends, and whose will I have diligently striven to make my pleasure for the last thirty years at least," he wrote. Losing his legal appeals, and facing certain death, he turned, in the last pages of his book, to those who had given him up. "I am not a traitor to my people, nor to my former friends and comrades who were with me on that dark day when the work of death was carried out in God's name, by a lot of deluded religious fanatics. It is my duty to tell the facts as they exist, and I will do it." And tell he did, though it did not save his life.

On a spring day in 1877, he was led to the Mountain Meadows. There, he gave up coat and scarf, asking that they go to someone in need. Then he sat on the edge of his rough-hewn pine coffin, almost, it seemed, trying it out. He rose and delivered his final words. "I do not fear death," he said. "I shall never go to a worse place than I am in now." He then spoke briefly of the man he considered a father. "I have studied to make this man's will my pleasure for thirty years. See, now, what I have come to in this day. I have been sacrificed in a cowardly, dastardly manner."

The firing squad assembled in the desert sunlight. Last pictures were taken of Lee. He asked that the executioners not miss the target. "Center my heart, boys. Don't mangle the body." Six months later, Brigham Young died, and so, seemingly, did the Mountain Meadows story.

IN THE opening lines of the book that Juanita Brooks says she was born to write, she goes out of her way to assure readers that she is a faithful Saint. As such, though, she could not ignore history; the daily diaries of the Mormon Dream were just too damning. "Anyone who is interested to look up my history will find that I am, and always have been, a loyal and active member" of the church, she wrote. The problem was a collective denial. "We have tried to blot out this affair from our history. It must not be referred to, much less discussed openly." Through the years, church authorities had discouraged Brooks, denying her access to many of the most vital documents. But she finally got inside church vaults and came away with evidence long hidden. Her book, *The Mountain Meadows Massacre,* was published in 1950. At first, the church tried to ignore it. But Brooks had put together an irrefutable case that the massacre was, at the least, a military mission, not a fluke of passion by a lone individual. She even printed the military logs. Upon publication, her greatest fear was that she would be excommunicated from the church. Fawn Brodie had recently published a definitive biography of Joseph Smith, *No Man Knows My History.* For that, she was banished from the church for life.

The question, which remains unanswered to this day, is who gave the orders to start the killing. Brooks concluded that Brigham Young probably would have disapproved, based on a letter in which he said the emigrants should be allowed to pass through Utah. But she did not let him off the hook. She said that his preaching and fear-mongering in 1857 set up conditions that made the murders possible. "In trying to understand it, one is led to think of other mass killings throughout our age, most of them done in the name of God and in defense of religion," she wrote. And she unearthed a letter in which Brigham said God is moving the Indians to kill the emigrants. "A spirit seems to be taking possession of the Indians to assist Israel," Young wrote ten days before the massacre. "I can hardly restrain them from exterminating the Americans."

Brooks' verdict on the father of Utah was this: "While he did not order the massacre and would have prevented it if he could, Brigham Young was an accessory after the fact, in that he knew what had happened, and how and why it happened. Evidence of this is abundant and unmistakable, and from the most impeccable Mormon sources."

In 1961, the Council of Twelve Apostles met in Salt Lake City and decided, based in large part on the findings of Juanita Brooks, to reinstate John D. Lee to full membership and blessing of the church. More than seventy years after his execution and excommunication, he was re-sealed. His descendants, more than a thousand people living throughout the West, including Stewart Udall, the former Secretary of the Interior, were ecstatic. The Apostles said nothing about the complicity of the church, only that John Lee was back in eternal good graces.

A WOMAN answering the phone at a number I had been given to call has disappointing news for me: Juanita Brooks is dead. I was glad to hear that Brooks had died in good standing with the church, her funeral held in the St. George tabernacle. Others remain less fortunate. Of late, the church has purged from its ranks writers and scholars deemed subversive, including D. Michael Quinn, a historian who documented Joseph Smith's dabbling in the occult. The gerontocracy that runs the $30-billion church empire cannot accept the idea that its founders were carnal, curious, occasionally prone to violence, but that story is imprinted onto the Great Basin, whether they see it or not.

Late in life, Brooks continued to campaign for a decent monument at Mountain Meadows. The church owed it to the dead, she said, and to themselves. A little marker had gone up near the creek bank in 1932. The Mormon Church later purchased the property and adopted a policy of discouraging visitors. The marker was torn down. On public land adjoining the church site, the Forest Service put up a plaque years later, but it was nearly impossible to reach; the access road was washed out and not repaired. The slab of Vermont granite on which I read the names of the dead is the most prominent marker to date. It must do, even with its cryptic account of what happened in the meadow in 1857. At the bottom of the granite slab, it says that the monument was erected by the state of Utah and by "the families and friends of those involved and those who died." It is the best evidence yet that some who carry the burden of this piece of the past are not afraid of it. No one understood this more than Juanita Brooks, for her grandfather had been with the killers in the meadow.

CHAPTER 8

Ostrich Boy

Highlands Ranch, Colorado

For a time again everybody wanted to live along the Front Range of the Rocky Mountains. A thousand people a week, a million newcomers in twenty years, they filled the high prairie from Fort Collins to Colorado Springs and marched up the mountains to timberline. They came first as visitors, gasping at the elevation, marveling at the sunset trim along fourteen-thousand-foot summits to the west, catching a Rockies game at Coors Field and arguing over whether home runs are cheap in the thin air. They imagined a life: skiing six months of the year, public school in a new building, a half-acre lot of their own. Mass migration to the blunt edge of the Rocky Mountains had happened so often that it became a predictable cycle of American history, dating to 1859. People were drawn by silver booms, coal bonanzas, cattle riches, oil gushers, military bases, a synfuels rush, real estate speculation. Arriving from the East, the Front Range was the first place to drop your past, leaving it in the Great Plains dust. All the booms were followed by busts: a sea of foreclosure signs, the wind blowing through half-finished skyscrapers, Denver in the rearview mirror. But this did not matter. There is no institutional memory in the West, only dawn.

This time around, they built not just ranch houses, subdivisions, or cul-de-sac communities named for the tribes that had long ago been driven from the area, but entire cities from scratch. Denver was a place to watch sporting events, eat authentic Mexican food, or conduct some state business in one of the capitol buildings. It renewed itself periodically, with people discovering the old stone homes and bike paths along the South Platte. But the serious sodbusting was going on elsewhere in the hundred-mile-long megalopolis stretching north to south or further west, two miles above sea level, in alpine enclaves where water was rationed and mountain lions would occasionally prowl the edge of a softball field. The new airport floated on the brown plains to the east, a self-contained world under full white sails, just outside the urban edge where the ground was being tilled for triplexes.

By the late 1990s, the fastest-growing county in America was just south of Denver—Douglas County. The wind blew at regular huffs from the Plains, making it hard for trees to take root. But homes had no problem finding a hold. The land wrinkled and folded up a bit in Douglas County, enough to give most every home a peek out the picture window to the spires of the Rockies. And it was here that Highlands Ranch, the biggest of the overnight communities in Colorado, came together. Staking out twenty-two thousand acres, the founders of Highlands Ranch envisioned perhaps ten thousand people in ten years. In five years they had applications for forty thousand and were on their way to ninety thousand—full construction. The homes were dropped, as if they fell from the air, on wide, curving streets. A garage was sometimes bigger than the entire house people had left behind. The architectural style tended to be a Rocky Mountain hybrid—usually three levels clad in beige or off-white, with bay windows, cedar decks, fireplaces, and huge central rooms stuffed with electronic appliances, called entertainment centers. Highlands Ranch is owned by a subsidiary of Philip Morris, the tobacco company; the few public spaces within the twenty-two thousand acres are no smoking zones.

Highlands Ranch had no reason to exist in a traditional city sense. It was not a port, a river confluence, a center of banking or commerce. It was ranchland, seasonal grass for livestock, empty in the way of the West where the tableland meets the mountains. But even as cattle country, it had no reason to exist either. So homes were perhaps a better use for the land. It took barely an acre to raise a single steer in the watered Mississippi River valley, but up to sixty acres near the Front Range. Still, Denver was long known as a cowtown. Buffalo Bill Cody is buried in the mountains just above the city. The image he created—a West of hoofed beasts at full gallop, buckskin-clad riders, and problem-solving by pistol—certainly did not go to his grave with him. To this day, Denver alternately promotes and rejects the image, as in the memorable 1985 headline from the leading newspaper: "War Declared on City Image as Cowtown."

Philip Morris housing contractors had yet to shoo away the last of the cattle from Highlands Ranch when a tall Canadian with an unusual plan arrived in 1992. Ken Turnbull had an idea that had been incubating in his mind for two years. A geologist, he had lived overseas for a time, then worked in Denver during the energy boom of the early 1980s, setting up his own business. He sold his company before the late 1980s bust. And by the 1990s, he came to Highlands Ranch, like many people, because he wanted to start a new life and do it in a place where there was no encumbrance of the past. Besides, he said, "My hands had become soft."

He had searched the length of the Front Range, looking for ranchland. He wanted it for a somewhat radical purpose. Cattle made no sense on open lands of the West in the modern age, when people were eating less beef, and fish from two oceans away could be in the neighborhood market twenty-four hours after being snagged in a net. Turnbull did not quite share Edward Abbey's description of cattle as "ugly, clumsy, stupid, bawling, stinking, fly-covered, shit-smeared, disease-spreading brutes." But he thought it had been a mistake to populate the West with European stock and then construct an entire system of subsidies and political support around them. He is a staunch free-market man: things should live or die, flourish or fail, on their own merits. Cattle, at the time Turnbull arrived in Highlands Ranch, seemed to be on the way out of the open West. By the market logic that he had studied, they were deficits on four legs. Throughout much of the 1990s, it cost on average $800 to raise a steer that brought only $660 at the market. But cattle stayed on the land in large part because of government welfare to stockmen and their beef, a taxpayer gift propelled by the image in many a mind that the West and cows were historic mates. Policy followed the old story.

Turnbull favored a different sort of exotic, a creature that he said he could prove had lived in Jurassic-era America. So he bought fifteen acres at the upper edge of Highlands Ranch and set up an ostrich ranch. Flightless birds, with eyes the size of tennis balls, eight feet tall, up to 350 pounds each, with just two grams of fat per three pounds of red meat, were the future, he proclaimed without a wink. Of course, many of his neighbors thought he was a crackpot. And some of the old cattlemen who had sold out to the tobacco company said he was doomed. Nobody would raise meat in the Denver metro area again, they said. It was time to move on and out, making room for the sea of beige homes. But Turnbull had done his homework. The land he bought was simply the wrong place for the wrong animals. "I showed these figures to my accountant: A single breeding pair of ostriches could ultimately produce 1.2 million pounds of low-fat, low-cholesterol meat," said Turnbull. "And he laughed. I mean he just started laughing out loud. Ostriches? Here? He said go back to the drawing board. There had to be a catch. So I spent another year asking questions. I could not find a catch."

Turnbull's gut instinct, and all the consumer and market trends, told him to stay with his plan. "Within a few years, there will be ostrich burgers in every McDonald's," he said. "Ostriches were made for the West."

Just as the new residents of Colorado were redefining what it meant to live in the West—lifestyle refugees, the demographic experts called them—Turnbull was in his way trying to redefine the archetypal Westerner, the one disappearing entirely from the range even as the image was soldered onto a high perch of history. If Kit Laney of New Mexico was ending the millennium determined to make a living like a Western man of the last century, Ken Turnbull was taking the same calendar pivot and going in the opposite direction, without any custom-and-culture protection or a dime in subsidies. He had logic on his side, but no mythic story to inhabit. What else were sacred cows good for, Turnbull reasoned, but for skewering?

He looked and sounded traditional enough for a high plains drifter: tall, angular, with lean features, sandy hair, a deadpan sense of humor. Had Turnbull come along 150 years ago, it's possible the dominant mythology of the West would be different. Bookshelves of paperbacks, vaults of film, dude ranches, those ordinances in Catron County—all might revolve around the bug-eyed, sharp-beaked visage of an ostrich moving over a dusty expanse instead of a cow. Imagine the Bierstadt painting *Emigrants Crossing the Plains*—the overlanders making their way through the mountain chasm toward the setting sun, wagon trains and walkers trying to match stride with their herds of ostriches. How might the West look at itself, or the world look at America, had one accident of history replaced another? Might we be singing around the campfire: Get along, you hose-necked feather dusters, get along?

A FEW YEARS into his project, Turnbull's ranch was crowded with birds—speedy, hyperkinetic, somewhat neurotic, exceedingly horny—and Highlands Ranch was crowded with people, who were doing their share for the Colorado population boom as well. The area could not build schools fast enough: children attended in shifts, going through the summer, with classes set up in vinyl modular units dumped on the bare ground. When Turnbull purchased his land, the main thicket of homes was off on the horizon, where the Philip Morris property faced Denver. But nobody expected that the bald land south of a city that had just suffered another devastating bust would take off as fast as it did. This surge of prosperity seemed different. The other Front Range booms were based in one way or the other on tearing up the Rockies. The coal and silver miners, the oil drillers, the water-snatchers, the shale-oil and synthetic fuels explorers—they all came armed with tools to rip up the land, and they left behind slag heaps of poison, half-built mountain roads, and communities saddled with debt and heartbreak. This time around, the boom was based on telecommunications, computer software, recreation—the new American West, they liked to say. Time and again, companies announced that the main reason for locating near the Front Range was because they wanted to be in the midst of all that Rocky Mountain country. The workers were skiers, hikers, rafters, fishermen, hunters, Sierra Club members first, and software engineers and biotechnicians second. The irony, of course, was that they came to an area where planning was anathema, and suburbs sprouted without logic or consideration to traffic problems or water supplies. The Brown Cloud, especially on stale winter days, kept the Rockies out of view.

Near Turnbull's property, the streets filled quickly with three-thousand-square-foot starter homes and spindly six-foot starter trees. The Philip Morris contractors, aware of the desire of their home buyers to be close to nature, named the streets and neighborhoods for endangered species. There was Spotted Owl Lane, Wildcat Reserve, Bobcat Ridge, Cougar Ridge. Turnbull's home was on the elevated edge of Highlands Ranch, about six thousand feet above sea level. He could look out on days when the wind blew the Brown Cloud away and see some of the big sentinels of the Rockies, from 14,255-foot Longs Peak in the north to 14,110-foot Pikes Peak in the south. And he could look up to where Buffalo Bill is buried and see a wave of homes rippling all the way down the slope of the mountains, through Denver and then south and east up to the border of his ostrich ranch.

The eccentricities of ostriches took some getting used to. Feeding them was not difficult. He gave them pellets of protein and fiber, a diet that would produce a mature bird in under two years. But they swallowed anything—car keys, kids' tennis shoes, cellular phones. They particularly liked shiny things. They ate sand and flecks of rock to aid digestion, so a silver watchband looked even better. When visitors entered the ostrich pens, they were asked to remove earrings, mufflers, hats—all potential ostrich appetizers. Turnbull shared stories with the other ostrich ranchers about what to do after a bird swallowed a glove or a sock (don't ever take your gloves off!). He constantly went over the ranch with a metal detector, searching for scraps that might find their way down an ostrich gullet. He built sheds that shielded the birds during spells of extreme weather. Any temperature between ten degrees and ninety they could tolerate, he found. The birds used their bundle of feathers for insulation in the winter, and fluffed it out into an umbrella for shade in the summer. Turnbull built a heated incubation shed for eggs, a nursery, and a barn. The chicks liked company; otherwise they sometimes panicked and refused to eat.

"So I went to Wal-Mart and bought one of these," he pointed to a simple mounted mirror. "An instant ostrich family." He had discovered one other ostrich trait: they are extremely stupid. When he noticed a pair that kept pecking at each other, he bought a rubber chicken and put it in a shed; it soon became the object of all vicious pecking. He did not want to experiment too much, though. What Ken Turnbull was interested in was proliferation, and for that, he let nature take its course.

"You have to appreciate the fact that they've been getting along for fifty-five million years without our help," he said. Their mating ritual was something to behold: a bit of strutting, some sniffing and circling, a big ruffling and swelling of feathers, then a mount. All the puffing and passionate unfolding of feather layers made a sound like a vacuum cleaner. They did this quite often. A single hen can lay up to forty eggs a year. Turnbull started out with four eggs and eight chicks. In no time, he had more than a hundred ostriches roaming the far edges of Highlands Ranch, their necks poking above the horizon of exurbia. Their appearance, alone, made Turnbull's piece of Front Range real estate a gawker's destination; the ostriches, of course, gawked back. The birds have enormous legs, with thick, muscled thighs and two heavy toes on each foot. They may not be able to fly, but they move faster than most traffic around the Denver metro area. With a top speed of more than forty miles an hour and a stride of fifteen feet, an ostrich in full sprint is impossible to catch, and much faster than a horse. Ostriches have very little hair on top, but a lot bunched up around their big eyes. Some have double chins. Squinting, a mature ostrich can look not unlike Alan Simpson, the former Senator from Wyoming.

It is impossible for another animal, such as a dog, to herd them. "They kill dogs," said Turnbull. "Stomp 'em to death." They also bite ranchers, as Turnbull's hands attest. Even so, he had taken to some of them. One bird, Claudia, was nine feet tall and a favorite; Turnbull, at age forty-eight, said he might grow old with Claudia, who could live to be fifty if well fed and healthy. At the same time, Turnbull recognized that he could not afford to get too attached to his protein. These birds were being fed, sheltered, and kept healthy so that they would end up on the grill.

"They eat half as much as cattle, and live four times as long," said Turnbull. "Plus . . . they're very light on the land. Smell that?" He sniffed. There was nothing but the whiff of fresh-cut lawns blowing in from the new homes of Highlands Ranch. "No smell. That's precisely the point. I can live here near all these people because I'm not driving away anyone with the smell of cow shit."

TURNBULL WENT down to the National Western Stock Show and Rodeo in Denver to spread the gospel of ostrich ranching and see how his competitors in the red-meat racket were doing. Not very well, as it turned out—the beef peddlers, that is. The annual event is often called the Super Bowl of stock shows, a strong-smelling, heavily leathered extravaganza of big folks and their hoofed investments. Cattle prices had dropped 35 percent in three years, and some cattlemen were not at all happy to see Ken Turnbull and a seven-foot ostrich at his booth. Nor, for that matter, did the cattle ranchers care for all the buzz over bison and elk at the show. The grandstands were packed for the elk auction, the first ever in Denver. Raising domestic elk for their antlers, which they shed every year, had started to take off, with pharmaceutical companies paying up to eighty dollars a pound for the ground-up dust of a discarded rack. In the global economy, it was a high-value Western export, ending up in drugstores in Asia, where men believe it keeps them virile and reduces blood pressure. As for bison— hadn't they been eliminated from the West more than a century ago? They looked good in Charley Russell sketches and on old nickels, but here, among the cattle, it was somewhat disconcerting to the cowboys. Buffalo were back, bigger than ever. The bison sale was the largest in the history of the event. One big yearling bull, the show's grand champion breeder, was purchased for $61,000.

At Turnbull's booth, crowds of people sampled his ostrich jerky (sweet, not too stringy), studied charts showing different cuts of the bird's meat, and peppered him with questions about how to raise and market the flightless birds. He talked about how the bird's skin made a soft leather, how the feathers could be used for pillows. Some people snickered at the ostrich boy—he didn't belong at the Western Stock and Rodeo show; ostriches had nothing to do with stock, rodeo, or the West. But Turnbull could not have been happier: just before the show opened, the Colorado Department of Agriculture certified the state's first slaughterhouse for ostriches. It was an enormous break for the two hundred or so pioneer big-bird ranchers in the state.

"The little seeds I planted are starting to grow," said Turnbull, sounding very much like a Johnny Appleseed of Ostrich. The cattlemen consoled themselves with numbers. America was a nation of beef-eaters, and that was not going to change, goddamn it. There were more than forty million cattle in America, compared with barely 150,000 bison on ranches throughout the country. As for ostriches, the cowboys sniffed: the birds looked ridiculous, they were foreign and exotic.

Cattle, as Turnbull said, had less of a claim to being native to the American West than ostriches. He had been going through Internet files, attending museum shows, consulting experts in the study of Jurassic-era fossils. He found considerable evidence, including an account of a skeleton in New Mexico, to indicate that when much of North America was a tropical savanna, ostriches had been part of the ecosystem. They evolved into one of the fastest animals alive as a defensive mechanism. They were likely wiped out in the Americas by the same cataclysmic event that killed off the dinosaurs—a huge meteorite, in the consensus scientific view. They remained in Africa. Egyptian royalty trained them to pull carts and rode them as the Romans rode horses, with gilded saddles and ornamented reins.

Cattle had come to the New World with the Spanish, arriving on January 2, 1494, along with those other exotic creatures brought to the Americas— horses. They were transported over the Atlantic during the second voyage of Christopher Columbus and landed on the island of Hispaniola. During Oñate's 1598 *entrada*, cattle came to New Mexico in large numbers, but the word "cowboy" had yet to make an appearance in America. The British, who coined the term, used it as a put-down, applied to Irish cattle-tenders. The Spanish word was *vaquero,* and it was from the Spanish that most of the cowboy terms came. *Rodeo* means "roundup"; a *stampeda* is a wild, rushing charge of animals; *chaparreras* are the leather chaps a cowboy wore on his legs; *la reata* is the rope lariat; barbecue is camp chow under the stars. When Ralph Lauren, the fashion designer, was trying to create a uniquely American line of clothes he went to Wyoming and came up with something called "Chaps," posing cowboys in eighty-five-dollar jeans. They sold well in boutiques in Europe, the ultimate source of cowboys and chaps.

Outside of New Mexico, cattle were background history for several hundred years; the natives, except for tribes like the Navajo, who took up sheepherding and some cattle ranching, preferred to eat what nature had so endowed the West with, the American bison. No detailed account of Western land is without some superlative-fatigued description of these herds, fast and thunderous on the Plains, equally stirring as they charged through mountain draws. They once roamed over 40 percent of the nation's surface. The furs made warm blankets, and when stitched together, a portable home. The meat was delicious; it could be dried and preserved, smoked, grilled, eaten raw, or ground up with berries and made into a high-energy snack bar of pemmican. Written accounts all came down to one theme: pure abundance. And it was because of the huge bison herds that the West was so often described by visitors from the East or Europe as an American Eden. Lewis and Clark simply stopped writing about bison, they were so ubiquitous. Consuming ten thousand calories a day, per person, hauling keelboats up the Missouri and Yellowstone, then walking on foot to the Continental Divide, the Americans sent west by Jefferson never would have made it past the prairie without buffalo. Fifty years after the Corps of Discovery came through Montana, Father Pierre DeSmet was astonished at what he saw—"thousands of bison, the whole space between the Missouri and the Yellowstone was covered as far as the eye could see." The irony is that the Catholic missionary called the land on which the bison lived, "unoccupied wasteland."

They were erased from the West in about twenty years. If it was not formal government policy to kill upwards of thirty million bison, then it was understood by many a cavalry commander that the best way to eliminate or subdue Indians was to get rid of their food source. But already, several decades before the wipeout of the two main Western bison herds, the Indians had accelerated their own hunting, after finding that bison robes brought money and trading goods. Following the Civil War and the arrival of the railroads, the slaughter was swift. Some hunters boasted of killing a hundred bison a day. Bill Cody said he killed 4,280 animals in eighteen months. In two years, from 1872 to 1874, more than 4.5 million were killed. Many a tourist shot buffalo from the window of a rail car. The accounts just a few years earlier of the great abundance were now replaced by equally same-sounding stories of the great waste. Carcasses were scattered all over the land. Skeletons were stacked, pyramid-style; one picture shows a man standing atop a veritable mountain of bison skulls. By 1873, the southern herd was gone. Ten years later, the northern herd, based mainly in Montana, was down to its last members, and so were the people who depended on them. A Blackfoot Indian, Almost-a-Dog, cut a notch into a stick every time a member of his tribe starved to death; his eventual total was 555 notches. One government estimate placed the number of bison left in America at twelve, though surely there were more. Late in the slaughter, Congress passed a law aimed at protecting what bison were left, but President Grant vetoed it—a way of retaliating against a handful of Indians who had recently begun to fight back.

Teddy Roosevelt arrived in the West in 1884, all teeth and spectacles on a horse, looking to get his shot at a buffalo. For days he rode over the Dakota Badlands, expecting to find the American Serengeti. Instead he found barren land, exhausted of wildlife. Roosevelt ultimately got his buffalo, a joyless task prompted by the demands of his own code of manhood. But the killing helped to make him a fierce conservationist, in the same way that seeing the fire die out in the eyes of a wolf he had shot moved Aldo Leopold. Another unlikely nineteenth-century green was the chief taxidermist of the United States National Museum in Washington, William T. Hornaday. He wrote the Smithsonian about the impending extinction of the great American animal, flabbergasted that such a thing was happening in a land that was supposed to be without limits. The reaction was utilitarian. "Since it is now utterly impossible to prevent their destruction, we simply must take a large series of specimens, both for our own museum, and for other museums," the Secretary of the Smithsonian, Spencer F. Baird, wrote back. He ordered the chief taxidermist west at once to find some bison, and kill and stuff them, before they were gone. Hornaday scoured Montana, hiring guides to help him look, but all he could come up with was a lone orphan calf, which he named Sandy. Taken back to Washington, Sandy posed for the capital press corps and died in the midsummer humidity of the Potomac River. Hornaday went on to write a series of blistering accounts of how his countrymen, "the game butchers of the great West," had brought bison to the brink of extinction.

With the bison gone, the government had to come up with some way to feed the people who had once relied on free buffalo herds. Thus were born the first major government subsidies of cattle. Significant numbers of people began to kill one another over cows as well. Indians were starving to death on the barren, bisonless reservations they had been moved to, in Oklahoma and eastern Arizona. Wards of the state, they were promised rations of beef by federal Indian agents. By 1880, the government was purchasing fifty thousand animals a year to feed the tribes. Providing those rations, through huge contracts, was a source of graft and ultimately folklore—of Billy the Kid and Pat Garrett, for example.

At first, the dominant cattle were hybrids from Texas. These longhorns were scrawny and ornery. And they had two other major problems: they carried a tick, which infected Herefords, the popular cattle brought to the West from Britain, and their meat was tough and gristly. As one cowboy put it, a Texas Longhorn was "eight pounds of hamburger and 800 pounds of bone and horn." Longhorns were quarantined, banned from most rail-shipment towns. The smaller, more docile, white-faced dogies became the dominant animal of the latter half of the cowboy era. The contrast between Herefords and bison was the difference between a redwood and a potted plant. Conditioned to a wet climate, cows bunch up along rivers and streams and will kill their water source with poop and poison unless moved. Bison spend most of their time on arid higher ground, going to a water source only for short intervals. In the winter, bison use their shaggy heads to plow through snow for forage; cattle whimper and bawl for human help. Bison can survive droughts; cattle need the equivalent of forty-plus inches of rain a year.

Moving beeves, as cattle were called, over open ground was said to be one of the easiest routes to riches in the 1870s and 1880s. The grass cost nothing, or so the owners and the government agents initially thought. Cattle chewed up all that feed on the public domain over which buffalo used to roam, and then were herded to rail depots for transport and slaughter. Establishing a tradition that, today, allows foreign-owned companies to extract billions of dollars in minerals from American public land without paying a dime in royalties, the United States opened the former bison lands to anyone with a head of beef. The point was to bring people west, for any reason, and to use the land, also for any reason. The Marquis of Tweeddale had 1.7 million acres. Large British investment houses bought enormous herds, and by the early 1880s more than 100 million pounds of frozen beef was being sent annually to England. The XIT Ranch in Montana, owned by a British conglomerate, counted fifteen thousand square miles of rangeland as its cattle domain—an area bigger than any of a half dozen states in the former British colonies. Inside wood-paneled clubs in Cheyenne and Denver, the owners read the *Sunday Times* from London, sipped gin-and-tonics, and purchased local sheriffs. In Wyoming, the stockmen-owned legislature passed a law making it a felony to possess a cow that was not branded by the owners' association. Basically, that meant any cow not owned by the monopoly was illegal. Rebellion by small homesteaders against this law prompted the Johnson County War, the biggest violent clash over red meat in the West. An army of hired guns owned by Wyoming stockmen started hanging, burning, and shooting people on a death list drawn up by the stockmen. A story of calculated violence and feudal power at a time when the homesteader was supposed to be king, the Johnson County War inspired one of the worst movies ever done on the West, Michael Cimino's bloated and interminable *Heaven's Gate.*

While the British were cornering their share of the market on the open lands, the ranch hands at the low end of the scale, the cowboys, were living the life that would define the West. Nobody glorified it, in written form or song, until well after the era was over. Then, the dime novelists made cowboys into something they never were. Cowtowns, among them Denver, Cheyenne, and Miles City, Montana, were places where the herders could shoot off their guns, get drunk, and spend their meager earnings at the end of a cattle drive. They were the source of many a John Wayne Western, like *The Chisholm Trail.* To police these violent, trail-end cattle ports, the towns hired violent, pliable gunmen. Marksmanship was not always their strong point. Bill Hickok, employed to patrol the streets of Abilene, shot and killed his own deputy by accident during the first gunfire exchange of his term. In the Johnson County War, one of the stockmen's hired guns accidentally shot his righthand man in the genitals. Other cowtown shooters showed undue modesty. Objecting to a newpaper account that he had killed six men who had kept him from a full night's sleep in Abilene, John Wesley Hardin asked for a correction, of sorts, insisting on accuracy from those writing the first drafts of Western mythology. "It ain't true," said Hardin. "I only killed one man for snoring." His plea went largely unheeded. Most writers followed the line from *The Man Who Shot Liberty Valance*—when fact and legend conflict, print the legend.

Dodge City, largest of the early cowtowns, banned guns within the city limits. Abilene, best known of the cowtowns, went a step further: its town leaders tried to ban cowboys. They had seen enough of "the evils of that trade," as they said in a petition. But that trade did produce a small, unique subculture, and a haunting American musical form, a blend of Spanish guitar songs and black blues, mixed with rural poetry. From "The Night Herding Song" came this verse:

> Snore loud, little dogies, and drown the wild sounds
> That'll go away when the day rolls around.
> Lay still, little dogies, lay still
> Hi-o, hi-o, hi-o.

And typically, the songs warned listeners away from the dirty job, as in this verse from the cowboy poet Gail Gardener.

> If you ever have a youngster
> And he wants to foller stock
> The best thing you can do for him
> Is to brain him with a rock.

For a time, I was among the youngsters who wanted to follow stock. At age fifteen, I hired on for a summer at a ranch near the Idaho-Washington border, a big spread run by a divorced woman, Jenny, and her three wild children. Like a lot of ranchers, Jenny was land-rich and cash-poor. She never told me what she was going to pay me when I signed on, but she said it would be worth my while. She milked cows, fattened cattle on the good Pend Oreille alfalfa, and kept a few horses as well. Some cows were pregnant when I arrived. Man, this was going to be the life. I dragged a musty canvas army tent from my family basement, and, with my friend John Buckley, set up camp down by a creek on the edge of the farm, shaded by willows. We smoked cigarettes at night, fixed up a motorcycle, and used it to herd the animals, chased farm girls. The second week, Jenny gave us pitchforks and shovels and walked us toward the barn. When she opened the door, I nearly fell back—the smell was incendiary.

"Clean the barn and that'll get you started," she said.

The barn was a foot deep in cow shit, slightly fermented. It took five days to clean. Three of those days I could not eat I was so sick. The next week one of the cows gave birth. In the elemental routine of farms, it was a momentous and graphic occasion—the willowy calf, encased in a clear bubble licked clean by her mama. The morning after, Jenny told me to get the small dozer and go bury a calf. The newborn had died. It was a sad ride to the woods, carrying the tiny dead calf in the bucket of the clanking old tractor. So it went that summer, up at 4:30 A.M. every day, bucking seventy-pound bales of hay, shooing stubborn animals, sunburned and bug-bitten, always smelling of animal essence. In late August, when I was set to return to Spokane for school, Jenny called me into the house to pay me. "You can have a cow," she said. Did I look like Jack the Beanstock? What was I going to do with a cow in the city? "Or five hundred dollars." The cow, she added, would be worth $800 in a year. I took the five bills.

Cowboys of the open range knew full well what I learned that summer: the job sucks. "We wasn't respectable and we didn't pretend to be," said Teddy Blue Abbott in his cowboy memoir. How it became one of the most romantic, glorified, and iconic roles in America will have to remain a mystery, and a prime debating point at those fractious conferences between New West and Old West historians. At least the argument usually ends under the stars.

What people on both sides of the cow debate agree on is this: just a few years after the bison were wiped out in the West, nature took its revenge on the animals that had replaced them. The Great Die-Up of 1887 hit most Western cattle states like a biblical plague. In the years leading up to it, Montana, Colorado, Wyoming, New Mexico, and the western plains had been grazed and stomped bare by the millions of domestic cattle, and the wild grasslands were turned over for agriculture. Barbed wire, invented in 1873, only made matters worse: huge portions of the range were fenced and given over to a single ecological use. But the money was good, and every year the herds increased. A popular book, published in 1881, was *The Beef Bonanza, or How to Get Rich on the Plains*. Basically, all you needed to do was plop some cattle on the land and wait for them to multiply, the book said. But what the sodbusters, the European cattle tycoons, and even the hardscrabble cowboys forgot was that the West was not England, and Herefords were not bison.

In the summer of 1886 there was no rain. The bunchgrass of the plains came up stunted, then failed. The overgrazed prairie was spent, the sod dusty and depleted. "Wrong side up," said a Pawnee Indian, looking over the old buffalo stomping grounds. A haunt settled on the West: beavers stored double the usual water supply, ducks migrated well before the summer was out, and otter and muskrats grew thick fur. In the fall, snow came early, with blizzards throughout the northern Rockies and prairies in the first weeks of November. It fell to twenty-five degrees below zero in Colorado, forty-six below in Wyoming, and sixty below in Montana. A brief thaw in January turned the snow to slush, and then it became an ice block in plunging temperatures. Barbed wire proved deadly; cattle ran up against it, snagged, and died—frozen beef on the line. They scratched at snow but couldn't get beneath the crust to find anything. They piled into drifts in little ravines, huddled together for warmth, and died en masse, not to be found until spring, when weeds grew up between their rib cages. Nobody sang songs about little dogies or wrote home about easy riches. It was a life-and-death struggle, through a six-month winter, for people and cattle. "A business that had been fascinating to me before suddenly became distasteful," wrote Granville Stuart, a Montana rancher, bison killer, and vigilante, who lost upwards of 85 percent of his herd. When the snows finally melted in April, the rivers flushed hundreds of carcasses downstream. The losses were astounding: many ranchers lost 90 percent of their herds. The disaster drove out many of the British investment houses and broke the backs of countless small cattle ranchers.

In the early days of settlement, the Indians demanded a toll of the wagon trains for passage through their lands. After the Great Die-Up, some Indians said the West itself had enacted a toll for the sin of wiping out the bison. And some cowboys started to tell the truth about what happened to land they all professed to love. In Great Falls, Montana, one day in 1923, the cowboy artist Charley Russell, a man whose work is still used to sanctify domestic beef, was the featured speaker at a booster-club luncheon. He had been a cattle herder during the Die-Up, but over the years, he became much more drawn to the original West. The room was packed for the great Western artist, whose image would later represent Montana in the National Statuary Hall in Washington, the only statue of a full-time artist in the Capitol Rotunda. After listening to the usual homilies about bringing life to the West, Russell walked to the podium. He usually worked with a little stick of beeswax as he spun his tales, fashioning a figure with his hands while he spoke. He looked out at his fellow Montanans. "In my book a pioneer is a man who turned all the grass upside down, strung bob-wire over the dust that was left, poisoned the water, cut down the trees, killed the Indian who owned the land, and called it progress," said Russell. The audience was stunned. But he was not yet done. "If I had my way, the land here would be like God made it, and none of you sons of bitches would be here at all."

AT THE Denver stock show, the cattlemen were drunk on doom and gloom, but those with a sense of deep history said the shakedown they were going through at the end of the twentieth century was nothing compared with what had happened a hundred years earlier. There were jokes about raising Rocky Mountain oysters—cattle balls, thick with testosterone, especially good in the Livingston Bar and Grill. There were suggestions from the ranchers to try llamas and ostriches, elk and bison, and even some talk that the whole cow thing had been a fluke, and all they needed was a twelve-step program to shake cattle dependency.

"What's holding us back now is the traditional cattle rancher and the grip they've got on the government," said Turnbull. "We're spending $110 million a year in tax money propping up and promoting beef." And up north, in Montana, descendants of the last free-roaming bison herd were being gunned down by the hundreds in a government campaign to keep buffalo from ever wandering outside the square boundaries of Yellowstone National Park. The cattlemen had gone to court to enforce the bison killings; they feared that disease might spread to cows, a long shot according to many biologists. There was not a single documented case of the dreaded brucellosis going from Yellowstone bison to cattle. But in a part of the West where government by a single view of history still ruled, the wild buffalo had to die to keep the unwanted cattle supreme. More than a thousand wild bison were shot, almost a third of the herd, the biggest killing since Bill Cody roamed the land. The irony is that brucellosis was introduced to the northern Rockies by cattle planted in Montana at the turn of the century.

But even as bison were being shot to protect domestic cattle, the cowboy-industrial complex was showing signs of age and weakness. In tourist haunts around Denver that used to make their money on cowboy-gilded images of a hard past, buffalo were ascendant. At the Fort, a restaurant of Old West pretensions and trading post trappings, fifty thousand buffalo entrees were sold in a year—nearly half its business. It had started as a novelty a few years earlier. People loved the meat. What's more, they had a healthy appetite for stories about how millions of bison used to blot the range. Maybe the evolution to a New West would not be so hard after all. To the north, Ted Turner continued his Noah experiment, buying the Flying D ranch in Montana, evicting cattle from it, and bringing in a herd of free-roaming bison that now numbers nearly four thousand. They cost half as much to raise as cows, and produce four times the income. A correction was clearly underway, with wolves and bison and cutthroat trout and even prairie dogs allowed back into their old home. A group of Indian tribes—Assiniboine and Gros Ventre among them—got together and did the same as Turner. Within a few years, two dozen tribes had brought seven thousand buffalo back to their former habitat. But they were not hobbyists, the Indians who live on the poorest land in America; for them, the buffalo were a path to prosperity. Beyond the reservations and ranches, people started to look at the former bison range, more than two hundred million acres of public land given to stream-fouling, helpless cattle, and wondered why buffalo weren't roaming in their place.

As the stock show went on, cowboys came to look at Turnbull's ostrich booth, and his meat samples went quickly. "Cattle eat seven pounds of feed to gain one pound of body weight," Turnbull told the curious. "Ostriches put on the same weight with just three pounds of pellets. They do more with less because they digest their food so slowly."

A few months later, Turnbull got more good news. A fast-food restaurant in California started to sell ostrich burgers. At $5 they were more than twice the price of a Big Mac, but Turnbull could sense the tide was changing. Then ostrich showed up on the menu at a White House dinner. A restaurant opened in the Highlands Ranch area, specializing in food of the New West; the big bird landed there as well. Turnbull's phone rang constantly. He spent the Front Range winter keeping his incubators warm and clean, showing off eggs the size of fruit bowls, nagging and feeding birds, and fixing up the place. One of his birds kicked him, but compared to a mule kick, an ostrich was better, he said. All around, the hundred-mile-long Denver megastate continued to close in, and Turnbull started to wonder if he was going to last, if maybe he might have to sell and move on like the cattlemen who had preceded him on this land. The winds were cold, as they always are in the meeting ground of mountain and prairie. The act of creation continued; birds got pregnant, eggs were laid—all of which made him optimistic. "To fail in this business," said Turnbull, "you really have to do something stupid."

The accessories of mythology, the narratives to go with the day-to-day living, were still taking shape. New ostrich ranches, clearly in transition but uncertain how to act or what to call themselves, were emerging all over the West. They reflected the cultural confusion. One was called Beefbird, a place where white-faced Herefords stared out at the new long-necked tenants. Another was the Cowboy Ostrich, a bird and a horse sharing the ranch logo.

Would bison never have been wiped out had the overland migration of 1843 to 1860 been one in which wagon trains were trailed by oversized birds on leashes? Unlikely. Would the new towns of the old buffalo range, in Colorado, Wyoming, Idaho, Montana, and New Mexico, have been any less lawless, any less full of shooters whose heads were stuffed with cheap whiskey, had the emigrants made their money selling ostrich steaks or slabs of emu to the miners rather than T-bones and burgers? Probably not. The towns rose and fell on the rush of the moment. There was always something to kill somebody over. Would the Great Die-Up of 1887, the ecological catastrophe of the open West, followed by the Dust Bowl of the 1930s, been easier on birds from Africa than it was on cows from England? Of course not. The mass death would only have looked more awkward. But after seeing Turnbull work his ostrich ranch, a hard job but not without some fun and a steady sense of renewal, I found it easy to close my eyes and see ostriches long-striding it across Monument Valley, and wonder how John Wayne and the boys would look riding herd on flightless birds.

CHAPTER 9

The Colony

Butte, Montana

He is the Copper King now, the Boss. Bill Murray, goofy, gangly, spindly-legged comedian, chaser of gophers, second banana to Rodney Dangerfield, sits in the owner's box at Alumni Coliseum overseeing his empire. People wave to him and make funny faces. He winks and smiles and keeps that hurt, hangdog look even when nobody is looking. It is a fine night for baseball on the cusp of the Continental Divide. The ragged clouds that were stuck in a trench of the Rockies have moved up and over the mountains, exposing the brown and broken town of Butte in sunlight that seemed incongruous. Twilight is more forgiving. There is no better patch of green in all of Butte than the diamond atop the hill, where the Copper Kings are playing Ogden, and the ale is home-brew. Of course, for more than a century, there was barely any green in Butte, and grass still won't grow on the dead land that makes up some of the most poisoned ground in America. But that is a thought beyond the universe of baseball.

Fly balls have more hang time here, more than a mile above sea level. For a power hitter, the Pioneer League is heaven; Cecil Fielder hit twenty dingers in 1982 when he was a Copper King for three months. Murray is looking for long balls from his Kings tonight and a good outing from one of his teenage pitching prospects, but little more. On game days, Butte is Bill Murray's town. "Hey! Murray's in Town!" is one sign on a railroad overpass. And draped across the stadium wall is a banner: "Murray's March Through Montana." When he visits to check on his team, he always does something nice, a gift to charity, a barbecue out along the first-base line, a good word to the local press, and a few jokes after a round of golf down by the slag heaps.

Robber Baron, King, Tycoon, Big Daddy, the Man—in truth, nobody in this feudal town can even approach such a title anymore. The real Copper Kings are all dead, leaving their legacy throughout the West, the crippled towns, the rivers that will run red for another generation, the old men on respirators. And in Montana, more than in any other place, they left behind a psychic blow so harsh that it continues to dominate the state's personality. This history is not easy to shake or replace, and harder still to inhabit; it hurts. Rockefeller, Hearst, Daly, Heinze, and Clark—they were Copper Kings. They owned Butte, and because they owned Butte, they controlled 40 percent of the world's copper production. They owned the greatest copper mother lode the world had ever seen at the very time the world most wanted and needed it—when electric lights and telephones became as common to a household as front doors. They owned the nation's biggest silver mine, one of the biggest gold mines, and nearly a million acres of timberland—and they cut freely on another million owned by the public. They had the biggest smelter in the world, just west of Butte, in Anaconda. They owned every major newspaper in Montana but one, and the power company, and the water company. They bought editors, archbishops, congressmen, senators. They even bribed grand jurors who were assigned to look into bribery. At one point, with the nation watching, they purchased a majority of the Montana Legislature—for a going rate of $10,000 per vote—in order to ensure a United States Senate seat for a Copper King. They had people they didn't like hung from railroad trestles, or shot by national guardsmen, or held in jail without charges. Five times, federal troops marched into Butte, and martial law was declared more than a dozen times. The first major posting of Omar Bradley, the World War II general, was in Butte, on assignment to keep fellow Americans in line.

But after more than a century it has come to this: Bill Murray, the only man left in Montana who can rightfully call himself a Copper King, has no more power than the ability to raise ballpark hot dog prices by a quarter or suggest trading a nineteen-year-old right-hander who still doesn't have anything more complicated than a fastball. This is progress.

Across the Bitterroot Range, south and west of Butte, another gimp-legged company town is holding a big parade, courtesy of its benefactor. Hailey, Idaho, used to be a railroad and livestock center. Basque shepherds drove their herds up into the Sawtooths in the spring and summer, and down to railheads in the valley at season's end, sending more mutton out to markets from Hailey than any other place in the country. Much of the nation's sheep production, for a time, was controlled by the little area just south of Sun Valley. Now the real estate around Hailey is more valuable as strutting ground for celebrities than grazing land for sheep. Hailey is a New West company town, and Bruce Willis owns it. The actor has a museum, a restaurant, a nightclub, numerous houses—entire blocks of the old town. He pays for the Fourth of July fireworks show, and the newspaper is full of comments on what a good man he is to keep the sidewalks clean and the museum open and the airstrip full of Lear jets. He and his wife, Demi Moore, send their kids to a local school. The parade moves through town, with an Old West theme, children and old-timers alike craning for a view of the movie-star owners. And there's Bruce Willis himself, on horseback, waving, a big cowboy hat covering his shaven head, that smirk-smile of his, scarf and chaps. As for his power, Willis, a Republican, star of *Die Hard* movies where he fends off entire armies of terrorists, got upset like a lot of his neighbors at the prospect of southern Idaho becoming a dump for much of the nation's nuclear waste. He helped to bankroll a ballot measure to stop the waste. In the election, he was outgunned by fellow Republicans who favor a nuclear presence. He could have learned something from the Copper Kings: they never lost unless it was planned.

Compared with the old models, the new company towns of the West are relatively harmless. Ralph Lauren gets a thing for Jackson Hole. Bruce Willis picks up where the railroad magnates left off in Idaho. Bill Murray is a Copper King. The towns may be mere accessories for film stars and fashion designers, but at least the new lords do not have the power to shape thousands of lives, ruin millions of acres, or control destiny for decades. Butte is on life-support. The richest hill on earth, they once called it, and that was not an exaggeration. But it was wrung out so completely, and given over so thoroughly to the interests of the Copper Kings, that the town lives today—barely—as a moral at the end of a horror fable. Some still wait for it to twitch and rise. So they have built a ninety-foot-tall Virgin in the mountains, Our Lady of the Rockies. She is fluorescent-white, feet glued to granite, overlooking Butte from a perch eighty-five hundred feet above sea level. Mary is lit by floodlights, so people can look up and see her at night as they ask for the miracle of civic resurrection.

Up in Helena, under the copper dome of the state capitol building, the governor of Montana, Marc Racicot, is giving a speech. He is young, a product of the timber-and-mining-company town of Libby, which has been in decline for thirty-five years. The governor is laboring to find some way out of a mountain of bad news: one of the largest corporate landowners in the state has pulled up stakes, closed its sawmills, and laid off hundreds of workers, having already logged off its most valuable stands of timber. Another big corporate presence, based in New York, has given up on mines that had kept several towns going in northwest Montana, the governor's old boyhood haunt. People are leaving the state. Montana is down to one congressman for an area that is bigger than Italy, stretching 535 miles east to west, with a population barely half of the metro area of Portland, Oregon. The pattern runs through Montana, more clear than any major river: cut and run, mine and run, take and run. It started almost as soon as whites came to the West. The fur rendezvous, where mountain men would hold days of unbridled dancing, drinking, and fornicating around the central mission of buying and selling animal pelts, was more a clash of business empires than a swap mart for entrepreneurs. Montana trappers joined the Rocky Mountain Fur Company, the regional, homegrown group. But this soon fell to the biggest fur monopoly in the country, owned by John Jacob Astor of New York City. No sooner had beaver started to be trapped along the Yellowstone and the Missouri than Astor, the richest man alive, the one person in the country whose name was usually preceded by the word millionaire, was taking the biggest share of the profits from Rocky Mountain skins.

So here is Governor Racicot, a Republican, trying to breathe hope into Montana, the pliant state. He knows it has a better side. But the insecurity, the beaten-down, held-down, controlled-from-afar sense has been there so long. It is as if the Copper Kings fathered a half million sons of futility. The choice, to most people coming of age, has long been: be a serf or flee. "None of us wanted to wear the copper collar," the writer Ivan Doig once said of his days growing up in Montana. Doig left, as did so many native sons and daughters.

"Montana now ranks forty-fourth in median income—right down there with Kentucky and Louisiana and below even Alabama," the governor says in his speech. Below Alabama! That should rouse them in Cutbank and

Lewistown and Miles City and Roundup. "How long will we be satisfied with the Extraction Mentality? We need to add value to Montana products. And who will control our future: the people who live here, or people in far away cities . . . ?"

The person who wrote some of those words, Andy Malcolm, has an office under the copper dome and keeps a summer cabin on the Yaak River, in the corner of Montana where another corporate presence based in a distant state has leveled so much of the forest that only a handful of the big bears that have always lived there remain. "If you want to understand Montana, and much of the West for that matter, you have to consider the dominant way people here think about the outside world," says Malcolm. "The view from Montana has always been: they're trying to screw us."

AT FIRST, they were welcomed. They were courted. They had money and grandiose plans and industry. And who cared if they came from London or New York or San Francisco. It was a huge piece of the country, bigger than any state but Texas or California, and nobody lived there. Nobody, of course, if you discount the natives. The Blackfeet in the north, the Crow, Arapaho, and Shoshone in the south, the Salish in the west—the bison-fed tribes of Montana, living off the surplus of a state so endowed with wildlife that it could feed all of Europe—had been pushed to the edges after the buffalo herds were crushed. Then, the first order of business was to give away much of the state. No territory in the West was more parceled up and handed out than Montana. The government wanted a railroad through Montana, a northern route from the Great Lakes to Puget Sound. It would carry people one way, and beef, minerals, and timber the other way. When Governor Racicot spoke of trying to break the "extraction mentality" of his state, he was referring to the flow of natural resources out of Montana, a one-way street for nearly two centuries. The resources, as imagined, always went out, but the people never came in. One of the first major actions taken by the United States in its territory of Montana was to hand over a huge portion of the state to a single railroad company. Trying to encourage development, the government made a deal in which the Northern Pacific could have a certain amount of acreage for every mile of track it built. In all, the railroad was given forty-four million acres, the biggest land grant in history. Throughout the West, the railroads got 174 million acres of public land—about equal to the size of Ohio, Pennsylvania, New York, and New England combined. Of this, seventeen million acres were in Montana. Instantly, the government had given rise to a land baron from afar, who controlled the state's choicest parcels of property—the lush river valleys and the most heavily forested slopes. And today, Montana is still fighting abuse of those lands, the unrestricted logging, the subdivisions along the scenic areas.

The first train entered Butte in 1881. It was still a mining camp, a repository for hormonal excess and primal greed, with a residual population of gold and silver prospectors, traders and merchants, whores, pimps, and buffalo killers. Early on, outsiders never had much good to say about the town. It was most often called, simply, "a deplorable place." A thousand people lived there, among them Marcus Daly. An Irish immigrant, he was in his mid-thirties when he arrived in Butte; the new country already had been very good to him as he made his way through the mines of Nevada. He was managing a silver mine in Montana for some outside interests when one particular hill in Butte caught his attention. The mine was called Anaconda, named by a former Union soldier for the way the Army of the North tried to wrap the Confederate Army in a snake grip, in the words of Horace Greeley. Daly thought the mine had potential, but he lacked money to develop it. He found help in a group of investors, men from New York and San Francisco. One was George Hearst, who had made enough money on his own from California gold fields to become a tycoon. One year after the railroad arrived, after Daly and his investors had just bought the Anaconda mine, a worker was scraping away three hundred feet below ground when he found what looked like a vein of copper. Daly examined it himself and was astonished. It seemed like nearly pure-grade copper, five feet wide, not the speckled mix that usually ran through the subsurface. This was an artery that would go from underground to the bank, with very little in between. They kept digging, following the vein, and it just kept getting wider and richer. At six hundred feet, the vein was a hundred feet wide. Daly and Hearst and a few outside investors now sat atop the richest find of copper the world had ever seen—more than four billion tons of red rock ore. Of course, they kept it secret at first. The Anaconda was barren, they told everyone, and promptly closed and sealed it. Then, they quietly bought up many of the neighboring mines around Butte. "The world does not know it yet," Daly said. "But I have its richest mine."

Their timing could not have been better. Alexander Graham Bell had invented the telephone, and Thomas Edison had created incandescent electric light. Copper was the perfect medium through which to run the electricity needed to power two of the biggest technical advances in civilization—communication and light. The new American age would have to come through Butte, or at least through the men who controlled Butte.

Copper ore still had to be shipped east, to be crushed and smelted. That meant Daly was a mere provider of raw material. So he decided to build his own stamping mills, where the copper would be separated and reduced to dust, and then, about twenty-five miles to the west, he constructed an enormous smelter to melt down the ore. This industrial complex soon became the town named for the mine. Anaconda, by the 1890s, was the biggest smelter in the world. Its smokestack, at 585 feet high, was the world's tallest brick structure. And Anaconda Copper, the company that ran it, was known as the Snake, or simply the Company. Daly and his cohorts bought up dozens of other mines. Soon, they had the biggest gold mine in the West, Homestake in South Dakota. To keep the furnaces burning at all hours, they needed coal; so they acquired some of the biggest coal mines in the country. To supply timbers that would be used to frame the hundreds of miles of underground tunnels, Anaconda joined the Northern Pacific Railroad in a deal that created the state's largest timber company, getting most of its wood by illegal logging of public land. They had seven sawmills working two shifts a day and a company timber town of their own, outside Missoula, called Milltown. To keep public opinion on their side, Anaconda started buying up newspapers, and soon, nearly a half dozen of the biggest dailies in Montana were mouthpieces for the Snake. The biggest paper, the *Standard* of Butte, had the largest circulation in the Northwest outside of the *Oregonian* of Portland.

The wealth that came out of Butte was prodigious. By the 1890s, cable cars lined the streets and a big brawny downtown section catered to thousands of miners and a handful of men who governed every aspect of their lives. Butte was well-built, chiseled and ornamented. Opera singers from Milan did a circuit of New York, Boston, Chicago, San Francisco, and Butte. The middleweight boxing championship of the world was fought in Butte in 1884—and given the audience, the fighters had to offer them their money's worth. The match, between Duncan McDonald and Peter McCoy, lasted two hours and thirteen minutes. When George Hearst died in 1891, he owned just under half of Anaconda. His son, William Randolph Hearst, came into a fortune of $18 million. From that money, largely derived from the ground beneath Butte, came a newspaper empire that spawned a war in Cuba and inspired the movie *Citizen Kane*.

Before New York was known as the city that never slept, Butte was

awake at all hours. When dark-eyed men came up from their shifts underground, they walked just a few feet and started drinking. There were 212
taverns in 1893 and sixteen gambling dens. The men poured down pints of
black Guinness and shots of Murphys. A bucket of beer cost a quarter—to
go. A shot was a dime. Once liquored up, a miner would wander another
few feet to Venus Alley, where more than six thousand prostitutes worked
during the peak years of the copper boom. Asians had their own brothels,
the most popular of which was called The Lucky Seven. The whores worked
out of "cribs," a mattress and wash basin in a single, small room. When
Charlie Chaplin came through Butte, what fascinated him most were the
cribs. More than twenty-five languages could be heard on the streets.
Underground, notices were posted in fourteen languages. Butte had a
Finntown, a Dublin Gulch, a Chinatown, a Dogtown, a Little Italy. The
city was full of Hungarians, Serbs, Italians, blacks, Croats, Greeks, Chinese—the polar opposite of monochromatic Montana today.

Butte was multicultural, yes, but clamorous with racial conflict. The
Chinese had made possible the greatest boom in the state, by building the
railroads, and made up nearly half the population of early Butte. But they
were not allowed to own placer mines or work underground. "The China-
man is no more a citizen than a coyote is a citizen and never can be," went
one Butte editorial in 1893. The Irish soon dominated, and they of course
hated the English miners, from Cornwall. Job notices at the Anaconda were
posted in Gaelic. St. Patrick's Church had three different units of the
Ancient Order of Hibernians. From one town in County Cork alone came
1,138 people to work the mines of Butte. By 1900, it was the most Irish city
in America—36 percent of the population immigrating from the Emerald
Isle to a brown hell in the northern Rockies.

Writers, politicians, actors, and others among the professionally curious
came from thousands of miles to get a look at Butte and sample a taste
of life at its most un-Victorian. There was a hermaphrodite named Liz the
Lady, who charged for a peek. One reporter called Butte "the most Western
of American cities, a place of tremendous disorder, of colossal energies at
play." An East Coast newspaper said Butte was "simply an outpost of Hell."
Carry Nation brought her temperance crusade at the height of its power to
the city, but Butte proved to be the place where the sobriety movement had
its last stand. First she was laughed at by a mob outside a bar. Then a brothel
madam kicked her to the ground, and likely would have stomped her to
death had not the sheriff intervened. Carry Nation never again entered a
tavern.

The city is perched on the side of a steep hill, five miles from the Continental Divide. There was no separation of homes and mines. The big coal-burning smokestacks spit their effluents of arsenic and sulfides down on the roofs and backyards of houses owned by miners and their families. Slag piles of mine tailings rose next to schools, next to churches, bars, on sidewalks. A visitor in 1917 compared the Anaconda smokestack to a volcano dumping a stream of heavy metal contaminants on anyone within a hundred miles. Everywhere, it seemed, the big elevator rigs loomed, the black headframes that rose 125 feet above ground. They held little cages that men locked themselves into for lowering deep into the guts of the earth. In the mines, the temperature averaged ninety degrees.

At its peak, Butte was an aboveground city of 100,000, and an underground city with a network of tunnels much more extensive than the streets. There were twenty-six hundred miles of crosscutting tunnels under Butte, and forty-six miles of vertical shafts. The city was perforated like a pincushion. When the men came up, on the many subzero Montana winter days, the steam from their wet bodies heralded their arrival, like a puff of smoke from a magician's stage.

In one neighborhood, the air was so thick with black clouds that it was called Seldom Seen. But so what if you couldn't breathe, if the streetlights were sometimes turned on at noon to light the soot-darkened city? It was the richest hill on earth, the Copper Kings proclaimed, the biggest city between Minneapolis and San Francisco, with ambitions to pass them both. At first, the miners were well paid. Daly had a soft spot for his fellow Irishmen, and early on he acceded to most union demands. The princely sum of three dollars a day set the standard, a huge wage before the turn of the century. But after the crash of 1893, unemployment loomed. A group of out-of-work miners commandeered a train and rode to Billings, demanding full employment. President Grover Cleveland sent in federal troops. It was the first of five times that armed soldiers of the American government would be used to keep Butte's miners in place.

Still, compared with other Western mining towns, Butte was, at least at first, an oasis of stability. In Idaho there was open war. Owners of the silver mines of the Panhandle tried to break the unions, slashing wages and firing anyone who wouldn't go along. The miners responded by blowing up the Frisco Mine near Wallace. Then they hijacked a train and went over to the rich Bunker Hill Mine, and blew that up. The explosion could be heard thirty-five miles away. Governor Frank Steunenberg declared martial law, and sent in National Guard troops to round up the men. The governor was assassinated in 1905. His confessed killer, an anarchist named Harry Orchard, told authorities that leaders of the American labor movement were involved, among them Big Bill Haywood. These labor leaders were kidnapped from Denver and taken to Boise, where they were tried for conspiracy in the death of the governor. A legal showdown followed, featuring Clarence Darrow, who defended Haywood and two others, against William Borah, the prosecutor and later senator. Darrow was victorious, and Haywood and his cohorts were freed.

The labor wars did not come to Butte until World War I, when wages were cut, hours increased, and the polyglot city in the Rockies was disparaged as an outpost of radicalism. Butte did have a socialist city government for a time, and it was the early nerve center of the Industrial Workers of the World, the leftist labor union. The Copper Kings took advantage of wartime restrictions against free speech and assembly and hit the unions hard. In Spokane, any union leader who stood atop a soapbox with a speech was arrested and thrown in jail. For good reason, the *Spokesman-Review,* editorialized. "They are notoriously and avowedly hoboes and bums," the paper said. Free speech was outlawed in Montana as well. The legislature passed a law making it a crime to join the Wobblies, or to write or say anything "disloyal, profane or scurrilous" about the government. In Butte, the I.W.W. leader Frank Little was snatched from his boardinghouse one summer night in 1917, tied to a car, dragged along dirt roads in the mountains, and hanged from a railroad trestle. In Miles City, another labor leader was beaten unconscious at an Elks Club. Many in Butte claimed to know who had killed Frank Little. But no one was ever charged with the crime.

Mail to the unions was intercepted at the post office and taken to the company's headquarters, where Anaconda men would pore over the correspondence, looking for inside information. A union hall was dynamited, reduced to dust. Wages dropped from three dollars a day to a dollar a day. Mass strikes were called. The company dispatched armed guards and Pinkerton agents against the pickets; machine-gun fire mowed down one group of miners, causing fifteen casualties. The Copper Kings called on the government, which sent in army troops. Now the richest hill on earth was under martial law. Soldiers with fixed bayonets forced the Butte men back into the mines. If there was ever any wonder about what sort of stories grandfathers in Montana told grandchildren about the bad old days of Butte—or how the state came to believe in the collective mantra of "They're Trying to Screw Us"—consider a two-thirds wage cut and a work order that came at the end of a rifle from one of your own countrymen.

The labor wars happened after Marcus Daly died. During his peak years as a Copper King, he had one persistent problem: William Andrews Clark, a pinch-faced, elfin man with a whisk-broom beard and standup hair. He hated Daly, calling him a tyrant, a pimp, a fat blowhard, and names that would make the women who worked the cribs on Venus Alley blush. Clark owned his share of copper mines around Butte, and he had his newspapers, smelters, and city blocks as well. He gave his miners turkeys on Christmas Day but generally stayed away from the underground men. His best-known line in defense of Butte came after an outsider disparaged the city's unbreathable air. "The ladies are very fond of this smoky city," he said. "There is just enough arsenic there to let them have a beautiful complexion." If he was kidding, nobody could tell.

Clark wanted to be the richest man in Montana; but more than that, he wanted to be a United States Senator. He had power, but no personality. "His heart is frozen," said one contemporary, "and he has a cipher in his handshake. He is about as magnetic as last year's bird's nest." Montana became a state in 1889. The year before, it had elected a representative, likely to be the next senator, by statewide vote. As a Democrat in a one-party state, Clark seemed a shoo-in. But his rival Daly had ordered that the two most populous areas, his company towns of Butte and Anaconda, vote Republican. He wanted a Republican senator to keep the Republican administration from prosecuting Anaconda for its massive and illegal logging operations on public land. The gambit worked, in that it delayed prosecution for a decade. Clark was incensed. For the next decade, there would be furious buying and selling of legislators, judges, and newspaper editors as Clark and Daly tried to foil each other's plans. Daly wanted the state capital to be his company town, Anaconda. He spent fifty-six dollars a vote in a statewide election, but lost. Clark gave free dinner and unlimited drinks to everyone in Helena, the eventual capital, as a reward.

The case that set the standard for bribery in Montana revolved around Clark's third attempt to win a Senate seat, in 1899. This time, he was taking nothing for granted. His men showed up in Helena with stacks of cash. In the legislature, which would choose the next senator, the Democrat Clark needed nearly a dozen Republican votes. Monogrammed envelopes—W.A.C. stamped on the fold—stuffed with crisp $1,000 bills were handed out to select Republicans. "What's the going rate for votes today?" they asked around Helena. The market settled at around $10,000 per man, but some held out for as much as $30,000. It was an astonishing display of corrupt frontier democracy, and it was like watching a hanging in the village square—everybody condemned it, but nobody turned away. One morally troubled state senator, Fred Whiteside from the Flathead Lake area, rose to shame his fellow legislators. He, too, had been offered $30,000 to send Clark to the Senate but had refused. "Let us clink our glasses and drink to crime," he said. "The crime of bribery as shown in the evidence here introduced stands out in all its naked hideousness, and there are forty members here who today are ready to embrace it." Clark won the Senate seat nonetheless, picking up his eleven Republican votes. It had cost him $270,000. Whiteside, the pesky moralist, was removed by his fellow legislators. And a grand jury in Montana that was assigned to consider prosecuting Clark for bribery found no evidence—after each juror was paid a purported $10,000 by Clark.

But in Washington, the Senate refused to seat Clark. The bribery evidence was too overwhelming. The facile Copper King found a way around it, though. Clark resigned. Then he had the Democratic lieutenant governor appoint him as the next United States Senator. There was, after all, a vacancy—his own seat. The Republican governor was away, but when he came home, he threw the appointment out. Clark dug in. The next year, 1900, brought another chance. This time, Clark would buy the legislature at the local level, making sure that enough of his people were sent to Helena, which would then send him to Washington. Nobody could prove open bribery with monogrammed envelopes. It was more like traditional American influence-buying. Clark barnstormed the state, holding himself up as the homegrown savior against outside interests. In part, he was right. Standard Oil, the Rockefeller dynasty built on monopolistic domination of the early oil industry, had bought effective control of Anaconda. Hearst was gone. Daly was sick. And now the biggest copper supply in the world was controlled by the Rockefeller family and a few major stockholders on Wall Street. "A foreign corporation," Clark's forces called the Snake. Allying himself with another Copper King who had used endless lawsuits to give himself a toehold in the Montana mining empire, Clark brought home his handpicked legislature. And as one of their first orders of business, they sent William Clark to the United States Senate. Less than a week later, Marcus Daly died.

Once finally seated as a member of the ultimate club in Washington, Clark abandoned any talk of representing the home-state workers and fighting the Rockefeller trust. He built a 121-room mansion in New York City, with thirty-one bathrooms. He opposed Teddy Roosevelt's antimonopoly initiatives, and he sidled up to his rival Standard Oil, now the most powerful of the Copper Kings. He helped to found Las Vegas, building a railroad with a pit stop at a desert watering hole that he happened to own. The county that holds Las Vegas would be named for the old graft-peddler and Copper King.

With consolidation under Standard Oil, the Anaconda Company was supreme. By 1910, one out of every six people in Montana labored in the Snake's two company towns, Butte and Anaconda. It paid almost nothing in taxes. When the last of the independent Copper Kings, Fritz Heinze, waged a counteroffensive by packing certain courts with his judges, the Rockefellers showed that they knew how to slap around Montana politicians as well as Clark or Daly had ever done. The Company ordered the governor to call a special session of the legislature, for the sole purpose of passing a law that would allow Anaconda to avoid any court of law overseen by judges not in their camp. A Butte area judge issued a ruling the Company did not like, so it promptly shut down all its mines, putting three-fourths of the wage earners in Montana out of work. Most of them had been living paycheck to paycheck. They now waited on the sidelines, with the gun held to the governor's head, as the Company blackmailed the state. The special session was called. And the special law ordered by the Company was passed. "Observers around the nation watched in awe as a 'sovereign state' was held up by a corporation," wrote Michael P. Malone, the historian of the Copper King years and now president of Montana State University. Never again would Anaconda be seriously challenged. By the 1940s, when the journalist John Gunther came through, he wrote that the proud state under the Big Sky was nothing but a played-out colony.

THE BASEBALL Copper Kings eke out a victory over Ogden on the strength of a few late-inning long balls. The next day by midmorning, uptown Butte, the part of the Hill that roared loudest and longest, is still asleep. Virtually the entire old business center, more than forty-five hundred buildings, a mound of saloons, hotels, and merchant fronts mixed in with the detritus of mining, is embalmed in a spooky National Historic District. The town leaders want to protect the slag heaps as well, freezing the poisons in a pose against the petrified buildings, the blackened cottages where children still play next to mounds of heavy metals. They look to the National Park Service for salvation: take us in, the ghost county with a surfeit of history. Their model is down below, in Anaconda, where ARCO paid Jack Nicklaus to design a golf course built over the old smelting works—it has black sand traps from slag piles, and the old 585-foot brick tower looms over the course.

Butte has a bigger historical district than Boston or New York or even the cradle of American democracy, Philadelphia. You can walk in the near-dead town and hear how the mayor was thrown from a second-story window, or what happened when the army stormed in to keep miners working, and how the entire water supply was turned green on St. Patrick's Day—an improvement, most people said. The streets are named Mercury, Quartz, Copper, Granite, Galena. No doubt about the intentions. No Elm Street, Oak Street, Spruce Street. No elms, oaks, or spruce, either. A few pawn-shops on the fringe unlock their doors. "We Buy Antlers," the sign says in one. "Hock It to Me" is the name of another; a window sign reads: "Fast Cash Guns."

Clark's mansion, where the king stayed while in Butte, is intact, a bed-and-breakfast now. Marcus Daly, in statue form, overlooks the city from the old School of Mines, now called the College of Technology. Clark proved to have more bathrooms in his mansion in New York, with thirty-one, com-pared to Daly's mere fifteen in his Georgian Revival palace in the Bitterroot Valley. But in postmortem posterity, Daly has got the better of his rival.

Anybody with money or sense has moved off the Hill, down to the less toxic Flats, where the streets have names like Friendly Lane and Fairlane Avenue. Those without money stay on the Hill in residential hotels, telling stories of the Company. Butte has lost two-thirds of its peak population.

What is strange is how all the main thoroughfares have half disappeared. Wide business avenues start in the west end of town, run straight for a few blocks, past a high school, a museum, a library, a hospital, a courthouse, and then fall off the earth. They are gone, along with the buildings, the homes, the cranes, the tunnels, the entire neighborhood of Dublin Gulch, and Meaderville, where the Italians lived. In their place is a fence; behind the fence is the end of the line for the Copper Kings, the second original sin of the American West. We, all of us—anybody who has ever used a phone or turned on a light—own a share of it. It is supposed to be a tourist attrac-tion, or so the brochures all say—the biggest draw in Butte. Come see the horror! The monster that ate Butte! The raped and plundered West! But it is summer, peak season in Montana, and as I walk through the tunnel to the big draw, I am alone. At the end, the light opens up, and there it is, more than a mile and a half wide: the Berkeley Pit. It takes your breath away. As with the Grand Canyon on first sight, so the Pit has a staggering effect. Nearly two thousand feet deep from the edge where I stand to the bottom of the sludge, the Pit is a six-hundred-acre stew of strong poisons: arsenic, lead, cadmium, mercury, sulfate. Dashiell Hammett, a Pinkerton guard on the Hill for a time, wrote a novel about Butte, calling the place Poisonville. The book's title was *Red Harvest,* but he only touched the surface. This harvest in the Pit grows every day, three to five million gallons of additional groundwater blending with the heavy metal stew, surrounded by tiers of scraped-away earth. The acid is strong enough to dissolve quarter-inch metal in a matter of days. A flock of snow geese, lost on their southern migration during a storm, landed in the Pit at dusk not long ago, seeking a momentary refuge. More than 340 died, their insides corroded by the lethal liquid.

By 1955, the Company couldn't afford to mine copper the old-fashioned way, burrowing deep under the Hill. Its competitors, Phelps Dodge being the biggest, were taking copper out of the earth in cheap Third World locations by simply ripping open a big gash in the ground. Similarly, the more logical, bottom-line way to do it in Butte, the Company's men explained, was to dig an open pit, to essentially turn the Hill inside out. The problem was that much of uptown Butte, and thousands of homes, were part of the Hill. The Company presented the dilemma to the community as a choice: let us cannibalize the city and it will die gradually, or we pull out and Butte dies a sudden death. Butte chose long-term pain. Some of the gallows were dismantled, the timbers caved in, houses scraped away, buildings torn down. One neighborhood after the other fell to the Pit. Then came the big streets, the stores, the hotels. They all went. The earth movers worked around the clock, trucks the size of houses, with eleven-foot wheels, cutting twenty-five hundred miles of terraced roads around the Pit. They didn't just chew at Butte; they ate the town in gulps. The hole grew to epic size. In 1974, after nearly a century, the Company started pulling out of Butte. They laid off half their workers in Montana. Open-pit mining was automated. Machines could do what the backs of immigrants used to do. Finally, the Company gave up altogether. Anaconda had been forced to hand over its big copper operation in Chile—nationalized by a socialist government— and the losses were staggering. The Snake was dead. Of course, the end was tied to a series of events more than 10,000 miles from Montana. People in Butte were the last to know, an old song, not unexpected.

Anaconda's operations in Montana were sold to ARCO for a fire-sale price, but the oil company had no idea how to play at Copper King. It clawed away at the Pit for six more years, then folded up the operation completely in 1983. The Hill was silent.

Butte had given a lot to keep electric lights shining, war machines moving, telephones buzzing. At least $22 billion in mineral wealth had been taken from the Richest Hill on Earth. The copper helped to make life easier for most everybody in the Western world. It helped to win two world wars. Then came the bill. When the Company, and later ARCO, stopped digging, they also stopped pumping water from the Pit. From then on, it became the ugly bath, growing daily. Water seeped from springs and wells deep in the earth, it came from rain and snow overhead, and it poured in from the big mining tunnels that had been crisscrossed beneath the ground. Aquifers were drained. Groundwater, coursing through bedrock, poured into the Pit. Engineers came up with dozens of ideas, Star Wars–quality plans to transform the liquid into something usable or less lethal. But there would be no way, they said, to control the amount of liquid in the Pit—which meant that it would keep growing. By 1985, the Pit held a 441-foot-deep lake of red liquid. Now, it is 900 feet deep, and rising more than thirty feet a year. By the time it reaches the 1,100-foot level, in the year 2020, it will overflow and start to run downhill, seeping into the alluvium and contaminating the water of the people who live in the Flats and beyond, killing what hasn't already been killed in the Clark Fork, the most eastern drainage of the Columbia River. Fishermen who snub the broken town of Butte will look to the Hill with some of the same trepidation as do pensioners living in the old hotels. The United States has declared the Pit and the mine waste down to Anaconda a massive Superfund site—virtually the entire county wears the scarlet letter of the Environmental Protection Agency's tag for ruined landscapes—the most polluted place in America, holding thirty billion gallons of poison.

Pit-Watch is the name of a little newsletter distributed to the people of Butte. Diagrams show what will happen when the Pit reaches something called Critical Water Level—the point of overflow. By then, according to *Pit-Watch,* somebody, perhaps at ARCO, perhaps at the federal government, perhaps even a friend of Bill Murray's with money and heart, will have figured out a way to keep the Pit from killing off the rest of Butte.

Above the Pit, to the north, I walk through abandoned neighborhoods, the land charcoal-colored, to an overlook. There is a tentative memorial here on Granite Mountain, something to show the world that more than a prime piece of Montana land was sacrificed to the Copper Kings. On June 8, 1917, a shift boss descended two thousand feet into a mine shaft to help untangle a cable. His light touched insulation and a fire started. Flames raced up the shaft, consuming the oily timbers, pushed upward by the draft. Then—

poof—all oxygen was sucked out of the mine, stolen by the fire, and everybody below was burned or suffocated. For some of the men, death was slow, over a period of hours. The last lines of Magnus Duggan:

"My dear wife and mother. It breaks my heart to be taken from you so suddenly and [un]expectedly but think not of me, for if death comes, it will be in a sleep without suffering."

James Moore wrote this to his wife:

"There is a young feller here, Clarence Marthey. He has a wife and 2 kiddies. Tell her we done the best we could, but the cards were against us."

The worst hard-rock mining disaster in American history took the lives of 168 men at Granite Mountain above Butte. At the half-finished memorial here, the names of the dead are etched on the ground, and a frayed Pepsi banner, the corporate sponsor, blows in the wind. A young miner and his family are sitting up there with me as the banner flaps around. He tells his kids to get away from the mines, from Butte, from a Montana ruled by somewhere else. But he himself is hoping to work on the Blackfoot River, where Phelps Dodge wants to mine gold and build a new pit. They are going to pay fifteen dollars an hour, he says.

"What good is the money when this place will kill you," his wife says.

The fire under the ground of Butte was only the most dramatic form of miners' death. Most men died from lung disease, silicosis; one study showed that 42 percent of the miners of Butte had this dread respiratory sickness.

"But look at how damn beautiful it is," the miner says, dragging on a cigarette and motioning to the mountains all around, off to where the statue of Our Lady of the Rockies is standing, well above the Pit.

MONTANA HAS never learned to say no. The people curse and swear off ever again giving their backs to distant tycoons with promises and cash. They will do as the governor says, break the extraction mentality, learn to master their own destiny, join the rest of the West in freeing themselves of timber and mining. But then something new comes along. There is a Butte in every Western boom, every rootless dream, every scheme presented as a forward-looking opportunity by senators who are only slightly less obvious than Clark was in his betrayal of the state. They believe a story, told in many forms, that sounds so good at first, and always has the same ending.

The frontier was closed, the historians and census takers said, in 1890, but Montana gave America one last shot at a land bonanza. The old buffalo grounds of eastern Montana, dry and windswept, arctic cold in the winter, frying-pan hot in the summer, were opened by the Enlarged Homestead Act of 1909. Anybody willing to improve land could claim a stake of 320 acres. The rush was on, prompted by railroads based in Chicago and New York. They pushed a vision of Eden on the High Plains. The immigrants came one last time, breaking the sod. In the end, Montana had more homesteaders than any other state; it was the last frontier of free farming. All told, 114,620 people filed claims on twenty-five million acres from 1909 to 1923. The state put out pamphlets promoting the opportunity. "There is no place where failure is so remote," they said.

And of course, their hearts were broken. The land was too dry, the weather too extreme. Half of all the state's farmers lost their land by the mid-1920s, and sixty thousand people left the state. Sections of Montana, today, have big, nearly bankrupt counties that are more empty of people than they were a hundred years ago. The last big homestead rush was a fraud. Still, when a new mine comes along, or some video from an agricultural center in Iowa promises a new miracle, or the time comes at the ballot booth to choose the old colonial pattern or to look within and try something different, Montanans lose their memories. They elect people who will not change the law that allowed the Copper Kings to take twenty billion pounds of metal from the ground without paying royalties, the one that will allow Phelps Dodge to open a new pit above the Blackfoot River and do it all on federal land for the 1872 price of $2.50 an acre. They know, as their grandparents knew, that somewhere not in Montana, it is happening now—They're Trying to Screw Us. But they don't trust the New West either, or what they perceive as the New West. They hear the new Montana residents make fun of miners, joke about cancer and "Butants," while buying mountain bikes and cell phones, forgetting how the copper got into those toys. They see the movie companies come to places like Libby and Livingston, throw money around for a few months, and then leave without much to show for it. "In the West, the mythic value attaches to the hard stuff," says the Montana writer and environmentalist Donald Snow. "Logs, haystacks, cattle brands, ingots. It's the moral supremacy of hardware."

The hope for the Big Sky country, the colony, is not for all the people who can't learn from history to wash out on a big demographic storm, replaced by enlightened urban exiles. You hear such talk in Missoula sometimes, or in Glenn Close's coffee bar in Bozeman, safely inside the zone to the west of the Crazy Mountains, where Montana's literary belt begins. But it won't happen. There is a reason why most of the real estate sold as ranchettes in Montana over the last two decades is not occupied. Visitors fall in love with Montana in the summer, slap their $10,000 down payment on the desk for a twenty-acre piece of heaven, then are bone-chill shocked by the fact that snow can fall any month of the year, and usually will. One study showed that 80 percent of newcomers to Montana move away within five years of arrival.

WHEN I was done with Butte and the Copper Kings, and done with Miles City and the barren homesteads overrun with tumbleweeds, I went out to a big graveyard downslope from the Pit. Just now, among the slag heaps and black gallows of old Butte, the living are still looking to hold on, heeding the call to dig in—like Acoma on the bluff, like Supai in the Grand Canyon, like St. George in the desert. I liked this place. I liked it for its toughness, for its black-lunged ghosts, for putting a ninety-foot virgin on the Continental Divide and hoping for a miracle, for having the gall to say that one of the most ruined landscapes in the West is worthy of the National Park Service, for a tavern called the Helsinki Inn, holding to precarious ground just a few feet from the Pit. The cemetery gave me hope. That miner could linger at the site of the worst accident in the history of hardrock extraction and be drawn to the mountains. And so here in the cemetery, the families of the dead could also look beyond what had brought so many of them to an early grave. The soil held bodies that died for Daly, Clark, and Rockefeller and people who had gone to the poorhouse on Northern Pacific promises of a good land there for the taking. On their tombstones were etched what they wanted to be remembered by: outlines of Montana, mountains carved into graveyard granite, the land that killed them. They loved this damn hard ground, for all its torture; when some way is found to make it love them back, Montana will be free.

CHAPTER 10

Light

Paradise Valley, Montana

O n the longest day of the year I want sunlight that follows me to bed and mountains without winter. The Going-to-the-Sun road would get me there, surely. It starts on the western floor of Glacier National Park, cuts into granite, ducks under waterfalls, and rises into the nosebleed section of the Rockies. It tops out at one of the few places left in the world where bears still eat people, semiregularly. When the road was finished in 1933, after seventeen years of construction, Indians in headdresses and Civilian Conservation Corps workers with whiskey flasks crowded together and sang "America." Glacier is north, perhaps too far for today, even by the standards of no-speed-limit Montana. What else goes straight up? Here's the Beartooth Highway on the map, crawling up to the heavens. I'm in Big Timber, breakfasting at the Road Kill Cafe. The cook is playing songs on the juke that make me think of the old joke about what you get when you play a country and western tune backwards: your wife comes home, your pickup truck works, and you stay sober all day.

The coil over the Absaroka-Beartooth Mountains winds to just under eleven thousand feet, then gradually drops into the northeast entrance of

Yellowstone. Longest day, highest road—a plan for the summer solstice. I will try to loop through the north end of the park and end up just outside the boundary in Paradise Valley, looking for Montana without tears. If Butte is the black hole of Montana, Paradise is the other side, one of the places in the West where you go to find light. Homeward bound, Captain Clark passed through the northern end of Paradise on the way to reunite with Lewis in 1806; as travel-weary as he was, Clark was spellbound by the bison herds shouldering along the Yellowstone. Teddy Roosevelt went there to jawbone about lumber barons and pound the bully pulpit for national parks. Even Maureen Dowd, the writer of American nuance who has managed to go through life without ever once sleeping outside in a tent, came to Paradise and found herself wondering—briefly—about the feeding habits of Yellowstone cutthroat.

Out of Big Timber, the morning is fine and the road straight. I push the car into a lather. I've got Eric Clapton on the tape deck, the Absaroka Range just to the south guarding Yellowstone, and the Crazy Mountains to the north, wherein dwell Crow Indian spirits. In the Big Empty of eastern Montana, you can drive for hours and not see another car. On the mountain side it is a bit more crowded. Still, ninety miles an hour seems to be the status quo on the interstate. I lose myself in the motion, the strobe lights of scenery flashing by, farms with rolls of hay, formations of clouds coming and going without pattern or purpose, waiting for the thermal lift of the afternoon to join a thunderstorm. You often meet people who say they are visiting Montana for one reason: to drive. In a day, you can pass through four seasons. The cafes are usually homey, and sometimes Gothic; the food is honest fuel.

My mobile daydream is broken by a big flashing blue light on my tail and a trooper representing the state of Montana out to greet me.

"Where's the fire?" he asks.

For as long as I've been driving in Montana, there has never been a daytime speed limit on the open roads. Even when the federal government forced everyone to drive fifty-five, Montana went its own way and refused to put up the double nickels. When the feds threatened to withhold Montana's highway funds, the state came up with a weasely law that made it a minor indiscretion to drive beyond fifty-five, punishable by a $5 fine, paid in cash to the trooper on the spot. It was not a speed limit, they insisted; going too fast was a fuel-conservation violation. Truckers and type-A drivers soon learned that you could make your way across Montana at a good clip with a stack of fivers on the seat. When stopped by a trooper, you just rolled down the window and handed the officer one of the fives, end of exchange.

Now, the fuel-conservation law is gone, and Montana still has no formal daytime speed limit on highways. What they have is a law that requires you to drive in a "reasonable and prudent" manner.

"You drive this fast in Washington State?" the trooper asks me, after looking at my license.

"No, sir. We have speed limits in Washington State."

"So do we. Reasonable and prudent."

We sit in his car and have a long, civil discussion about reasonable and prudent. I ask: reasonable and prudent to whom? To a sixteen-year-old, this is a far different thing than it is to a ninety-year-old. He says it applies to the road and the weather conditions, not the age of the driver. Then we talk about politics for a while. He's mad that Montana has only one congressman now, and "that idiot for a senator," his words, describing the farm auctioneer Conrad Burns, voted among the dumbest legislators in Washington. He likes Pat Williams, who's from Butte, and is sorry as hell that Pat stepped down, giving the lone congressional seat to anybody who can run television ads round-the-clock in Billings, Helena, and Great Falls. A lobbyist is the latest to do that, and holds the seat. I ask about the Grizzlies, who stumbled somewhat after winning the small college football championship for the University of Montana in 1995. We are just at the edge of the Seattle Mariners radio zone, where it blurs into Colorado Rockies territory. The trooper, who lives in Milltown, is an M's fan. But he spends most of his free time working on his house and watching osprey snatch fish from the Clark Fork.

This is going much better than my last encounter with a Montana trooper, when I got a taste of summary roadside justice. I'd been pulled over in the Bitterroot Valley by an officer who claimed I had passed another car illegally. He hadn't seen it, but he was told by someone that I had broken the law. Not so, I claimed. "That'll be thirty-five dollars," he said, pronouncing me guilty on the spot. I protested. He said, "You have the money or not?" I reached into my wallet: twenty-eight dollars was all I had. "Then I guess you'll be spending the night in the Ravalli County jail," said the trooper. I asked him if we could find a cash machine. He tailed me to the nearest bank, which was closed, its ATM broken. "I'll take the twenty-eight dollars," the officer said, "and let it go at that." There's a reason, I guess, that state troopers of Montana still wear the patch of the old vigilantes, the 3-7-77 that was pinned on victims, the dimensions of a grave three feet wide, seven feet long, and seventy-seven inches deep.

This time, after thirty-five minutes of visiting, the trooper takes his book out and writes me a ticket for ninety dollars. He's smiling all the while, and I don't hold it against him. "We just don't have much of a tax base here in Montana," he says.

I EAT lunch in Red Lodge. Grilled cheese sandwich, huge pickle, potato soup, coffee, a slice of berry pie—and change back from a five-dollar bill. Already, I don't mind contributing to the tax base of Montana. Outside of town I saw a billboard with these words: Whoa, Dude. There Is A Speed Limit. Red Lodge is a version of Butte before it fell completely into the clutches of the Copper Kings. It was a coal-mining camp, grimy and cold, with all the ethnic stew that boiled up in Butte. But it freed itself of coal's dominance and survived, looking to the giants of the Beartooth Range for sustenance instead of underground. Even with a few boutiques and espresso stands, the old town front still wears overalls. Italians, Finns, Indians, Irish—they have their neighborhoods in Red Lodge. Skiers come to town when they need some vertical relief late in the year, after everything else has closed.

The Beartooth Highway is the road where car radiators go to die. Guy in the gas station tells me that it's so cold up in the higher reaches of the road that radiators will freeze in the midst of a boilover. Now, that can't be true? The road is open only about four months a year. Some winters, thirty-five feet of snow falls on the Bearteeth. My ears pop on the way up and my head is lighter. Listening to the Pretenders, I can't hear the engine strain. The road switches back and forth, steeper than the grade on some Rocky Mountain summit trails, edging up along the contour lines. The walls along the road are granite. Snow is about two feet deep along the side, at first. Near the top, the snow is ten feet deep. I can tell because there are marker poles planted along the road, showing the depth. At the Beartooth Plateau, the road is essentially a tunnel without a top, boring through the snow. I find a little turn carved in the snow, next to exposed rock, and park.

Top of the world. A summit plateau at the edge of the Absaroka-Beartooth Wilderness, which holds much of the water supply for the northern Rockies. Wyoming and the caldera of Yellowstone one way, Montana and the plains the other way. The Absarokas have hundreds of lakes, sharp granite summits, twenty-nine mountains above twelve thousand feet. Froze-to-Death Plateau looks intriguing, as does Phantom Glacier. Most of it is tundra, above the timberline, sprouting wildflowers as it gorges on daylight. There is no bigger expanse of land in the lower forty-eight states at this high an elevation; it is the roof of the West, pressed against the sky. Wilderness, it says on the map. And that is a formal term, not an adjective. The law behind it says wilderness is "an area where the earth and its community of life are untrammeled by man, where man himself is a visitor who does not remain." The sun is blinding. But it is also the day of the big turn from spring to summer, so I need some green, some color, water that is moving rather than frozen.

I take my time shifting downslope, fleeing winter, into the first stands of high alpine spruce, then the lodgepole pine, signature trees of the Yellowstone area. Lakes and tarns, half-freed from the lock of Rocky Mountain cold, appear. The huckleberry bushes are leafing out. A few lupines and columbines have blossomed, splashes of lavender and blue against the green of the mountainside. Down, down, winding along the impossible road, into Wyoming, the cowboy state, license plates with a bronc getting busted. Highest mean elevation of any state in the nation, above six thousand feet. A certain amount of ambivalence about Yellowstone still exists in Wyoming. Goddamn nature park and waffle-stomper playground. In Wyoming, people second-guess and tut-tut the Park Service the way pundits in Washington blather on about congressional follies and White House blunders every Sunday. The big fire of 1988, well, of course it was the fault of the Park Service, with that horseshit let-burn policy of theirs. Wolves in the park? What the hell were they thinking? We got sheep and cattle to raise around here, you computer-geek biologist bureaucrats. And what's with this plan to restrict snowmobiles in winter? Got to make a living in the cold months in West Yellowstone, Gardiner, and Cooke City.

I'm in Cooke City now, northeast gateway to Yellowstone, a little one-time mining town that used to be called Shoofly—a better name. Cooke City, home to ninety people in the winter, three hundred in summer, was given several chances to die and never took it up. Snowmobiles are stacked and parked for the season. In winter, they invade in such numbers that park rangers get dizzy and nauseous at the entrance gates. Two thousand snowmobiles equals 1.2 million cars in exhaust output, giving Yellowstone the highest carbon monoxide levels in the country during the winter. And Senator Conrad Burns is going to make damn sure that the carbon monoxide level stays that way, the daily paper from Cody says. The air is so bad during the snowmobile flock-ins that park rangers in West Yellowstone pump in their own air to the entrance booths.

I hear piano music, non-honky-tonk variety. A woman in Smokey's green is reading under a tree and sipping a Coke. Windows are open in the damp upper rooms of sagging lodges. Every door has a rack of antlers over-head. A few people walk the wooden boardwalk, no place to go. Just a few feet above town the blackened trees from the big fire form a line. Most people thought Cooke City would go in a poof, the old wood fire-hazard. But they watered down the roofs and fought the blaze in hand-to-flame combat. It was dark, suffocatingly smoky, and broiling hot. The yellow-shirts brought in reinforcements, and air power as well. The fire hopscotched away, moving up the mountains towards the Beartooths.

More recently, Cooke City has appeared in datelines around the world. Above town, the stories go, is a time bomb. A Canadian-owned mining company has staked a claim to federal land in an alpine bowl. They want to bore deep into the ground, haul out a mountainside of ore, leach it with cyanide to bring the gold out, then store the waste for eternity in a huge tailings pond—their own little version of The Pit. Only a layer of plastic would keep the mine poisons—in a lake ten stories deep and the length of a dozen football fields—from leaking down into groundwater and ultimately into Yellowstone, land of a thousand small earthquakes a year. The Canadian company, of course, would pay no royalties for a venture on American public land that could imperil the world's first national park. They call the project the New World Mine, but it's very much an Old World giveaway.

One summer President Bill Clinton, following the divining rod of a poll taken by advisor Dick Morris, came to Yellowstone during his vacation. Americans, Morris told the president, wanted to see a chunky-looking guy with pasty legs hanging around campgrounds and eating burgers, just like they do during their holiday. Dutifully, two years in a row, Clinton went to the Grand Tetons, just south of the park. Most of the time, he had a pained look on his face, riding horses, getting sprayed by cold water on the Snake River, swatting deerflies. He was puffy and sunburned. Clinton's idea of green is Astroturf, the kind he used to have in the back of his pickup truck in Arkansas. In the Rocky Mountains, he looked like all he wanted to do was play golf, and damn that Dick Morris for using my vacation for a five-point bounce in the polls. Chelsea Clinton and her mother went to see the wolves in Yellowstone; they heard a howl and were enchanted. The president thought golf, golf, golf, burgers, golf, and to hell with Dick Morris. He was in Homer Simpson mode. When he arrived in Yellowstone the second summer, Clinton heard the usual woeful story of the Canadian-owned mine that threatened the American crown jewel.

"How can the logical mind approve this?" said the park's feisty and politically savvy superintendent, Mike Finley. After all the reporters had been alerted that something was afoot, the president declared his intention to stop the mine, to swap some land in Montana in place of the alpine bowl above Yellowstone. The Canadian mine company, owned by a subsidiary of the Seagram liquor dynasty, could go carve up the earth and leach it with cyanide on some other piece of American public land, less scenic, less known to participants of poll surveys. Sighs of relief went out from coast to coast. Even some newspapers in Wyoming, where they eat Democrats for camp appetizers and hang Interior Secretary Bruce Babbitt in effigy as a civics lesson for the kids, applauded Clinton. So, for the time, it appeared that the bomb above Yellowstone was defused. And Clinton, safely re-elected, could stay out of the mountains.

IT IS so cold along Soda Butte Creek I can't tie the little nymph onto the end of my fly line. I'm inside the park, walking along the edge of the creek. The water is high, bloated with snowmelt, but there are a few pools and riffles where trout are sure to be feeding. It's early afternoon. I've gone from breakfast at dawn in Big Timber, a ticket on Interstate 90, lunch in Red Lodge, a heart-stopping haul over the Beartooth Plateau, in and out of Cooke City to safety in Yellowstone. I'm still looking for that first-day-of-summer warmth. The elevation here is just below eight thousand feet. When I wade into the stream, my head feels as if it took a shot of novocaine from a foot-long needle. With the nymph finally attached to my line, I work the stream for a while. My casts aren't very good. I can't see the stinking lure, which is supposed to be a subsurface bug, struggling to live. I prefer dry-fly fishing on lazier water. Casting for an hour, I get one strike and that's it. Skunked. And now it's starting to snow. Not just flurries, but a regular whiteout. Those lazy, crazy days of summer in the northern Rockies. I get under a tree, seeking protection. The storm drops an inch of snow on the ground in twenty minutes, then moves on, leaving the land smothered and sunlit. I hear the crunch of wood, loud snapping sounds. It startles me. Just ten yards away is a moose, with nostrils as big as my fists, chomping away on the side of a large tree. He is eating twigs, bark-skinned branches, leaves—the whole fibrous woody feast. Yellowstone, they call it the American Serengeti.

WHAT THEY used to call Yellowstone was a liar's landscape. The stories the mountain men brought back East were otherworldly and unbelievable. You boys have been without human contact for too long, the rational listener would respond, accustomed to an earth where rivers did not flow backwards, or boil at a constant temperature of 210 degrees. The French were the first to spread tales. They lived with the Mandans, the tribe of destiny, so integral to the success of Lewis and Clark's expedition, but wiped out by disease as a consequence of a decade of multicultural socializing. The French came up with the name Roche Jaune, which first surfaced in 1795. The land was the color of gold, yes, but not the substance. So Napoleon saw all the Missouri River drainage as expendable. Americans wonder why the French seem crabby and charge people extra just to sit down in their cafes; consider the historic giveaway. The majority of the American West, most of it unmapped at the time, was sold to the United States for $15 million.

Lewis and Clark missed Yellowstone. They followed the Missouri to its source, then picked up the first trickles of the Pacific drainage and rode the water to the ocean. On the way back, Clark deviated down to the Yellowstone River, where it picks up at the north head of Paradise Valley. But the most unusual land formations of the continent were never seen. A veteran of the Corps of Discovery, John Colter, was not interested in going East and dining off his memoirs, as most members of Lewis and Clark's expedition did. At least not yet. He said goodbye to his transcontinental traveling mates and backtracked up the Yellowstone River. For the next five years, he walked over fields of cacti and blistering earth, through snowdrifts of twenty feet and muddy bogs. In the winter of 1807–08, with just thirty pounds on his back and snowshoes on his feet, Colter slogged through Yellowstone and Jackson Hole, a thousand-mile journey, he claimed. When he at last returned he told of hot springs and geysers, waterfalls and wildlife, wedding cakes of sulfur-smelling crystal, and a lake at the base of a broad, sunken volcano. His critics called it "Colter's Hell," and him a liar. He may have fudged the part about tramping through all of Yellowstone in winter with a mere thirty pounds on his back, but the other stuff was true. And much later, the wordsmith Rudyard Kipling, teller of fantastic tales, could not improve on what Colter had said of Yellowstone. "It's a howling wilderness of three thousand square miles, full of all imaginable freaks of fiery nature," Kipling wrote.

The nature writer, whether Mark Twain at his self-deprecating best in the Sierra, or John Muir at his mystical peak, rarely gets much credit for altering the course of events. Western historians, new and old schools, dismiss the romanticizing, the anthropomorphizing, the exaggeration. When

Terry Tempest Williams went to Congress to rhapsodize about the red rock country of Utah not long ago, she was snubbed by her state congressional delegation. Nature poet—what the hell does she know. Thomas McGuane is rarely listened to by anyone with tax money to spend in his home state of Montana. Muir, at least, was given a camping trip with Teddy Roosevelt; but T.R. was already sold on saving Yosemite. Yellowstone National Park, the creation of which was unprecedented, the idea of which was an American gift to the world, owes its foundation to storytellers with pen, ink, and silver oxide. When the stories about Yellowstone ceased to be disregarded as yarns, America realized it had a treasure and it had a culture that would be linked to the wild. All of this evolved over time. And some of it was simple nationalism. The British had dismissed reports of megaflora and towering geysers as "Yankee inventions." Well. Bring Mr. Kipling over here, and we'll show him a thing or two.

Rumors of Yellowstone grew and multiplied throughout the nineteenth century, long after Colter's wanderings. It was the Loch Ness monster of the West: a lot of people claimed to have seen some parts of it, but almost all of the descriptions were reality-challenged. By 1871, Congress had decided to send a formal expedition out to map, sketch, and photograph the rumors. A similar thing had been done with the Grand Canyon two years earlier, with John Wesley Powell at the head. For all the government support of industries that worked to kill the better parts of the West, from bison to wild rivers, there has always been another tradition: subsidized serendipity. Of course the explorers with presidential seals on their compasses were directed to specific ends. But they were paid to wander, roam, sniff, sketch, listen, take a close look at the country, and try to grasp it in all its dimensions. A Pennsylvania geologist, Ferdinand Hayden, was put in charge of the Yellowstone trip, financed to the tune of forty thousand dollars. He was well supplied with food, horses, mapping equipment, a platoon of soldiers and assistants, scientists, and, most importantly, a painter, a photographer, and a writer. The landscape painters Karl Bodmer and Albert Bierstadt had already captured some of the essence of the West that had escaped other travelers. Religious zealots, prospectors, homesteaders, city builders, railroad surveyors, Indian killers—they had been widely promoted and were ubiquitous. The painters were more interested in light, color, the contours of the land and its inhabitants. John James Audubon spent more than half a year at the headwaters of the Missouri in 1843, sketching drafts for what would become *Birds of America*. Bierstadt painted the Rockies on his first Western trip in 1859, and then on a second trip in 1863, one that took him to

Yosemite. Some of his paintings did give an undue glow to the otherwise harsh and killing walk across the continent by emigrants. But his best work captured the West of grandeur.

In Yellowstone, Hayden's survey found the headwaters of the Snake River, the geyser that would later be known as Old Faithful, and the extraordinary stair-steps of white at the terraces of Mammoth Hot Springs, formed by calcium carbonate. Hayden, short and full of bounce, was called "Man Who Picks Up Stones Running," by the Indians. He was a geologist in rock heaven. Yellowstone has the highest concentration of active geothermal features in the world and the largest geyser. Three times in the last two million years, Yellowstone had experienced a monumental eruption, reshaping much of the West. The core of Yellowstone is a collapsed volcano; all around are windows into the molten interior of the earth—mud pots and geysers, hot springs and fumaroles. Hayden's expedition was in a land that seemed to be still forming, alive, and was overrun with bison, antelope, wolves, bighorn sheep, elk, pikas, grizzly and black bears, trumpeter swans, and osprey. Colter had told no lies; he simply never had anything to back up his claims.

Hayden returned with proof. His expedition painter, Thomas Moran, recorded some of the color and detail of Yellowstone. Moran was the son of immigrant handweavers, and he was self-trained. He captured the spray and energy of the waterfalls, the way the rivers pushed through the yellow-colored rock, the breadth of valleys grazed by thousands of bison, the mountains at sunset. Later critics called his work, and that of Bierstadt and others, the propaganda arm of monumentalism—landscape as power. Which meant that landscapes without big central monuments, be it prairie grass or old-growth forest, were inferior by comparison. The argument has merit, but the academics who ruminate on this topic miss a point: people do not make intellectual attachments to land. They become passionate because something clicks, some esthetic connection. They get a dose of religion, sometimes from a monument, sometimes from the angle of light at dawn, but it is seldom rational in its origin. John Steinbeck toured the country for *Travels with Charley: In Search of America* in 1962 and sounded like a schoolboy trying to explain what happened to him after going through the Big Sky country. "I am in love with Montana," he wrote. "For other states I have admiration, respect, recognition, even some affection, but with Montana it is love, and it's difficult to analyze love when you're in it." Yes, but would it love him back?

Moran's painting of the Grand Canyon of the Yellowstone, depicting the waterfall that plunges a thousand feet over brightly colored rock, dazzled Washington. It was the first American landscape, by an American artist, to be purchased by the government. Equally convincing were William Henry Jackson's black-and-white photographs, most of which were later destroyed in Chicago's Great Fire. Hayden added his own words from his diary, appealing to nationalism. "We pass with rapid transition from one remarkable vision to another, each unique in its kind and surpassing all others in the known world," he wrote.

The national park idea was formalized the next year, 1872, when President Grant signed the law establishing a sanctuary of more than two million acres. It was termed "a pleasuring ground for all the people." But it started something. Instead of the government giving away the West, or trying to remake it, or disparaging it, the land was cherished for simply what it was— America in the raw. To protect the new reserve, the army was sent in, and for better than thirty years, they were the first national park rangers, chasing poachers, shooing out prospectors, giving directions to women in corsets and men in suits who had taken the railroad down Paradise Valley to experience something akin to the American version of the grand tour. There may have been no better use for the cavalry in the West. The British, snubbers and disbelievers early on, were among the first to show gratitude and to realize the significance of what had happened in the American West. "All honor to the United States for having bequeathed as a free gift to man the beauties and curiosities of this wonderland," said the Earl of Duneaven on a visit to Yellowstone in 1874. More than 120 years later, in the mid-1990s, members of a strident new Congress proposed closing some national parks, and getting rid of all public art—in a single legislative bill. They derided park advocates as nature freaks and elites who wanted to lock up the land. "Waffle-stomping, Harvard-graduating idiots," was the phrase used by Congressman Don Young, head of the House committee that oversees most public land issues. The promoters of wilderness and parks, cast as somehow un-American, out of sync with Western tradition, were defensive. They should have boasted of their lineage. Yellowstone owes its existence to a mountain man, a geologist who could write, and a painter. None of them went to Harvard.

I TRY to dash through the Lamar Valley. I've been there a dozen times, but I can never pull myself away. In early evening all manner of creatures great and small come together in this banquet hall of nature. Trout rise for bugs. Osprey and eagles swoop for trout. Pronghorns bounce, as if on springs. Hundreds of buffalo graze along the valley, joined by their calves. Unlike cattle, bison know how to drink from a stream without destroying it; their hooves are thin, and they don't lie around in turd-covered mudflats, aswarm with flies, waiting to be herded off to the next meal. But they have to be on their toes; the weaker ones do, at least. The new Yellowstone wolves have discovered, like their predecessors of a hundred years ago, that Lamar Valley is a good place to hunt. A healthy bison can run just under forty miles an hour, at top speed. Wolves have to lie low, watch and wait for a tired old buffalo to stumble. There are plenty of wolves in crowded Italy, including some in the Abruzzi forests not more than an hour from Rome. But trying to bring them back to the original national park took more tax money, caused more litigation, and produced more political obstructionism than anything the government has ever done with endangered species. None of the arguments put forth by wolf opponents have been borne out: the cattle and sheep industries have not been hurt, no private land owners have suffered an egregious breach of property rights, no children have been snatched by fairy tale predators. All of this was part of a phony debate. The big issue—what the West should be like and who would control it—was never brought out into the open. Some people are afraid of wolves, even in a huge national park, because it means they no longer control the plot line from which flows public policy.

With the return of bison and wolves, the century-long era of the sterile West, drained of certain wild animals and dominated by domestic stock, may be down to its last days.

This is not to say that nature-balancing has been an easy task. Playing God, as Yellowstone biologists have done since some of the last grizzly bears and bison were given a home in the park, has been fraught with problems. Tourists used to file into grandstands to watch the rangers feed garbage to grizzly bears; this produced a generation of welfare-dependent big animals, who didn't smell all that good either. Weaning them of dump scraps was an epic fight. There are far too many elk in the park, but until wolves were brought back, there was no predator. In hard winters, thousands of elk died of starvation; I saw them pawing the doors of houses in Gardiner and staggering around Main Street looking for handouts. Nonnative trout are crowding out the homegrown cutthroat in Yellowstone Lake. And what about humans, long a part of the Yellowstone ecosystem? The Indians set fires and chased bison off cliffs. Now, snowmobiles make convenient paths in the snow for bison to exit the park, at which point they are shot dead by the long arm of the cattle industry.

"**GOD DAMN!** That is just the goddamndest thing I've seen!" The man next to me has an accent from someplace warm, and he's blue with chill. He can't take his eyes off the Lamar Valley, him and about twenty-five other people gathered to watch the evening animal frolics. He has his binoculars trained on a flock of pronghorns, which seem to be dancing around a big bull buffalo.

"Take a look." He hands me the binoculars. His fingers are drained of blood. The guy is about six feet five inches tall, with another six inches of cowboy hat. He seems hypothermic. He needs a sleeping bag, a car heater, or at least a coat. He tells me he's from Houston. "Wife and two of the kids are back at the hotel," he says. "In the hot tub is where I left 'em. That's my boy over there." He points to a surly teen, also freezing.

"You better do something about that chill," I say.

"I got some of this." He shows me a half-empty pint of Yukon Jack, the black sheep of liquors, as their slogan says.

"Sip?"

I demur, with miles still to go in the twilight of the longest day.

"When we left Houston it was a hundred and five degrees, I shit you not," he says. "Been hot and humid for months. We'd had enough. Had to get somewhere cool. We just threw a bunch of T-shirts and jeans together and got in the car. Ever been to Houston in the summer? Humidity is one hundred percent."

They looked at a map and decided: why not see Grand Teton, Yellowstone, and Glacier, the crown jewels, and do it all in a couple of days? At worst, they thought, it might get down to seventy degrees at night—relief. When they they arrived in Yellowstone, yesterday, they ran into snow outside Canyon Village, where the elevation is just under nine thousand feet.

"Shit my pants," he says. "Car nearly went off the road. The kid, that one over there, is laughing. What's the deal here with this weather?"

The cold talk has focused my mind, anew, on the primary goal: to find the light. I move through Lamar Valley, up to Mammoth Hot Springs, park headquarters. Fort Yellowstone, where the cavalry was based until 1916, is still intact. Elk lounge on manicured grass and prune trees that look as if they don't need it. The road winds down to a warmer climate, the driest part of Yellowstone, the edge of Paradise Valley. The grass is amber, the sky mostly clear. Perhaps two hours of daylight are left. I exit the park under Roosevelt Arch, the big stone monument named for T.R. "For the benefit and enjoyment of the people," the inscription on the arch reads.

Gardiner, the Montana town that borders the park at the north entrance, is jumping. Heavy with fresh runoff, the Yellowstone River roars under a bridge in town. The sound would cure any insomniac. It is the longest free-flowing river in the West, picking up all of that Yellowstone Park high plateau snow, water from the Absaroka-Beartooth wilderness, and swooshing through the grand canyon dropoff that so impressed the Senate in the nineteenth century. It tumbles down roche jaune flanks, then forms the main valley of Paradise before it scoots half the length of Montana and empties into the Missouri. There are hot springs and religious wackos and a string of mildly bashful Hollywood heavies hidden throughout Paradise. A number of horse ranchers, river-raft expeditioners, fishing and hunting guides, and writers live there as well. It's a good mix. Not that they get along. But at any time of the day you can look up at the sky and feel there's enough room to disagree.

An old stone-block building that looks like a jailhouse but is now a theater, is playing *Tombstone.* Much as I like the story in all its incarnations, I decide to skip the movie and walk the myth. But the cowboy and sourdough story of the West is not selling well along the wood-planked main tourist street of big-buckled Gardiner. Shops are crowded with people buying wolf pictures, wolf tapes, wolf books. The other big sellers are landscape paintings—jut-jawed mountains and noble ungulates posing in good weather. Just once, I'd like to see a picture of a hyperkinetic pronghorn with froth mouth, or maybe a postprandial griz. Russell Chatham, who lives up the road in Livingston, is big in Paradise. You look at his series of paintings, *The Montana Suite,* and realize he's got the same sense of the Big Sky country in his bones as had those Butte miners who had the mountains chiseled on their tombstones. Another painting, *Paradise Valley in August,* is the opposite of monumentalist sentiment: the land is hazy, inglorious, and looks hot. In prison with a such a painting, a lifer would not feel confined. Chatham is self-taught, just like Charley Russell of Great Falls and Thomas Moran. How did they learn? You can see a lot by watching, as Yogi Berra said.

I order a buffaloburger and fries, to go. The meat is sweet and juicy. I watch the swollen thunderclouds break up in the Beartooth Range, a great show of energy and drama. Afterward, I stroll along the river, Electric Peak in the near distance, aglow with solstice light at 9:30 P.M. I know a place in the other direction, a river that runs bathtub-hot year-round, with natural pools set in big rocks and a view facing a thick flank of mountain. I have sat in those waters and listened to elk during the fall rut, at a time when fire was still moving across much of Yellowstone, and the skies were full of smoke. This evening, I just want to hear the river in Paradise Valley and move fast enough to keep warm.

I feel about Montana now the way you feel about good friends at the end of a lengthy dinner. Of course, I've been walking at a good clip at the end of the longest day, with a buffaloburger inside of me, my pulse up, so it could be the endorphins talking. But I think not. What happens here, and in the other best places of the West, is subtle persuasion—the land as lobbyist. It worked its wonders with that garden-variety life-form of politician, state legislators, in 1972, when they rewrote the Montana Constitution. "We the people of Montana, grateful to God for the quiet beauty of our state, the grandeur of its mountains, the vastness of its rolling plains . . .," it begins. This is a boast, by way of stating the primary values—the grand, the vast, quiet, and God—at a time when Anaconda Copper's grip on the state was in its last days. And it worked time and again with Wallace Stegner; at his most pessimistic, he could always find a Paradise Valley, and so he never gave up on the West. It snagged Steinbeck and Thomas Moran and that Texan slipping into hypothermia while he sipped Yukon Jack and watched buffalo do nothing more than chew grass on the longest day of the year.

CHAPTER 11

Top of the Food Chain

Bitterroot Mountains, Idaho

Articles of adventure: neoprene waders and a Gore-Tex coat, a half dozen bagels and a reading light with extra batteries, a dome-shaped tent and a sitting chair that collapses. Polarizing sunglasses that allow us to see through water and a purification pump that lets the water go through us without leaving a trace. Juice to make mosquitoes wince and horseflies think twice. More than twenty-five square feet of Forest Service map, representing about nine million acres. A Swiss Army knife that holds a fork, a saw, scissors, three blades, a screwdriver, a corkscrew, a toothpick, and a firestarter of dubious utility. Never go into the back country without the ten essentials, they say in those places where they sell the ten essentials. We have the basic ten and then the worthwhile stuff: garlic, sweet onions, red peppers, a marinade mix, meat, apples, eggs in an unbreakable container, whiskey, red wine, beer. Our shirts are made of a substance unknown to nature, but they keep water off the skin, and—in a pinch—can be torched to induce damp kindling to flame. We have an inflatable pillow, a mattress of foam and air pockets, a sleeping bag for three seasons, good to twenty degrees. And what happens below that threshold?

We have light reading, Jane Smiley's *A Thousand Acres,* weighing barely more than a folded T-shirt, and heavy reading for a tent-lashing-storm, *A Soldier of the Great War,* a book that will take us through a three-day blow but will double in size with moisture. All of this must fit into what we can put on our backs. We have made some sacrifices, trying to keep the Information Age at home. No cell phones. No radios. No portable global positioning systems to bounce off the satellite when lost. We're packing a compass.

"Thro' thickets in which we were obliged to Cut a road, over rockey hill Sides where our horses were in perpetual danger of slipping to Ther certain distruction & up & Down Steep Hills," was how William Clark described the first American entry into Idaho and the drainage of the Pacific. "The greatest difficuelty risque & c . . ." They had left a nation of five million people on the orders of a president who believed the highest mountains on the continent were in Virginia. Lewis and Clark traveled 7,689 miles between 1804 and 1806, and the only place that really seemed to scare them, where they were on the brink of starvation, was in the mountains of the Idaho-Montana border—the Bitterroots. "The country is so remote and rugged that nearly two full centuries later it remains basically uninhabitated," said Stephen Ambrose in his chronicle of the Corps of Discovery.

When low-wattage loners, toy soldiers with mildewed grudges, and early-retired Los Angeles police officers seek a place where they can hide from the rest of the world, inevitably they come to the mountains of Idaho. When anglers, hunters, hikers, and river-rafters look for Alaska without going north, they also come to Idaho. The same state that has more armed paranoiacs than any other also has more white-water river miles, thirty-two hundred, than any other in the Lower 48. The state that sent a militia sympathizer to Congress could not be just flat, boring, and humid; it has sixty different mountain ranges, more than two hundred peaks above eight thousand feet, fourteen million acres of wild land, the largest granite foundation in the world in the Idaho batholith, and a most wondrous central artery: the River of No Return. The two extremes are drawn to the same place, perhaps for the same reason—cover.

We shoulder our packs and take final inventory. Extra water bottles. Oysters in tins of olive oil, sardines in mustard sauce. A blister remedy called Second Skin, and a nasal-blocking aid known as Snore-No-More for sleeping in tight quarters. Edam cheese and Costco warehouse bricks of orange cheese—"for nachos," my younger brother, Danny, says. Soap, with an environment-friendly seal of approval on the front. Three small stoves. Canisters of kerosene. Extra whiskey, a dash of tequila, some limes. Wool gloves. Baseball hat. Topographical maps, trail maps, maps of the river. Toilet paper. Medical bag with antiseptic, gauze, tape, snake-bite antivenin, and ibuprofen. Most important: graphite fly rods, reels blessed by somebody royal in England, vests with fourteen pockets, and three dozen fake bugs—all hand-tied by my other brother, Kelly. We are going into native cutthroat habitat in the heart of the Bitterroots for one reason: to fish until we drop.

"It's the wildest country I've ever been in," says Kelly. "And it's the best fishing. Every cast a strike."

"We won't see a soul," says Danny. "You'll feel like the first person who's ever been there."

They make me promise I will never write about it. I bargain, and they hold their ground. We reach a compromise: if I do write about it, I will not name the river. I can say, without giving anything away, that it is in the broad, overgrown, western drainage of the Bitterroots, and that it is public land—not considerably changed from how it looked in that late summer of 1805 when Lewis and Clark were trying to follow some of those mountain streams to the big ocean. A famous painting of the expedition, *Lewis and Clark in the Bitterroots,* by John Clymer, shows men knee-deep in snow, rifles in hand, descending the steepest of forested slopes, trailed by a horse on which sits someone shivering in a Hudson's Bay Company wool blanket.

No snow today. It is hot, mid-eighties, a bowl of blue overhead, three shades of green at eye level on the forest horizon. The ground crackles underfoot—pine cones, twigs, leaves from last fall. The wildflowers, lupine, Indian paintbrush, and columbine, are in third-act histrionics. The first huckleberries are ripening. My pack rubs against my shoulder blades and along the bones of my hips; no matter how I adjust one of the half dozen or so straps, the weight is never completely comfortable. The ballast problem is caused by tonight's dinner; it will be my turn to cook on the first evening, and I'm carrying a surprise. But it weighs too much and is sloshing around inside a plastic container. Danny is the youngest in our family of seven kids. I'm the oldest boy. Kelly is in the middle. We brothers no longer fight like we used to, and we have pretty much settled on avoiding any discussion of why the college that I am loyal to, the University of Washington, usually beats the college of their tribal bonding, Washington State University, in an end-of-the-season football game called the Apple Cup. In their Cougar view, all Husky fans are elitist, Brie-eating Seattleites who look down on them as hayseeds with cow shit on their shoes. They are rural and slow and have just a bit too much affection for farm animals. We are pampered, pushy, latte-sipping weenies. I had given Danny a backpacking espresso-maker for Christmas, lightweight and compact, partially as a joke. He refused to bring it along, saying it violated his Cougar ethics. A Cougar brings Nescafe and spills it on his shirt, where it joins decades-old bits of dried chili and Dinty Moore Beef Stew. What we do now on back-country trips is cook competitively.

"As we had killed nothing during the day we now boiled and eat the remainder of our pork, having yet a little flour and parched meal," Lewis wrote as he and three members of the Corps ascended the foothills of the Bitterroots, soon to leave behind the land Jefferson purchased for three cents an acre.

We hike through a forest of larch and spruce, an easy trail, under laissez-faire Forest Service maintenance. The path finds the river, shadowed by old cedar trees, fir, some white pine. In the hottest part of the day, the pack is clammy; it feels as if it's tied to me by a guy wire. But we're making great time, three miles an hour, almost. The water looks dreamy, swift and clear in parts, pooling up in others. A little breeze flutters along the river. The trail seems to end, but my brothers know another way, guided by habit. We go up steep rocks, down a flank that would be treacherous if wet, over scree marbles and big talus. We stop at an opening, level and grassy. There's a granite-ringed firepit, plenty of flat tent space, logs for stools. The river music, white noise for sleep, is at perfect volume.

"We lucked out," says Kelly, dropping his pack. He's red and sweaty and as happy as I've ever seen him. "We got the best spot on the river." Our arrival sends an osprey away. The bird is a close cousin of the bald eagle, a superb predator, swooping and diving for cutthroat. In the narrow river valley, the osprey looks oversized, with a wingspan the length of a picnic bench.

"I hope he saved us some fish," says Danny.

Just below our camp the water forms a deep pool after sliding over stair-step falls. We edge up to a small cliff, strip down, and dive in. It's exhilarating, the water cleaning the trail dust and sweat away, and it's numbing. We swim up into the white water and play there, battling the current. Near shore, Danny wedges cans of beer in the river, held down by rocks. In early evening we take our fly rods and walk upstream. I have on old leather tennis shoes; it's too warm for waders. Danny takes a water temperature reading and pronounces it just right at fifty-seven degrees. I tie on an elk-haired caddis, a medium-size dry fly, and start working a stretch of the stream. I'm thinking like a fish—or at least how I think a fish would think in the hunt for fresh-hatched nymphs. My bug, in theory, has just come off the floor of the river, floated to the top, and is preparing for a few days of life out of water. We take turns at being the first to hit a hole as we move. I cast upstream, trying to land the fly in the place where the air bubbles from the current meet the slow water of the pool—the gravy train, Kelly calls it. The bug lands a little short of where I want it, but that's okay. I've got enough slack out for a short, decent ride. One second, two, three, and—splash!—a nice-size fish rises for the caddis.

"Got one!" and I'm acting like a teenager in the thrall of first sex, all aflutter, heart pounding, hands moving awkwardly. The reel makes a zinnnng, zinnnng sound. I land the fish. It's a beautiful, midsize, west-slope Bitterroot cutthroat. A native. There are no planters in this part of the West. Kelly cautions me to keep the fish in the water, remove the fly carefully and quickly, kiss the trout on the snout and let him go, making sure he's not too disoriented. While I'm doing this, Danny gets one on the line, and then Kelly connects on his first cast. The light is angled, summery, filling the valley with holy luminescence. All through the evening until the stars appear we catch fish and let them go.

"Caught 528 fish, most of them large trout," Lewis had written a few days before going into the Bitterroots. The Corps had feasted on cutthroat. It would be their last good meal for some time.

AT DINNER, I pull out my surprise. At home, I had cut strips of lamb from a leg bone, cooked it lightly over a grill, and then packed it in a sealed plastic container. All evening, since we hit camp, the lamb has been marinating in a sauce of soy, wine, sugar, lemon, and rosemary. I unveil softball-sized Walla Walla sweets, the best onions in North America. You can bite into a Walla Walla sweet as if it's an apple. I cut them into pieces. Then I take the peppers, red and yellow, and slice them up. I run metal skewers through the meat and vegetables, and then set them over low, orange coals of the fire.

"What the hell is that?" says Kelly.

"Dinner," I say. "Lamb shish kebab."

For a side dish, I have a rice pilaf, mixed with scraps of the sweet onion and peas. I take out a packet of dried mix, add water and olive oil, stir it up, and present it to them, next to vegetables and pita bread.

"Hummus mix. We're eating Middle Eastern tonight. Dig in."

Danny has cracked open one of his beers, but he seems dissatisfied. It's not very cold. I pour him some red wine from a plastic water bottle. It's not very cold either, which is how we want it. I turn the kebabs one rotation over the fire. They are nicely grilled, sizzling with juice and marinated blood. We talk about our siblings, three sisters and another brother, and sports, and Helen Chenoweth, the CongressMAN, as she calls herself, from Idaho. She comes from the wildest part of the Lower 48, the drainage of the River of No Return, and she hates the wild. There are no grizzly bears in the Bitterroots, the Sawtooths, anywhere in Idaho, though the Fish and Wildlife Service and plenty of outdoor-loving Idahoans are trying to bring them back. Chenoweth says the bears are "manic-depressive" and don't belong in the wild because they might scare away people who come to Idaho on their vacations. Keep them in zoos, she says.

"Maybe the bears need counseling," says Danny, who is not a doctor or a shrink but works with manic-depressives and psychotics in a public hospital in Coeur d'Alene, helping them through sports therapy.

"I'm going to try a hopper tomorrow if this weather stays hot," says Kelly. He is focused, locked in pursuit; he will not talk about anything but fishing. "A hopper is cool, because it's big enough, you can see the action."

The lamb is done. The outside is flame-licked to a nice crust and the inside is pink. Using my wool gloves to hold the skewers, I give my brothers their dinner—full plates of flayed and marinated leg of lamb, with sweet onions and peppers, grilled over a pine and alder fire, a rice pilaf on the side, a little Chianti out of plastic to wash it down.

"Needs a sauce," says Kelly.

"I have one." And out of a side pocket of my pack I produce a little plastic film vial containing mint sauce, which I had made up in advance.

"This is unbelievable," says Danny. "You hiked all this stuff in. Top Ramen would do it for me."

"I've got salmon fettucine for tomorrow," says Kelly.

"What kind of salmon?"

"Alaskan King, baby. Copper River King, to be precise. Should we hang our food?"

"Why? There are no grizzly bears. No predators. We're king of the valley."

Lewis and Clark identified 122 animal species or subspecies previously unknown to science, including cutthroat trout. They gave a detailed account of grizzly bears, which they first encountered on the eastern side of the Divide, on the High Plains. A griz has huge balls, Lewis wrote, "the testicles suspended in separate pouches from two to four inches asunder." The Corps hunters shot a grizzly bear, but it kept coming toward them. "It is astonishing to see the wounds they will bear before they can be put to death." They fired repeatedly, "five balls through his lungs and five through various parts," but the bear would not slow down, swimming for twenty minutes until it finally died. The Indians, Lewis noted, would paint their faces with war paint when preparing to hunt the big bears. In California, where grizzlies once lived in what are now San Francisco and Los Angeles, the Washo Indians used the same word to describe both bears and white people. The last grizzly was killed on the Plains in 1890. They were driven to the highest, coldest, most barren ground in America, until all that remained of grizzly bears in the West were a handful in Yellowstone and Glacier national parks.

In Idaho, there are a few woodland caribou up north, and bighorn sheep roam around the Owyhee Canyons in the south, dodging Air Force planes on practice bombing runs.

AT DAWN the valley is a different place, the chill from the river hugging the ground, having left a film of moisture on the outside of the tents. Sleep was deep and long; I was lulled by the river. We make coffee, scramble some eggs, eat fruit bars, and then stuff our packs with apples and cheese for a day of fishing.

"These beers are cold," Danny says. He's stumbled into a Cougar moment: the night temperatures have chilled the beer, meaning the only time he can really drink them is in the morning. Time of day has never been a problem for Cougars in the past. He laughs, puts three of them in his pack.

"I want to take you guys to Dollywood today," Kelly says.

Dollywood is the name he's given to a series of pools far upriver, near the headwaters, where Dolly Vardens, the big bull trout of the Rocky Mountains, are said to dwell. The biggest Dolly ever landed in Idaho was thirty-two pounds. They live to grow to such a size because they won't rise for just anything. They are smart, wary, and plentiful here, though approaching extinction in many other rivers of the West. We predators will have to be stealthy and present them with flawless bugs to lure them out of Dollywood. We follow a trail upriver, flushing another osprey away from breakfast. I nibble on a few huckleberries, dewy and crisp.

"Hungary as a wolf," Lewis wrote of one of his early mornings approaching the Bitterroots. He had eaten nothing the day before, save some wet mix of flour and berries. They had entered the most densely forested, chaotic, and vertical part of their journey across the continent thus far, and the food was nearly gone. He had his men divide a few pounds of flour into rations. They were with Shoshones, hoping to find the Pacific drainage, still following the letter of Jefferson's order, to seek out "the most direct and practical water communication across this continent for the purpose of commerce." At the end of the day, the Indians took pity on the Corps and gave them cakes of service berries and choke cherries. "Of these I made a hearty meal," Lewis wrote. The next day he sent one of his hunters out for food. He killed a deer, and as he was dressing it the Indians gorged on the innards. The Indians did not touch the meat, only the organs. "Some were eating the kidnies the melt and liver and the blood running from the corner of their mouths, others were in a similiar situation with the paunch and guts," Lewis noted. The whole scene looked carnal and primitive to Lewis, the Virginia gentleman. He ate a hindquarter of venison, cooked over the fire. "I really did not until now think that human nature ever presented itself in a shape so nearly allyed to the brute creation." He may have over- looked what the French do with geese, ramming food down their gullets to engorge the livers for *foie gras.*

They found no game in the Bitterroots, except a few grouse. Even the Shoshones were beginning to starve. Finally, they were forced to kill and eat one of their horses. They called the area of this meal Colt Killed Creek. Snow fell. They inched west, realizing there was no simple passage across the continent, not a river or an easy portage. Unable to descend the Salmon River—the River of No Return—because it was too turgid, they had gone into the thickly wooded mountain country. Pained by hunger, they killed another horse. "A coalt," Lewis noted in a brief passage, "fell prey to our appetites." Clark designated the area Hungery Creek, a name that remains to this day, the spelling corrected.

The water is a little rougher upriver from our camp, the pools small but deep. Our casts have to be precise. Kelly's hopper has no takers. The fish know better; it's not warm enough in the day yet for grasshoppers to be floating downstream. I'm superstitious, sticking with the elk-haired caddis. In the faster water, it sinks. Kelly lends me a little vial of fluid that keeps flies afloat. Still, the fishing is slow for me. Danny can do no wrong. All morning I hear the zinnnng of his reel and look upriver or down to see his bent rod and the trout splash in the river.

"You're ready for Dollywood," says Kelly.

We find some shade and eat salami, apples, cheese, and wet cookies, and drink one of Danny's beers, now warm. It all tastes great. Kelly, in his predator mode, is off chasing bugs. He comes back with a sample of what's hatching on the river.

"Let me see that thing of yours," he says, grabbing my line, then biting off the caddis. "There's nothing like that out here today. You think these fish are stupid? Try a royal coachman."

After lunch, my luck changes. The west-slope cutthroats love the coachman. I'm slaphappy with fish, stripping in line all afternoon. After a while, I keep count, a bad habit from a lifetime of fact-gathering. In two hours, I catch twenty-seven fish. The last one is the biggest of the day, over twenty inches, and fat. That's it for me. I don't need Dollywood. I'm sated. So is Danny. Reluctantly, Kelly folds. Besides, he has to cook. At camp, he gives us tequila and an appetizer of smoked fish on crackers. Danny adds chips and orange cheese. Kelly cooks like he fishes: eyes on the prize, always aware of his next move, the picture of self-confidence. It takes him a while to complete his masterpiece, but it's worth it. We eat under a sky dense with stars, windless, leaning against a stump. Salmon fettucine, in a cream sauce of garlic and butter, fresh salad of Spokane garden greens, with a white wine from a plastic bottle, chilled by the evening temperature drop.

"Needs basil," I say.

"I've got it," he says, reaching next to his cook kit, to a little mound of fresh leaves.

Lewis killed a coyote, which he mixed with leftover horsemeat and crayfish. "I find myself growing weak for the want of food and most of the men complain of a similiar deficiency and have fallen off very much," he wrote. They were deep in the Bitterroots, having traveled about 150 miles through thickets of old growth.

Day three for us is still hot, but the water temperature has not risen in our valley. We have not seen another person. Kelly is pushing Dollywood again, but Danny and I want to go downstream, cut a cross-country path through the woods, and then work our way back. Our campsite is full of deer this morning; obviously the word has gotten out about the chow. We decide to hang the food to keep critters away. We pack our rods in cases, load up with lunches, and hike. It's a slog through bramble, alder, and willow in low marshy areas, pine up high. We contour gradually downward, following the valley. I feel utterly disconnected from anything outside of this river drainage and drawn to a simple world of gravity, river flow and sky. The canyon walls are too steep, in parts, for a trail. In other sections, though, we follow a faint path, used by deer and chasers of fish. At an oxbow in the river, we're confronted by a big pile of fallen timber, blown and washed down the river during the storms of late spring. A clean, sandy beach is off to one side. Crossing over a log, I see something in the sand, very clear and incised.

"Take a look at these tracks."

"Not deer," says Danny.

"Not bear," says my other brother.

The tracks form a pattern that shows a big loping stride, that of a four-footed animal. There are two lobes on the leading edge of the heel pad and toes of elongated ovals.

"Mountain lion."

"What?"

Danny looks at me and smiles. "Boy, you are in cougar country."

"A big tom, judging by the prints," Kelly says.

Cougars are six to eight feet long, from nose to tip of the tail, and weigh up to 180 pounds. They are extremely secretive, stalking their prey without so much as a crunch of leaves betraying them. When they attack, they usually go for the central vein in the neck, bleeding their victims dry. Unlike grizzly bears, who seem to lose their taste for meat as the summer wears on, cougars are lusty carnivores year-round. They are long gone from Europe. They used to live everywhere in the United States, but now their range is limited to the West, and Florida, where there is a remnant group of panthers, a subspecies. Westerners have long had mixed feelings about these predators. The Indians in the north, particularly along the coast, seldom put cougars on their totems. One of the first orders of business of the provisional government of the Oregon Territory of 1843 was an assembly called to organize a way to get rid of all wolves, grizzlies, and cougars. Teddy Roosevelt was afraid of cougars, saying they were "as ferocious and bloodthirsty as they are cowardly." Once they were nearly gone, people missed them— sort of. Voters in Oregon and California passed citizen initatives outlawing most kinds of mountain-lion–hunting.

"Tells you something," says Danny, looking closely at the tracks in the sandbar.

"What?"

"That we're not alone."

Unlike wolves, cougars are not group hunters; they are solitary predators. A single lion can control a territory as large as four hundred square miles, marking it with piles of leaves or needles scented with its own scat or urine. Usually, they eat deer, elk, and squirrels. In a few cases, more recently, they have gone after joggers. In California, a cat attacked a forty-year-old marathoner who was running in the foothills of the Sierra and nearly cut her in half. It was the first death by mountain lion in that state in eighty-five years. In Colorado, an eighteen-year-old runner was killed by a lion. About two thousand cougars a year are killed legally by hunters. I still want to hunt fish, but now I feel one notch lower on the food chain.

After eleven days of wandering through the Bitterroots, Lewis and Clark were saved by the Nez Perce in the Clearwater River drainage. The Indians welcomed them with salmon, roots, and bread mixed with camas bulbs. Though still five hundred miles from the ocean, they could taste the Pacific. What a feast they had. "I cautioned them of the consequences of eateing too much," Clark wrote. But the hunger was too great. For days, the Americans gorged themselves on the local bounty. They ate until they were sick, and then they ate some more. "It filled us so full of wind that we were scercely able to Breathe all night."

My legs are scratched from the cross-country slog, but we finally get back into our rhythm. The fish are a little smaller downriver, the big ones having gone to the colder, deeper water upstream in this week of hot weather. My coachman is still doing the job. But the fish are not hitting every cast. Maybe that is because my concentration is diffused. I glance at the brush and at the shore quite a bit, taking in the light and the color, and looking for tawny brown fur and almond-shaped eyes, following me.

At night, back at camp, Danny is cooking. He has a beer popped and his little Coleman burner is going at full speed.

"Ramen?"

"Three different kinds. All in one pot. It ends up that way anyway."

His chow is fine, washed down with beer. He's got some peppermint schnapps for desert, which he pours into hot chocolate. He thinks I don't like it, I can tell. He's wrong.

"Nothing's keeping me from Dollywood tomorrow," says Kelly.

"What about that cat?"

"He's got to eat too," says Kelly.

Cougars mainly hunt at night, from dusk till dawn.

"You're supposed to fight back if one attacks you," says Danny. With bears, the conventional wisdom is to play dead, rolled up in a ball. These ten-foot bruins will paw you over, experts say. Despite the fact that your heart is beating two hundred gongs a minute, and you're sweating buckets, they'll conclude that you're dead. All I can think of is the "Far Side" cartoon where two bears come upon campers, face down. "I just love it when they play dead," says one bear to the other.

With mountain lions, you're supposed to stand up tall, hold sticks in the air, and look big. Just don't run. I have been thinking about this since we spotted the cougar tracks. If confronted, I'm going to wave at the cougar my ten-foot fishing rod with a royal coachman at the end of it.

"Satellite passing over," says Kelly, head slightly propped up as he looks at the night sky. "You could check your e-mail if you'd brought the battery-powered laptop with cell phone."

"That's as lame as it gets," says Danny. "A cell phone in the wilderness."

"Yeah," I say, taking a swig of schnapps and cocoa, looking away. "Lame." I have a confession to make to my brothers. Last year, my editors at the *New York Times* had asked me to keep in touch one weekend, just before I headed off on a three-day backpacking trip in the Cascades, into the William O. Douglas Wilderness east of Mount Rainier. Even after decades on the Supreme Court, Douglas used to head for the alpine lakes of the Cascades, near his boyhood home, and disappear—the business of the nation's High Court be damned. We walked a long ways into the wilderness to a basin sheltered by boulders, and I lost myself in the details of a hike, observing the rock, watching the sky, listening for wildlife, thinking about all the worthless stuff at sea level, shrinking in significance with every step. On the second morning, I got up early and set out to find a place that would be high enough to give me a direct phone signal out. I climbed for two and a half hours to a summit ridge, my mind in the world of paragraphs, editors, and the tight ecosystem within the building on West 43rd Street. At the top, I dialed out with my cell phone and was connected to New York. A national desk editor came on, pleasant and gossipy. "Your story's been held for lack of space," she said. "Check when you get back."

"You need help," Danny says.

"I'll take you to Dollywood tomorrow," says Kelly. "That's about as wild a country as you can find in America."

Maybe. But there is no place in the Lower 48 that is more than twenty-five miles from a road. When I tell this to my brothers, they don't believe me. I had read this in *Sports Afield,* a magazine that is full of advertisements for gear to keep you comfortable while preying on fish and game. The rage in the outdoor world, judging by the ads, is the global positioning system, a handheld device that bounces a signal off a satellite and gives a map reading of the sender's location. They were refined during the Gulf War. "When it comes to blazing trails, nobody does it like Magellan," it says in a typical ad. "Combining a 12 parallel-channel reception with superior tracking in dense cover and 24-hour battery life. You always know where you are with a Magellan GPS."

I unfold the Forest Service map, and we scan the squares of central Idaho with our flashlights. We chart distances from deep in our valley, from nearby summits, from side channels in the heart of the Frank Church River of No Return, as the biggest wilderness in Idaho is named. A long day's hike would get us to where Lewis and Clark ended their ordeal in the Bitterroots. But much of that area, around the town of Orofino, is a ruined landscape, the site of a monstrous dam that was built for no other reason than political pork, killing the once great steelhead runs of the north fork of the Clearwater River. It is the town that produced Helen Chenoweth. Little fish-and-bait shops, with yellowed pictures of steelhead ghosts, are rotting along the river near Orofino. They try to hold on, waiting for some miracle return of big steelies. At one such shop, Guns 'n' Gear, the owner keeps a chart showing the decline of steelhead throughout Idaho, a death watch. On a hill above Orofino is a state mental institution, just a few feet away from the local high school—home of the Maniacs. The regional icon of Orofino, adorning the football stadium and the side of the school, is a drooling psychotic in a straitjacket.

In other directions, the map is less cluttered with the products of modern Idaho. But there are enough logging roads cut into the woods that the twenty-five-mile statement seems to hold up. This is an awful thought about a place that is supposedly the largest roadless area in the contiguous United States, a place people visit because human beings need to keep some sense of the wild. But we know there is another marker out in the Bitterroots tonight, a border established with leaves and cougar scat, staking territory. Despite the schnapps, I have a fitful sleep, which is how it should be in some places.

CHAPTER 12

Homecoming

Joseph, Oregon

G athering in the buttery sunlight of a late-September afternoon, a band of men in cowboy hats and John Deere caps went looking for a hanging post in Joseph, Oregon, not long ago. It was the kind of day to get out of their way, and most people did, leaving the streets to the eighty or so men determined to take care of things in a way that certain people in this valley have always settled their more intractable problems. Defiant with hanging rope and vigilante bluster, they came to declare that the Old West would not die without a fight.

The little town of Joseph is tired-looking, somewhat chapped by the weather, but fragrant with the smell of freshly cut hay or big cottonwoods after a rain, it still puts up a pretty face most days. It sits in a high alpine valley near Hells Canyon, the deepest cleft on the continent. The shoulder-to-shoulder flank of the Wallowa Mountains, snowy and blue and much too tall to be rising out of the prairie of eastern Oregon, tends to overwhelm anything that people have tried to do with two-stories of stone or wood down in the valley. The peaks are of such heart-stopping beauty that you feel like tipping them after taking their picture; they are ecoporn, in virtually any pose.

But for all its natural radiance, the Wallowa Valley is also a place where the crosswinds of history can blow hard and sharp, bringing a hint of some distant bloodletting over power and land. Running people out of town is an old habit. Chief Joseph, the mountain of nearly ten thousand feet, shadows over the valley. Chief Joseph—the man, the myth, the industry—casts other shadows. The Nez Perce leader is everywhere, his face on the logo of the weekly newspaper, the *Chieftain*, on banners advertising Chief Joseph Days, on windows and coffee mugs and bank murals. But that Joseph—the one everyone knows about, the one whose piercing nobility seems to burn through the pose of the Edward Curtis photograph, the one who outfoxed some of the best Civil War–hardened generals of the United States Army— he is not here in the land of his birth. His father is. Old Joseph, his body mutilated by the great-grandparents of some of the people who marched down Main Street with a hanging rope, is buried at the foot of Wallowa Lake, in a small cemetery. Young Chief Joseph is buried in the chalky volcanic soil of the Colville Indian Reservation, in Washington State, where he was exiled after the war of 1877. Young Chief Joseph met with two presidents, Rutherford B. Hayes and Grover Cleveland, kept two wives, and was called by Buffalo Bill the greatest Indian that America had ever produced— a compliment he considered meaningless, as it turned out. The dusty grave was the end of the line for a man who spent his life trying to hold on to this valley, as his father had asked him to do on his deathbed. Banned in life from ever returning to the Wallowas, Young Joseph was also banned in death.

Ten years after the Nez Perce were driven from the Wallowas, thirty-one Chinese gold miners were attacked in an ambush. It started as a robbery. But after stealing $50,000 in gold, the thieves decided to kill every one of the Chinese miners in order to protect themselves from incrimination. In that sense, they were right. Though six Wallowa County men were charged with the murders, three of them were acquitted by a jury of friends and neighbors; three others fled and were never found. Wars have been fought in the West over less loss of life, but nobody was ever brought to justice for this mass killing. Nor are there any plaques or historical markers in the valley to commemorate one of the worst massacres of the nineteenth-century American West. And Oregon schoolchildren, rightly steeped in the struggle of the Americans who walked across a continent to settle on the Pacific slope, know nothing of the slaughter that took place within sight of wagon-trail ruts. The killings, the evidence of Chinese life, the story in all its elements, was never set down in the ritualized way that Westerners establish lore about themselves, and so it did not exist.

The targets on this September day were a pair of local men, both in their mid-forties, white, and both rooted in the Pacific Northwest. The marchers walked past the sign at the entrance of Joseph—This Little Town Is Heaven to Us, Don't Drive Like Hell Through It—and beyond all the new store-fronts, more than a dozen galleries, places where bronze statues of Chief Joseph sell for $5,000 and coffee comes with Italian soda flavors. On Main Street, in the center of town, Dale Potter strung two ropes over a makeshift gallows, beneath an American flag. Then he hung two stuffed dummies, the heads tarred and feathered. A little cheer went up among the hanging crew as the figurative life went out of the victims.

One of the dangling dummies was labeled Andy Kerr. He is a small, bearded man, a prominent person in Oregon, who had only recently moved from Portland, where a million people live in the metro area, to Wallowa County, where the population is seven thousand. Kerr looks like a spotted owl, the celebrated nocturnal bird that has been the source of so much contention in the Pacific Northwest. He has a talent for speaking in such loaded sound bites that it was said by reporters that if Andy Kerr did not exist, someone would have had to invent him. He knows how to use an active verb, most often as a weapon. The other dummy was given the nametag of Ric Bailey, a former logger, friendly and self-deprecating. He came to the valley in 1977 and fell in love with what he saw. Since then, he has been trying to make Hells Canyon into a National Park.

The hanging-in-effigy did nothing to affect the timber mill that was closed recently by Boise Cascade, the county's largest private landowner, taking a third of the entire payroll of the town of Joseph with it. Nor did it have the slightest influence on cattle prices, which were nearly half what they'd been just a few years before. But how do you hang an invisible, ephemeral thing like free market forces or a corporation like Boise Cascade? It's much easier, said Dale Potter—later, when he was away from the mob—to go after an easy target, in this case, a pair of guys who are seen as a threat to the traditional rural lifestyle. The hanging allowed people in the valley to blame someone else for all their troubles.

"These rural people are pretty simple and unsophisticated," said Potter, a semiretired salesman who traces his family lineage in the valley to the 1880s, about ten years after the Nez Perce were kicked out. "They aren't part of the laptop-computer crowd. They know bad things are happening, but they don't know how to defend themselves. I had to do something spectacular to get people's attention. And boy, did I ever."

Potter had been helped in his crusade against change by *The Chieftain*, which put out a special report on plans for "The Re-wilding of the West." It was accompanied by a very ominous-looking map of the three states in the Columbia Plateau, showing little islands where people would live and a large blotted-out red area that would be returned to nature—re-wilded, as it were. Judging by the map, it looked like the Red Menace all over again.

After stringing up likenesses of Kerr and Bailey, the crowd moved on to a weekend of hard talk about those forces swirling around the West, trying to make the map red and the land wild. You could not legally hang Kerr and Bailey, one speaker said; but you could certainly make life miserable for them. For one thing, they could urge all businesses to boycott them—just refuse them sales or service. All the big names in Wise Use, a movement dedicated to the idea that environmentalism has brought America to its knees, had been drawn to tiny Joseph for the weekend, for a price. Ron Arnold, a Seattle-area writer who coined the term Wise Use, gave a speech titled "The Dangerous Agenda of the Nature Conservancy," referring to an old-line conservation group whose board of directors includes General Norman Schwarzkopf, the Gulf War leader. Another speaker, Carolyn Paseneaux, a member of the Wyoming Legislature, gave a talk on the Endangered Species Act, "the atom bomb of the war on the West," as she called it. Understatement does not travel to these symposiums.

Potter had hoped that at least three hundred people from the valley would sign up for the weekend sessions. But only a hundred or so paid the forty-five-dollar fee. It was a bust, Potter said later. "I lost five thousand dollars bringing those speakers in," he said. "I'm still paying for it."

WHAT PROMPTED ranchers and timbermen in the Wallowa Valley to string a rope around the straw neck of two of their neighbors is the same thing that people have always clawed over in the West—the public domain.

Dale Potter may call those who work the land simple and unsophisticated. What he seems to be saying is that they are dumb and hick. But they know much more than he gives them credit for. They know the New West is inevitable; they just don't know what their role will be in it. They fear change. They do not want to become bit players in a new economy, flipping buffaloburgers for mountain-bikers from the city. When a new sporting-goods store opens on Main Street, what comes to mind are unctuous urbanites in Lycra. They see the huge, glass-chested homes on the hill, the architectural sketches for Elk Trail Estates going up on the glacial moraine of a lake where they always took their kids fishing, and they cannot find a place in this future for themselves. Hunting for hope, they revert to the past—which at least is predictable.

Andy Kerr got into trouble because he spoke directly to this insecurity. Understatement, also, does not know Andy Kerr. He gave a speech in the heart of eastern Oregon cowboy country not long after he moved to the Wallowas. "The future is clear," he told the ranchers gathered at a Rotary luncheon. "Soon, this county is going to be selling more espresso than barbed wire."

Kerr had taken up residence in a large log home in Wallowa County, which is about as big as the state of Delaware, and where cattle outnumber people by a six-to-one margin. Having forced some of the nation's most powerful timber companies to retreat from a binge of clear-cutting that had left large sections of the Oregon Cascades naked of forest cover, Kerr had turned his sights on the arid eastern side of the mountains. Big ranches controlled most of the public land in the dry half of Oregon—reliably serviced by a congressman with the second-biggest district in the Lower 48—but their century of dominance had taken its toll. Salmon had vanished from streams overrun by cattle, water had been drained from marshes that were once magnets for millions of migratory birds, and bighorn sheep were dying in Hells Canyon, from a disease biologists traced to domestic livestock. Kerr wanted nothing to do with a slow transition from Old West to New; he wanted history to hurry itself along, casualties be damned.

"Advocating better grazing of the arid West is like seeking better beating of little children," Kerr had written. "Better grazing is boring to work on. Abolition is much more interesting."

Kerr said he rejected the stark choice between "old land abusers" and "yuppie scum." Typically, these sides are presented as the only two choices for how to live in the West, two extremes, both unattractive. But Kerr, like many Westerners, had no idea what form the middle ground might take. So he waged his war on one side, and flourished like the people on the other side who are paid to stir up residents of depressed towns like Joseph.

After his speech to the cowboys, Kerr was lucky to get out of Rotary alive. There were hisses, some gasps and insults, and later—headlines. His comments grew, magnified in each retelling. Soon he was a pariah. Restaurants refused to serve him. Anonymous callers threatened his life. A rock shattered a window of his house. The manager of a gas station told him to get his gas somewhere else. Bumper stickers called on him to leave town. Kerr professed to be unruffled, telling people that his wife and he had brought "three mean dogs and a gun collection" to their new home. He intended to stay. He had a right to live in the Wallowas.

To deal with people like Kerr, and others with no political agenda but who had moved to the Wallowas because it was so beautiful, or because it inspired art and poetry instead of hamburgers and two-by-fours, the county commissioners came up with an ordinance. Like Dale Potter, the commissioners had long ago cemented their minds to the Old West; virtually everything new was seen as a threat. They drafted their own version of the Endangered Species Act. In their customized take, the law would protect loggers and ranchers, not bighorn sheep and salmon; it was modeled after the ordinance passed by the Catron County commissioners in New Mexico. In their minds, Wallowa County was just about perfect back when Walter Brennan, the stuttering character cowboy of so many films, had a ranch in the valley, and perhaps it was.

At the time the commissioners tried to turn back the clock in the Wallowas, the county had already lost two-thirds of its population of fifty years ago. The three commissioners, all sympathetic to the ranching and timber lobby, declared that Wallowa County—not the federal government—had control over the millions of acres of Forest Service and BLM land in their region. They could do with it what they wanted, they asserted. Any federal action, like restricting grazing in Hells Canyon National Recreation Area to protect bighorn sheep, could be ruled null and void by them, they asserted. They could do this, they believed, because the government had failed to respect the traditional culture of the land.

The traditional culture, as they defined it, was a narrow thing, belonging to perhaps a hundred entrenched white families, and it was nearly gone. In all the Hells Canyon National Recreation Area, only a single commercial sheep rancher remained. Throughout Wallowa County, there were only forty-six ranchers and, after the Boise Cascade closure, two small timber mills. But the commissioners did not see anything before or after the cowboy and the logger; some of them were cow-centric in the extreme.

"I dare you to name one object that isn't associated, somehow, with cattle products," said Arleigh Isley, chairman of the Wallowa County Commission, when I spoke with him. "Name one. Everything you use in this world, just about, comes from cattle."

The ordinance would not protect the two herb farms that opened in the valley, or the artists coop, or the microbrew pub, the jazz festivals, or the writers workshop—all of which were starting to bring money into the valley, without any help from the government or special ordinances. Nor would the law do anything to stop the rich from moving in, plowing up pasture for exclusive developments, or having their way. A southern-style mansion went up on the lake, to nearly everyone's chagrin. A big condo development was planned not far from Joseph's grave. The valley was slipping away, becoming another Golden Ghetto lost to the homogenizing forces of the gilded West. The old guard tried to hold on to a nineteenth-century fantasy, legislating clear-cutting and salmon-trashing for beef that nobody wanted, passing on Walter Brennan homilies written on a movie-studio backlot. The more fair-minded people in the valley, genuinely struggling with one century slipping away a hundred years later than it should have, while another century pressed down on them without much warning, wondered if anything could really save the Wallowas.

Ric Bailey refused to be run out of town after he became a hanging object. Many businesses boycotted him, as the Wise Users had suggested, but just as many welcomed him. He kept up appearances around Joseph, his home of twenty years, sending out flyers on bighorn sheep deaths in Hells Canyon, playing poker once a week in public—his back to the wall. And instead of making himself scarce at public meetings, he became more of a nuisance. "No lynch mob is going to drive me out of the Wallowas," he said.

At one meeting of the commissioners, where they were drafting the traditional-culture law, Bailey stood up to make a point.

"If you're going to base your decisions on who's been here the longest," he said, "you had damn well better talk to some Nez Perce Indians."

There was a name rarely mentioned in any way except as an historical oddity. What did they have to do with anything? a commissioner wondered. For a visitor entering the Wallowa Valley, the only official notice of an Indian presence is a sign outside one of the smaller towns: Welcome to Enterprise—Home of the Savages.

"They've been pissed off," Bailey said, "a lot longer than you have been."

ONE OF those Indians, Earl (Taz) Conner, is a direct descendant of Old Joseph, and he is one of the few native people to be seen in Wallowa County on a regular basis. He was working for the Forest Service when he was approached by a community leader with a suggestion. The commissioners had ignored Bailey's idea of talking to the Nez Perce, as they did with everything Bailey said. But quietly, other whites in the valley began to give a second thought to the vanquished tribe. Every year, by the thousands, visitors from an ocean away made the hard trip to the Wallowas, asking about the long-dead Indians. In Europe, there are Chief Joseph clubs, dozens of them in Germany alone. The name is gold. But in the Wallowa Valley, it has always meant something else.

Taz Conner got his nickname when he was a toddler and he liked to hop around to the razzmatazz sound coming across the radio. He grew up as an outsider, a Nez Perce among Cayuse and Paiutes in the dry Umatilla Indian Reservation in central Oregon. He joined the Navy, did two tours of Vietnam. It was only when he left the Pacific Northwest that he realized what it meant to be a Nez Perce.

"I was in Spain, and this guy said to me, 'You're Indian, right? What are you, Sioux? Apache?' I told him I was Nez Perce and his face lit up. He said, 'Nez Perce! Chief Joseph!' "

Wallowa County was suffering the highest unemployment rate—near 20 percent—of any county in an otherwise booming state, and one in six lived below the poverty line. The Pacific Northwest was on a roll, building the prototype of a global economy, one that whole countries could only imagine. There was one glaring exception to the general prosperity: those areas such as the Wallowas that were tied to an imagined past. In this island of failure in far northeastern Oregon, out of desperation, a handful of people now turned to the Indians. And Conner was the only Indian with anything other than a spectral presence in the county, though he lived in a neighboring region.

"This man from the community development office, he thought the Nez Perce could save this county," said Conner. "How's that for irony—asking us Indians to return after booting us out in 1877?"

AFTER LIVING in the Wallowas for perhaps a thousand years or more, the Nez Perce were given thirty days to pack up and leave in the spring of 1877. Thirty days to say goodbye to the dead. Thirty days to gather up thousands of head of cattle and prize horses. Thirty days to close up all residences for all time. Thirty days to look again and then no more. Then they would be off—babies, toddlers, teens, grandparents, the hotheaded, and the passive, about 750 people in all, the followers of Young Joseph. In their place would come ranchers lusting for the waist-high grass, dairy farmers looking for free land, merchants with tourist plans for the lake. The Nez Perce would not receive a dime for their land. They would simply have to walk away, give it up. And they would have to do so knowing they had a treaty, barely twenty years old, that promised the Joseph band of the Nez Perce that they could keep their home in the Wallowas for as long as the waters of the Columbia rolled to the setting sun, a treaty signed by the president, backed by the Senate. Imagine holding a deed to a house that you have lived in your entire life—and then a stranger comes along and orders you out, without compensation. That was the Nez Perce predicament of 1877.

"We have respect for the whites," said Earl Conner's great-grandfather Ollokot, a son of Old Joseph, who had died in 1871. "But they treat me as a dog." Ollokot had reason to be perplexed. In all the disparaging history written about American Indians, the Nez Perce had stood out as a breed apart. The shorthand description of Indians for most of the nineteenth century had them pegged as squat, filthy, poor, with no future. Not the Nez Perce. They were invariably described as tall, handsome, prosperous, athletic, industrious, articulate. "The most friendly, honest and ingenuous" of all tribes, Sergeant Patrick Gass of Lewis and Clark's expedition had written.

Clark himself fathered a Nez Perce child. He called the tribe "expirt marksmen and good riders." During the months that the Corps of Discovery spent with the Nez Perce, they staged horse and foot races, shooting contests, games of skill and chance. The Nez Perce won almost everything. The Pacific Northwest might well be part of British Columbia or Russian Alaska or belong to some other sovereign, had not the Nez Perce opened their arms to the first Americans to cross the continent. Had they bumped into the Blackfeet, perhaps the most feared tribe of the West outside the Sioux and Apache, Lewis and Clark might well be footnotes instead of names of counties and high schools in the West. It was their luck to stumble, at their lowest point, upon a tribe whose "hearts were good," as Lewis wrote. The whites gave the Nez Perce medallions with the likeness of Thomas Jefferson and some tobacco—both largely worthless items from a place, Virginia, that might as well have been Jupiter. The Nez Perce gave the whites canoes, horses, women, shelter, and food. And what food it was: chinook salmon, the fresh fall run from the Clearwater River, elk steak cooked in a stew of camas bulbs—the garlic of early Northwest cuisine. And for dessert, four kinds of berries, topped with honey. At the time, the Nez Perce numbered perhaps six thousand, living in dozens of bands, in what are now three states of the Columbia River Plateau. The whites numbered no more than three dozen, and possessed good blankets, cooking utensils, and guns that could have given the Nez Perce an edge over their traditional enemies, the Blackfeet. In a swift, ugly moment, the Nez Perce could have wiped out Lewis and Clark, or at least stripped them of their goods and sent them packing. Instead, they smoked with them, ate with them, made love with them, raced with them. Then they gave them canoes and showed them how to find their way to the big ocean. They promised to hold on to some of their goods through the winter, and to give them enough horses in the spring, when they returned for the trip home.

And what's more, in the spring of 1806, when the rain-soaked, somewhat dispirited Corps of Discovery returned, the Nez Perce kept their word. Horses and goods were waiting. The horses were not the lame, half-mule rejects that other tribes tried to pawn off in trades. The Nez Perce had refined the practice of selective breeding of fine horses; the Appaloosa is perhaps their best-known product. For all the toffs in Virginia horse country, the plantation gentlemen who bored many a dinner party with details of their own animal husbandry, Meriwether Lewis had some news from this distant corner of the wild: the Nez Perce method of horse-breeding, he wrote, "is preferable to that practiced by ourselves."

And so a pattern developed for most of the nineteenth century, from the early encounters with muddle-headed Christian missionaries to the rescues of confused and frightened Oregon Trail travelers and lost trappers—the Nez Perce were guardian angels. They liked the Americans, or at least had enough self-interest in them to take pity on them. The Boston men had better trading goods than the English or French. They came, at first, without missionaries, unlike the Spanish. Seldom did any American letter back home describe a Nez Perce as anything less than glowing. "They are certainly more like a nation of saints than a horde of savages," wrote Washington Irving, in his account of Captain William Bonneville's epic roaming around the West. Bonneville, the first white to see the Wallowa Mountains, was hungry and lost (a pattern for Americans stumbling upon the Nez Perce) when he found a band of Joseph's people living in the splendid setting in 1833. Old Joseph was then called by his pre-Christian name, Tuekakas. And how did they react to Bonneville? They gave him "the hospitality of the golden age," Irving wrote.

The stage was set for what the nations of the Pacific now aspire to: free trade, based on mutual respect of treaties and sovereignty.

Even when other Northwest tribes declared war after a fraudulent treaty conference in 1855 had opened Indian country to settlement, the Nez Perce fired not a shot nor an arrow. Indians from other tribes were being killed for sport, their leaders lured into truce conferences and then hanged. The Nez Perce resisted the conflict, because they had a very clear document, the treaty that explicitly stated that no white could be allowed on Nez Perce land without Indian permission. Joseph possessed his own parchment map, showing the boundary lines. "The line was made as I wanted it—not for me but for my children that will follow me," Joseph said. "This is where I live and this is where I want to leave my body." And to make the point clear, he established a line of poles planted in rockpiles, so that stray cattlemen, prospectors, or other potential trespassers would not be confused.

Alas, this story, whether it takes place on prairie, mountain, or seacoast, has only one ending, a familiar one. Prospectors and cattlemen ignored the treaty. The grass was good in the Wallowas. And on the Idaho reservation, gold was discovered. A flood of miners, with their instant whorehouses, instant liquor mills, instant land claims that would later be defended by politicians as the most sacred of property rights, overwhelmed Nez Perce land. The treaty, they told Congress, would have to be rewritten, the Nez Perce moved. Joseph and a few other bands refused. The Idaho communities, the more Christianized Indians, living among the boom of miners, caved in. A new document in 1863—later dubbed the "thief treaty," or "the fool's treaty"—was signed by some of the chieftains and some white Christian missionaries. It reduced the Nez Perce holdings to one-tenth of those in the original treaty. The Wallowa band would have to go to Idaho, to live among those who had sold out their land.

Old Joseph was so furious at this betrayal that he tore up his Bible and renounced his Christian name. He told his sons Ollokot and Joseph to do the same. Young Joseph's Indian name, Hin-mah-too-yah-lat-kekht, meaning Thunder Traveling to Loftier Mountain Heights, was evocative, but a mouthful. He was still called Joseph. Some members of his band returned to an old religion—the Dreamer faith, led by a shaman named Smohalla, who lived in a hovel on the Columbia River, not far from what would later be the birthplace of the atomic bomb. The Dreamers went on vision quests, seeking spirits through dreams, trances, fasts, and extended periods alone. By returning to a purer life, the Dreamers believed, they could banish the white man, and they would be rewarded. Digging a hoe in a meadow or burrowing into the ground for gold was seen as a desecration of the earth.

"You ask me to plough the ground!" Smohalla said. "Shall I take a knife and tear at my mother's bosom.

"You ask me to dig for a stone! Shall I dig under her skin for her bones.

"You ask me to cut grass and make hay and sell it and be rich like white men! But how dare I cut off my mother's hair."

Just as the Irish clung to Catholicism at the lowest point of their long subjugation, and early Mormons held to a much-ridiculed faith as they were driven out of Illinois, the last best tribe of American Indians looked to a familiar God for help.

Old Joseph would not budge from the Wallowas. "Always remember that your father never sold his country," he told his son Joseph, just before he died in 1871. "This country holds your father's body. Never sell the bones of your father and your mother."

Young Joseph did not sell. An army commission assigned to look into Joseph's claims sided with the Nez Perce, but to no avail. Joseph likened the treaty of 1863 to naked theft. "Suppose a white man should come to me and say, 'Joseph, I like your horses, and I want to buy them.' I say to him I will not sell them. Then he goes to my neighbor and says to him, 'Joseph has some good horses. I want to buy them, but he refuses to sell.' My neighbor answers, 'Pay me the money and I will sell you Joseph's horses.' The white man turns to me and says, 'Joseph, I have bought your horses and you must let me have them.' "

Today, when there is talk about property rights at the angry Wise Use rallies in towns like Joseph, or in public hearings chaired by Representative Helen Chenoweth or Senator Phil Gramm of Texas, the indignant never mention the biggest and most flagrant violation of all.

After the Nez Perce were told to get out, the whites were emboldened, rushing in to take the prime land in the valley even before the Indians had gathered up their stock. Two settlers entered an Indian hunting camp, got spooked, and then shot and killed a Nez Perce man. The Indians cried out for justice. The government said they would take care of it, bringing the men to trial. But there was one insurmountable legal problem for the Nez Perce: it was against the law for an Indian to testify against a white. Without a witness, the killers went free. And so, with this final indignity burning inside them, the Nez Perce retreated down into the deepest river-carved canyon in the world, heading for an uncertain fate as they crossed the swollen Snake. Hells Canyon, the whites called it. Of course.

"Bereft of their own culture, their strength, self-respect, and dignity, they became a subjugated and lost people, a second-class minority in their own homeland," wrote Alvin M. Josephy, Jr., the preeminent historian of American Indians.

The prospects of an Indian treaty being honored in nineteenth-century America were no more likely than Abraham Lincoln's coming back from the dead. And 1877 was a particularly bad year to be pressing for an aboriginal claim. The year before, George Armstrong Custer had blundered into the lopsided defeat at Little Bighorn. Sitting Bull and a large band of Sioux had escaped to Canada. The army was not about to let another Indian war sully its image. Besides, the battles with native people were said to be over; it was mop-up time, with some ill-trained conscripts chasing Apaches and other renegades in the Southwest.

But there was a heartbeat, still, in the Nez Perce even as they retreated. Joseph's followers envisioned a new life in Canada, perhaps among the Sioux. There was very little time for debate, however. Avenging the death in the Wallowas, and other slights, a few Indian warriors killed some whites—one the local whiskey merchant, the other a man known for siccing his dogs on Nez Perce children. The settlers, occupying Idaho land they had only recently taken from the more docile and Christianized Nez Perce, demanded that the army take immediate punitive measures. A young captain was sent by General Oliver O. Howard to chase the Indians. Howard, mindful of Custer, told Captain David Perry not to get whipped. "There is no chance of that happening, sir," Perry replied.

In White Bird Canyon, not far from what is now the moribund town of Grangerville, Idaho, Captain Perry sent about ninety troops down the bare valley at dawn to round up the Nez Perce. His trumpeter was the first to die, a bullet in the chest before he could even bring lips to bugle. Then, a dozen soldiers were knocked from their mounts. By midmorning, the entire platoon was in retreat. They were sprinting uphill, literally running for their lives. At the end of the day, thirty-four soldiers lay dead. The Nez Perce lost not a man.

Telegraphs carried news of this second "massacre," this Little Bighorn all over again. The nation was stunned. And so it went throughout the summer, on a seventeen-hundred-mile chase over Lolo Pass in the Bitterroots, which the starving Lewis and Clark company had crossed seventy-two years before, down Montana's western valleys, up the Snake River and into Yellowstone Park and then over a high rock pass that had been labeled impassable, and north, into the fall snows, within a day or so of freedom in Canada, where it all ended with a wounded, wailing band of Indians in a frozen coulee, surrounded on all sides. Most of those details are familiar, but a few points seem all the more remarkable with each passing year.

The Nez Perce knew nothing of war, save a few long-ago skirmishes with other tribes, but they were unmatched marksmen. They could shoot bighorn sheep from a half-mile vertical flank; mounted soldiers in blue were much easier. They were motivated, fighting as any patriots would for their home and lives. While the army was a unit composed entirely of soldiers and suppliers, the Nez Perce were a traveling town—barely a third of them warriors. The rest were elderly, or children, or babies, or mothers, carrying their life possessions, their two thousand horses, their dogs, their tipis, their food—everything. They could not just sprint up a hill or march to a position at the sound of a horn. The only real battle in which the army did significant damage, the Battle of Big Hole, was a surprise attack on a sleeping camp; children and old people were the main casualties. And even in that battle, after the warriors roused themselves, they put General Howard's men to flight.

As Alvin Josephy has pointed out, the Indian fighters of General Miles and General Howard, memorialized in bronze since the late nineteenth century, hailed by the Daughters of the American Revolution, were in reality a rather hapless and mediocre army—beaten time and again in this, one of the few Indian wars that had some actual pitched battles. The army had superior manpower and superior firepower, with Gatling guns and mountain howitzers, and still it was routed all summer long by a retreating band of natives with families in tow.

During the war, the Nez Perce remained honorable. They paid for goods along the way, buying coffee, sugar, tobacco, flour, and other food with gold dust from white merchants. They were betrayed by numerous Indians, notably the Crow in Montana, the Shoshone in Idaho, and their own Nez Perce brethren in the Lapwai Reservation—something the more militant revisionists tend to forget. After the surrender, each of about thirty Sioux and Cheyenne scouts were given five Nez Perce horses per man for their service on behalf of the army.

Inside Yellowstone Park, the Nez Perce kidnapped a handful of campers, but only for protection. The tourists were released with a tale to last a lifetime. And it was just outside the park that one of the most astonishing escapes occurred. The Nez Perce went up the Lamar Valley—today, the haunt of large bison herds, elk, and the transplanted wolf packs—and then veered north. With the press following every move, General Howard at last breathed a sigh of relief; the Indians were trapped. During the war, Howard was known to the Nez Perce as General Day After Tomorrow. But now he was advancing from the rear, certain of at last catching his prey, and General Miles's troops from the east were closing in from the other side. The canyon to the north was so narrow a horse could barely get by. There was simply nowhere to go, unless the Indians sprouted wings. But backed up at Canyon Creek, the Nez Perce families shinnied up a rock wall and slipped away.

Three weeks later, Joseph surrendered in order to save what was left of the families. Unlike other Indian leaders, he had the sympathy of much of the non-Indian world by this time. The Nez Perce War, "on our part, in its origin and motive, was nothing short of a gigantic blunder and a crime," the *New York Times* wrote in 1877.

Miles, after rounding up the tribe, said, "They were a very bright and energetic body of Indians; indeed, the most intelligent that I had ever seen. Exceedingly self-reliant, each man seemed to be able to do his own thinking, to be purely democratic and independent in his ideas and purpose." He sounds patronizing. But compared with comments by other generals, he was a booster. Ten years earlier, General William Tecumseh Sherman had said of the remaining free tribes: "The more we can kill this year, the less will have to be killed the next war. For the more I see of these Indians, the more convinced I am that they all have to be killed or maintained as a species of paupers."

The press had dubbed Joseph the "Indian Napoleon," but in truth he was not the military mind behind the war. He was an organizer, an eloquent speaker. At six feet two inches, his regal bearing drew many a camera. But the many flattering words and haunting poses did little to help him. He was sent to Oklahoma Territory, to the dry, leftover country, the wasteland reserved for defeated Indians. There, more than a hundred Nez Perce, once the most healthy and prosperous tribe in the Pacific Northwest, died in the heat. Among the dead was a descendant of the first white man to sing praises to the Nez Perce, Captain William Clark. So far from the blue Wallowas, from salmon, elk, and water never more than day's remove from snow, the Northwesterners called Oklahoma Eeikish Pah—the Hot Place.

Joseph later met two presidents and was treated like a grand celebrity during a tour in New York, but he never got an acre of his land back. Until the end of his life in a little shack among Dreamer faithful at the Colville Indian Reservation, he made a simple request. "Let me be a free man. Free to travel, free to stop, free to work, free to trade where I choose, free to choose my own teachers, free to follow the religion of my fathers, free to think and talk and act for myself." It was an old American refrain—what Thomas

Jefferson had asked the King of England to grant the colonists, and what the Acomas in New Mexico had asked the Spanish to give them.

INDIANS, Earl Conner knows, are best appreciated by Americans in the past tense. We love underdogs in story form. We are less sure of Indians with lawyers, Indians who go to court, Indians who want something other than our sympathy. An Indian can put on a headdress, and it usually does him no good in the halls of Congress or a court of law. It's just the opposite for cowboys. A few of the ranchers in Joseph put on their cowboy hats, slipped into their snakeskin boots, and went before congressional hearings, where they begged for protection from the forces of time.

But all the cowboy posturing, the bills introduced in C-Span prime time by protectors of property rights, could not bring the Wallowa Valley back to the days of daguerreotype glory. The last years of the twentieth century ticked by. Andy Kerr and Ric Bailey kept their homes. The rodeo—known as Chief Joseph Days—continued as the old-guard high holiday. But more than ever, what the tourists wanted to see were the Nez Perce camped for a few days near the rodeo site. And downriver, a small miracle hatched at the confluence of the Wallowa and Lostine Rivers. Earl Conner, the great-great-grandson of Old Joseph, stood on ground that was one of the last places where the Nez Perce had slept before being driven out, and he was welcomed home.

Conner had recently lost his right foot to an infection, and his kidneys were failing him, but on this day, with the summer winds as sweet as a blackberry milkshake, he felt young and free of pain. All around him, other Nez Perce were arriving. Joseph McCormack, a fifth-generation descendant of Joseph, moved to the Wallowas—becoming the only full-time Nez Perce resident in the county. At the river confluence, the Nez Perce were planning to dance, to feast on salmon and elk, to play drums, renew aquaintances.

And when it was all over, some of the longtime residents of the valley had a gift they wanted to give the Indians. These men, a social-studies teacher, a few small business owners, a retired contractor, a historian—all of them white—wanted people to know they had nothing to do with the hanging-in-effigy crowd.

"We're not all like that," said Terry Crenshaw, who lives in Wallowa, a town just downriver from Joseph. "If you look at what's been going on in this county, you can see that the logging industry suffered because they shaved the damn forest bald. It's as simple as that."

A few years earlier, during the yearlong celebration for the 150th anniversary of the Oregon Trail, Crenshaw and a handful of other people began to meet and talk about that other trail, from the Wallowa Valley down to Hells Canyon through two other states and ending near the Canadian border, the one the Nez Perce followed in 1877. A Nez Perce National Historic Trail, along the route of the war, was in place—drawing the curious to the battefields where Howard went after Joseph. History was Crenshaw's passion. "I always knew they lived here for centuries, but it was so curious that they were not here now," he said. "They should at least feel like they're welcomed back."

It took a century for dominant sentiment in Wallowa County to arrive at such a conclusion, or for a white man like Crenshaw, who teaches history to children of the valley, to say such a thing without fear of harassment. After Young Joseph was exiled to the Colville Reservation, he came back to the Wallowas on a one-day mission, and all but begged the settlers to let him buy a little home not far from his father's bones. There was a big turnout for him in town, pictures snapped and published in all the papers of the West, the mayor greeting him, everybody wanting to slap the chief on the back. But things were too unstable, the town leaders said in 1904, to let Joseph back, to even allow him to buy a home. He died that year, one night while staring into his fire. His father's bones were dug from a field that a farmer wanted to plow. Somebody broke the skull from the neck, and it ended up in a dentist's office in Baker, Oregon. In 1926, the bones of Old Joseph were buried at the foot of Wallowa Lake, where they remain.

Over the years, a few Nez Perce occasionally came back to the valley, as happened during the rodeo, to ride on the parade grounds or set up tipis near Joseph's grave. They never felt at home.

"The whites thought of us as drunken Indians," said Soy Red Thunder, another descendant of Joseph. "They wanted us for their cowboy festival, but they were highly indifferent."

But then a handful of Nez Perce and Terry Crenshaw and others began to meet, trying to figure out some way to give something back to the tribe. They raised money, through grants and donations. It wasn't, of course, an entirely charitable act: the Nez Perce, as merchants had found out, were good box office—like wolves in Yellowstone and bison in Montana. Guilt was a factor. Those whom the government had crushed to make the old myth live could not be brought back without finger-pointing and pain. Some longtime residents felt not unlike modern Germans, struggling with how much guilt to carry or ignore. During the Oregon Trail celebration, state officials had found that something called "heritage tourism" was very profitable. People did not want to merely know about the past; they wanted to touch it.

Finally, with nearly $200,000 in hand, the Wallowa group made plans to purchase a tract of land atop a little nub known as Tic Hill, just above the Wallowa River. The white rancher who offered to sell it to them said it was a great honor to know it was going back to the Indians. The hill would belong to the Nez Perce. They would build a cultural center, a place for visitors to see a real live Nez Perce, while looking down at the source of all the fighting. To the whites, many of them at least, this was as solid a commercial boost as the valley could get short of a new sawmill. With the announcement of the cultural center plan came some new businesses, restaurants, carpentry jobs. News traveled across the Atlantic, and soon the Chamber of Commerce was getting inquiries from Germany and France: when I can come see a Nez Perce in the home of Chief Joseph?

To the Indians, it was something else. They did not see themselves as tourist props. "We look at this as a homecoming," said Red Thunder. He lives on the Colville Reservation and practices the old religion. The band has about a hundred and fifty members.

At the river confluence, Joseph's descendants prepared to dine on Wallowa salmon and Wallowa elk. The bounty was not dead—yet. The Indians used to catch steelhead trout and thirty-pound chinook salmon in the rivers, using a *wallowa,* a fishtrap. When a series of dams all but killed off the great salmon runs of eastern Oregon, in its place came a multimillion-dollar apology, as legal mitigation—a fish hatchery. In the manner of modern American things that draw on the name of whatever it is they displaced, the hatchery was named for one of the leaders of the Nez Perce war, Looking Glass. (A salmon-killing dam on the Columbia is named for Chief Joseph.)

So now the Indians sat under the Wallowa sky on a summer night, next to fires and tipis, and ate a fine meal of elk steak and salmon fillets, joined by hundreds of people from the valley. Among them were some folks who had lived their entire lives in the Wallowas, knowing all along they had built houses on stolen ground. The laws, whether passed in Congress or the town of Joseph, could not make loggers come back or ranchers rich again. Still, the lynch mob in cowboy hats and John Deere caps had a point. Bringing back the Old West might save them after all; they just had the wrong Old West.

CHAPTER 13

Nuevo West

Sunnyside, Washington

T he asparagus fields had been picked for the day, the orchards pruned and sprayed, and now it was time for church or drink on Saturday night. Not yet twilight. Mount Adams still held the sun in the Cascades, far to the west. The Yakima River was higher than anyone had seen it in almost a century, its waters fat and fast through the canals and irrigation ditches of the valley. Rattlesnake Ridge and Horse Heaven Hills, brown and beige most of the year, were pool-table green. The Indians on the big reservation went out in the late light to see if any spring chinook salmon were fighting the high water, and the rodeo cowboys in Toppenish let their Appaloosas run until they were in a nice lather. The first call to the Yakima County Sheriff's Department, on a night when you could expect some gunfire, a meth-head driving into a ditch, a domestic assault or two, came after six P.M. Just beyond the new Wal-Mart, at the throwaway fringe of Sunnyside, a crowd of people were stirring near the intersection. What had been only a few dozen people at first had grown to several hundred. Kids. Teenagers. Familes. They lit candles and played music and danced. Some kneeled in the gravel. Almost all of them spoke Spanish. The object of their attention was a Washington State Department of Transportation sign, green and white with directions on one side, silver and blank on the other.

"Apparently people have seen, on the back of the street sign, the Virgin Mary," said the Yakima sheriff's sergeant, calling in the report. "I'm looking at the sign now. I don't see anything."

The next day at dawn, people were still at the foot of the road sign, in temperatures barely above freezing. The valley came to life, people moving to harvest the stalks, backs still sore, hands with three levels of spring blisters. The asparagus-cutting machine did not stop for Sunday. Churches throughout the valley were abuzz with talk of the wonderful thing that had happened at the intersection of the Yakima Valley Highway and State Route 241. The new bishop, Carlos Sevilla, spiritual head of sixty-four thousand Roman Catholics, did not know what to make of the shrine in his midst. In the two-thousand-year history of the church, only seven sightings of the Virgin, Mother of Jesus, had received official validation. But in twelve hours in Sunnyside, Washington, many people had seen the apparition, and they wanted the bishop to say, yes, it was a miracle—a visit by Our Lady of Guadalupe, in the image of concentric lines of pink, blue, and yellow on the back of the highway sign. Here she is with us, Father, they said at church. Here she is, 466 years after the Virgin appeared to the Aztec convert Juan Diego in Mexico, almost four hundred years since the Spanish put their colony in the upper Rio Grande. She had never appeared this far north, a valley on the arid side of the Cascade Mountains that draws visitors with murals of bronc-riding cowboys and the slogan "Where the West Still Lives."

Sunday's headline across the front page of the valley's biggest newspaper, the *Yakima Herald-Republic,* was a banner six columns wide: "Miracle or Happenstance?"

They came then in wheelchairs, on crutches, on motorcycles, on bikes, on horseback, in low-riders. From cherry orchards in Oregon, from hops fields near Hanford, from the vineyards along the Columbia River and apple farms near Lake Chelan, wherever food was grown and Spanish-speaking people were paid to tend it and pick it, from there came the believers. The Virgin was a blast of *esperanza*—hope. She was dark-skinned, as in Mexico. She held her hands together in repose. Look closer, the believers said, and you might see her crying. No, she was not in the valley to express sorrow, others said, but rather to say it was all right to live in this far-northern place. It was the Lady of Guadalupe, yes, the Virgin who had spoken to Juan Diego in his native Nahuatl language and later convinced the doubting bishop. The rebel Emiliano Zapata, whose picture was on the window in the new video outlet in Sunnyside, used to carry a little card of this Virgin tucked into his headband, as did his followers. She was a favorite of outlaws, liberators, and farmworkers.

The crowd on Sunday afternoon swelled beyond a thousand. Although the atmosphere was festive, it spooked the police. They did not know what to expect—a rumble, a riot, or just a fairly unusual traffic snag. A dance group, Las Matachinas, performed in front of the sign, on ground that used to be scrub-steppe like the rest of the eastern Washington desert, ground where an Anglo cattle king named Ben Snipes grazed his big herds more than a century ago, ground now given over to a Burger King with bilingual menus and a drive-through espresso booth and some of the most intensively irrigated farmland in the world. The sheriff was perplexed. He called the State Patrol, and they called the Washington State Department of Transportation. After an urgent round of meetings among bureaucrats, the order was passed: get this goddamn road sign out of here. An engineer from the state arrived. He waded among the crowd and stared. He saw nothing, except the directions to Sunnyside and Vernita Bridge.

"Maybe I'm unenlightened," the engineer said.

The troopers decided to close the intersection, barring traffic from the corner. Still, people arrived on foot. Then an officer from the Sunnyside police, Chico Rodriquez, came to assist the sheriff's deputies and state troopers. Rodriquez made his way through the worshippers and the curious to get a close view of the road sign. But, unlike the sheriff's deputies or the engineer from the state, he had no trouble seeing what the others could not.

"It's the full figure of the Virgin Mary," he said, explaining the outline to other cops. "The full figure."

The engineer was put on hold. A mumbled round of discussions followed, three different police agencies trying to figure out what to do now. No time for donuts. New plan: the road sign would stay put, for the time being. Why mess with a miracle? And down the road, in the village of Granger, poorest town in the state of Washington, the phone lines lit up at radio station KDNA, Radio Cadena for the Yakima Valley. Everyone wanted to talk about the Virgin. Most of them believed. The host and station manager, Ricardo Garcia, was somewhat skeptical, but the phenomenon delighted him. He came to the Yakima Valley in 1962, from the Tex-Mex region around El Paso. In the border country, the West that has been in American hands for barely 150 years, the Virgin had long made reprise visits. But not here, in a state the Spanish had sniffed at in the sixteenth century and briefly tried to colonize in the eighteenth century. Spanish sailors were the first Europeans to set foot in the Pacific Northwest, in 1775. Sixteen years later, a little fortress was built along the storm-lashed coast, but New Spain in the Far West lasted only four months. Now, in the final decade of the twentieth century, the language of conquistadors and vaqueros could be heard in nearly every Western valley with a crop.

"This appearance of Our Lady of Guadalupe was overdue," said Garcia. "Long overdue. From now on, I expect you will see a lot of her in this valley."

IN THE FALL of 1847, American troops occupied Mexico City, having marched deep into the land that had been forcibly taken by Spain. The United States had conquered Mexico. Now what? President James K. Polk, an expansionist of the British Empire school, wanted to take over the entire nation and absorb it into the swelling Union. His plan brought reactions of horror: *these* people could never be Americans, it was said. Not quite a century and a half later, 112,000 people, the largest crowd ever to see a professional game of football, jammed into a stadium in the capital city of Mexico to see two American teams play a sport founded in the Ivy League. The border between the two countries moved even as the game was played, with the Colorado River shifting ever so slightly in the Mojave sands. On the American side, a presidential candidate raged that the brown tide north had to stop, and vowed to build an impenetrable curtain along the 1,952-mile length of the border. Putting on a black cowboy hat and clutching a rifle in Tombstone, Arizona, Pat Buchanan pointed to the south and said, "No way, José!" On the Mexican side, letters from Sunnyside, Washington, arrived in the province of Michoacan, telling of jobs and miracles in a valley full of more apples than any place in the world. The funnels of humanity at El Paso and San Diego—two former Spanish mission towns—had been clogged by border guards, but it was nothing to squeeze under a torn fence at Nogales, Arizona, and follow a family map and word-of-mouth to the north. The first fifteen dollars earned, in Nogales, could be had by selling a pint of blood; it amounted to half a week's wages for some.

The dilution of a singular culture and the creation of something altogether new, a process that has been under way since a Moorish slave, Estavanico, and a Franciscan priest, Fray Marco de Niza, went searching for what the Spanish called the Northern Mystery, continues, as ceaseless as the

Sonoran winds. Political lines on the map have come and gone in the West. What has remained in place has always defied official cartographers. It has also proven to be some of the most elusive of moral high ground.

The Latino West, born in conquest and subdued by later defeat, was nearly erased for a time. It has come back, changed, and now is poised to dominate even the most remote reaches of its long-ago domain. Perhaps the reason it never died or was blended to the point of invisibility is because it belongs. It is as much a human element of the West as Monument Valley is a physical feature. New Mexico, once a six-month journey from its sovereign headquarters in Mexico City, seems a more natural fit with the American West than it does with its old colonial masters. But many people think the West is not big enough for two cultures with equal holsters of shame and glory. A lot of Westerners fear the epic morph. They don't recognize their main streets, their menus, the schools where mariachi bands have replaced marching tubas. The Cinco de Mayo parade draws bigger crowds than pioneer days.

"We get these calls, 'They're in the swimming pool at the racquet club, they're in the city park, they're shopping where we shop,' " a police detective from Park City, Utah, Rod Ludlow, told *High Country News.* This ski town, in a state that used to belong to Spain and Mexico, was supposed to be one of those Anglo refuges, full of people who feared what was happening in Los Angeles, Denver, and Phoenix. The new arrivals from Mexico, *cholos,* are lumped with longtime Latino residents as wetbacks, foreigners, spicks in the eyes of others. They are also vaqueros, campesinos, padrones—archetypal Westerners.

For those who think that the West is becoming Mexico North, it is worth remembering that Mexico was nearly America South, a state that would be bigger than Alaska, and certainly as intriguing. The war with Mexico had, for the Americans, been swift and almost casualty-free. On a pretext that Mexicans were not paying back debts to American interests— and then after a skirmish on the disputed border—the Army of the West had moved into New Mexico. With nary a shot being fired, they took over Santa Fe on August 18, 1846. The New Mexican militia did not even fight. Instead, under Governor Armijo, they gave up the territory to the Americans in a few days of flag-adjusting and low-grumbling sycophancy. El Paso, downriver a few hundred miles, fell to an even smaller contingent. The governor was bribed, it was said, otherwise why would he have caved so quickly? The upper Rio Grande, imprinted with the footprints of Coronado, Oñate's misguided colonists, and generations of Franciscans, was now under the control of a general with the first name of Stephen and some volunteers from New England.

But the New Mexicans had been trading with the Yankees for some time; they had socialized at fandangos, intermarried, and for the most part did not fear the Americans. They had long-standing grievances against the central government in Mexico City, nearly two thousand miles to the south. The territory was Hispanic and Pueblo Indian. The colors would not change, it was said at the time, only the flag.

In California, the war followed the same pattern. The American Navy, which sent ships to the coast, met little opposition. Meanwhile, John Charles Frémont—the Pathfinder, as he called himself, in the wake of his best-selling maps—went after settlements in the Sacramento Valley. A Swiss-German polygamist, John Sutter, was trying to build a fiefdom at the confluence of the Sacramento and American rivers. Fleeing legal, marital, and monetary entanglements that stretched from Europe to Hawaii, Sutter had been welcomed in California. He obtained a fifty-thousand-acre land grant from the Mexican government, carved from a neighbor's empire, the nearly 500,000 acres of one of the richest men in the West, Mariano Guadalupe Vallejo. But Sutter had no sooner started sleeping with thirteen-year-olds and laying the foundation for New Helvetia than Frémont's land-hungry army marched into the valley and tossed him in jail. Then they tramped onto the grand Sonoma *rancho* of Señor Vallejo, and he was arrested. From there, it was on to San Francisco. Ten cannons guarding the harbor were no match. Frémont took the village merely by walking in. He renamed the sheltered salt water the Golden Gate. Monterey fell two weeks later. "Henceforth, California will be a part of the United States," American naval commanders announced from the Pacific shore.

Not yet. In the south, the *Californios* took a toll. They lived on large *ranchos,* grants from the government, and golden farms that grew from the missions established by the Spanish in the late 1700s. Life was good for the *Californios,* though they also had considerable problems with the central government in Mexico City. At one point, in 1836, they had declared their independence. What they wanted now was the same thing the New Mexicans desired: property rights, keeping the deeds to the land grants, a degree of self-governance. Into Southern California came American troops in full war cry. There was no talk of an easy transfer of sovereignty. The *Californios* struck back. Led by the brother of Pio Pico, Mexico's last governor of California, they took over the garrison of Los Angeles, a murderous cow town that had been held by a few American mercenaries. Then they defeated soldiers under the command of Stephen Kearny, whose Army of the West had waltzed into Santa Fe. That was it, though. Kearny regained his footing, and California fell to the Americans. It was surrendered in January 1847.

Now, from a base in Mexico City (after American soldiers had marched into the heart of the country), all of Mexico was essentially under U.S. control. A question raged in the Congress: should this enormous territory become a part of the United States? Even in a country that had consumed unimaginable pieces of North American real estate from decaying European monarchs, such a question seemed preposterous. Should Mexico, a land of eight million people, of Indians, Spanish, and mixed-bloods, of Catholics and miracles, of arroyos and jalapeños, be folded into the former British colony? Certainly, much of the land looked worthwhile. But the people—"degraded, mongrel races," in the words of one editorial in Ohio—could never be Americans, according to the consensus view. So the United States settled on taking a very large piece of Mexico instead of absorbing the whole country. In the Treaty of Guadalupe Hidalgo, signed February 2, 1848, Mexico gave up one-third of its land; with the loss of Texas, a decade earlier, it shrank by half. For the territory that would become the states of California, Arizona, New Mexico, Utah, and parts of Colorado and Wyoming, the price the Americans paid at treaty time was $15 million. Together with the Louisiana Purchase, virtually the entire American West was bought for $30 million.

The Americans had much to offer. They would honor Spanish and Mexican land grants, they vowed. Anyone (except Indians) living in the old Spanish colony could become an American citizen. And they brought a different approach to property ownership. The Spanish, in a legacy of feudal Europe, tended to give out huge sections of land to titled men, veteran soldiers, or well-connected opportunists. The grants led to a landed aristocracy, wealthy padrones whose serfs, usually Indians and mixed-blood Mexicans, worked the *ranchos*. In California, just after the war, Mexican land grants covered fourteen million acres. The Americans also gave away state-size pieces of turf, mostly to railroads in the 1860s. But for individuals, there was the prospect of a small homestead to anyone who wanted to prove up the land—the Jeffersonian ideal in the brown squares of the newly American West. Also, rather than rely on the benevolence of a wealthy landowner, income for public schools was to come from a parcel of every township set aside for public revenue. The two great dreams of every Mexican migrant who shows up in the asparagus fields of Sunnyside today were within reach just after the Mexican-American war: property ownership and education.

But the larger goal of the Americans, seldom stated in official government policy, was to lay an Anglo blanket over the Latino West. The odds against bleaching the demographic landscape looked considerable. In 1850, the census counted just over a thousand Anglos and fifty thousand Latinos in New Mexico. Only a few decades earlier, the assimilative imperative had gone the other way, as Anglos tried to become more Latino. Thus, Jonathan Temple arrived in the semidesert town of Los Angeles in 1827, fresh off the boat from Reading, Massachusetts. He liked the climate and the Mediterranean setting. There was plenty of opportunity. Temple set up shop in town, and within a few years became a Mexican citizen and changed his name to Don Juan Temple. Then he married Señorita Rafaela Cota. In what is now the area around City Hall, in downtown L.A., Temple built his large home. After the war, in 1850, the census of Los Angeles counted a town that was 80 percent Latino. But over the next two decades, Don Juan may have wanted to change his name back to Jon. By 1880, the Hispanic population of the city was down to 1 percent. Across the West, the *ranchos* and Spanish land-grant holdings fell to swindle, purchase, or coercion. Rancho Rodeo de las Aquas was bought for five hundred dollars; it became the city of Beverly Hills, and courted Iowa immigrants. Rancho Cerritos was transformed into Long Beach. Out of the southern end of Rancho Malibu was carved the city of Santa Monica. In nearby El Segundo, the new civic leaders boasted that their town, despite its name, was a place with "no negroes or Mexicans." A century later came places like Rancho del Oro, a new exurb in Southern California, billing itself as "a completely walled community."

Of course, as soon as Hispanics began to recede, like bison and Indians, they grew in stature and romance—the Western historical glow of the rear-view mirror. The old *rancho* and mission life was elevated to a mythic idyll. Red-tiled roofs and adobe walls rose in new Anglo neighborhoods. And those much-feared Mexicans, the political *bandidos,* were cast as the last of a daring breed. Just before he was hanged, Tiburcio Vasquez was interviewed by sympathetic reporters, posed for a formal portrait, and was the recipient of fresh-baked pastries brought to his jail cell by the Anglo ladies of Los Angeles. He was the last caballero, it was said, a brown-skinned Robin Hood, fitted for a place in history that would make the new residents of California feel comfortable enough with the recent past. By 1893, the year that Frederick Jackson Turner made his bell-ringing statement that the frontier was now closed, one of the many pamphleteer-journalists of the former northern provinces of Mexico celebrated the old border country as "the new Eden for the Saxon homesteaders."

But in fact, the Anglos living the good life in the valleys with lyrical Spanish names soon discovered what the Hispanic padrones long ago knew: an empire in the sun was best built on the back of cheap labor. So, the border opened. And between 1890 and 1920, 10 percent of Mexico's population—1.5 million people—emptied out of the home country and came north. It set a pattern, still unbroken, of Mexico providing cheap labor for a neighbor it could never match in economic might. The Mexicans picked cotton in Arizona, tended cattle in New Mexico, and were everywhere in the fields of California, fast becoming the world's dominant industrial agriculture region. Early on, stories emerged of harsh treatment, disease-breeding campgrounds, horrid conditions, and meager wages. The only difference between the new outrages and those of a century earlier was that now Latinos were the victims. It had been the Spanish, after all, who had introduced the pattern of hiring poor farm labor—usually Indians—paying them a pittance, and keeping them in line with beatings and threats. They used Yokut Indians in the Central Valley, Modocs in the north, Chumash along the coast. Natives who dared to rebel were hunted down—as in 1829, when a posse led by the beloved Vallejo went after a group of Indian rebels. Vallejo, incidentally, was no friend of the Chinese, calling them "clouds of Asiatics" and "a threat to the moral and material development" of all who lived in California.

In the twentieth century, Mexicans were welcomed in the West as long as prosperity reigned. The farm depression, which hit America before the rest of the country came tumbling down following the crash of 1929, put an end to the first great immigration wave. Then whites from the broken lands of the Great Plains, where rain failed to follow the plow, poured into the Central Valley of California and the fruit orchards of the Pacific Northwest. In less than a decade, from 1929 to 1937, a half million Mexicans were sent home. And along the border, guards with machine guns patrolled the line drawn by treaty. Latinos who stayed, who had gained citizenship, or were the descendants of people who had lived in America for decades, faced a new set of rules. In the 1920s, Los Angeles segregated Hispanics from whites in the schools. And the city police department espoused a view that Mexicans were inherently criminal, that they had a racial disposition to break the law. Throughout the West, a peculiar form of vagrancy statute appeared: "greaser" laws. Anyone who looked Mexican, and had no visible means of support, could be thrown in jail. Thousands were. And for a time again, the new Edens from Colorado to Castroville, from Sunnyside to Salt Lake, were free to pursue a certain destiny.

When World War II brought a labor shortage, the border guards suddenly disappeared and greaser laws went unenforced. Any Mexican in good health was welcomed. But no sooner had the war ended, when another sweep of the land came about, designed to remove virtually every noncitizen Mexican from the West. It was called—formally, and not just in private— Operation Wetback, launched in 1954 by Eisenhower's attorney general, Herbert Brownell. By the time it was over, more than a million Mexicans had been deported. Los Angeles, which had seen its Latino population rise to 20 percent by 1930, was an Anglo enclave again by 1960, with less than 2 percent of the population Mexican-born. "The so-called wetback problem," proclaimed Joseph Swing, the Immigration and Naturalization commissioner, "no longer exists. The border has been secured."

A WEEK before Labor Day, almost half a century after Operation Wetback was conceived, the town of Jackson Hole, Wyoming, was hit by a crisis. It was the height of the summer tourist season, with throngs of people eating ribs under the antler arches of the main city park, strolling in the meadows of the Grand Tetons, fishing the Snake, and at night, eating spicy food and sleeping between fresh sheets. But in a few hours, the city merchants were seized by panic. Overnight, the work force disappeared. There was no one to wash dishes. No one to make beds. No one to clear tables. No one to take out the garbage. No one to work the graveyard shift at the 7-11. No one to clean the wooden boardwalks in the morning. A team of federal agents and local police had made a sweep of town, arresting 151 Mexicans who were without proper documentation. They were promptly put on a bus for deportation. Hotel and restaurant owners were livid.

"I'm upset. I'm pissed off," said the manager of the Westerner Family Kitchen. The restaurant had to shut down for a while. They tried to hire enough Anglos to reopen, but it was not the same. "I've hired a total of six Anglos and only two of them actually showed up for work. That's why we hire Mexicans. Excuse the term, but most Americans are lazy."

Another merchant called the Jackson police, asking if the officers who participated in the biggest immigration bust in Wyoming history were going to come down to her motel and make beds. She had lost her maid service and her guests were furious, and a little grungy as well. Calm down, she was told. You know how this goes. It'll all blow over. And sure enough, within a few months the Mexican work force returned for the ski season, as they had throughout other mountain towns in the West. They lived more than a hundred miles away, across the Tetons in Idaho, in rusted, leaky trailers, and showed up every morning, no matter how icy the roads over the pass, to keep the wheels of winter vacations going. Merchants in Aspen thanked God that immigration authorities did not target them; the most famous ski resort in the West would likely shut down without its Latino work force, the twelve thousand people who live down the Roaring Fork Valley from Aspen, out of sight.

Operation Wetback was supposed to cleanse the West of Mexicans. But the Latino West grew back, reclaiming the boundaries of the nineteenth century. In the old northern provinces of Mexico—including half of Wyoming and half of Colorado—almost three-fourths of the landmass now has a Latino population of between 9 percent and 40 percent of the population. In all eleven Western states, more than half the land has similar demographics. In California, Latinos will be 40 percent of the population within fifty years, which means there will be more election-day historical pivots like the one that happened in Orange County in 1996, when Bob Dornan, the copper-haired former radio talk show host, a congressman whose nickname is "B-1 Bob," was bounced by a Latina accountant. There are now more people of Mexican ancestry in Los Angeles than in any other city in the world outside of Mexico City. And the city's most-watched local newscast is in Spanish, with English subtitles. In the entire United States, by 2009, Hispanics will be the largest single minority. By 2050, when the United States is a nation of four hundred million, one in four Americans will be Hispanic. Much of the West, ahead of the rest of the country, is living the future now. Entire valleys, counties, cities have, almost overnight, become majority Latino.

FOURTH OF JULY. In Sunnyside, the bank temperature sign reads ninety-six degrees. In two languages, it welcomes clients. You know you are in the Pacific Northwest because the roadside fruit stand just off the highway has big block letters spelling out four words: Apples. Peaches. Cherries. Espresso. The one-stoplight town is scrubbed for the summer season, park grass trimmed. A new Safeway has opened, and across the street, Tienda del Pueblo has been doing a brisk business offering sugary pastries from Mexico and cactus ears from Arizona. They have sold out their supply of Lady of Guadalupe candles. The Chinese restaurant is sporting a new sign in Spanish—Comida China. Down Main Street, there's a big mural of the heroic West, cowboys moving cattle against the leathered hills of the central Washington desert. In front of the mural, a crowd of campesinos eat tacos sold by a vendor on wheels. Sid Egley's clothing store, "Work and Western," has gone from traditional cowboy wear to more Mexican styles, and is doing its best business in a decade. I drop into El Conquistador for lunch, on a side street bedecked with American flags. A passel of rodeo cowboys, sunburned and blond, their spurs still on their boots, are gathered in one corner, sucking down beers and laughing. Hispanic families, dressed as if for a wedding, are seated at long tables. They had been to see the Virgin, a young man explained, and after lunch, they would celebrate the Fourth of July at the rodeo. In the borderlands, around Deming, New Mexico, and El Paso and Nogales, I had seen signs on businesses which read, "American owned." Here, there are no such statements of defiant nationality.

Once sluggish and midwestern, Sunnyside is changing by the day. The accelerated pace has produced a tension that is out of place in a town this small. But it has also given the sleepy valley a sense of drama. The drip, drip, drip of history is on hyperdrive here, all sparks and noise. With the first real heat wave of summer, and everybody gathering for the four-day party on the rodeo grounds, the police fear trouble—a rumble or two, some gunfire.

Sunnyside is where much of the West is headed. The Yakama Indians have lived in the valley for centuries; two-thousand-year-old petroglyphs are scratched into the rocks just above the valley. Now, the largest tribe in Washington State lives on a 1.4-million-acre reservation, sharing stores and parks with the new arrivals from Mexico. With dry heat in the summer, and annual rainfall of just eight inches, the desert interior of Washington was a paradise for sage grouse, but no place for Anglo farmers looking for another green home like the Willamette Valley. Ben Snipes built a little slouching cabin in 1881, a sometime home while he ran his cattle over the hills. Then came irrigation, the canals that tapped into the river, and the valley grew gold on trees, becoming the world's biggest apple producer. In the 1930s, Dust Bowl refugees harvested much of the fruit. By the 1960s, it was mostly Mexican labor.

In ten years time, from 1980 to 1990, the Hispanic population in Sunnyside went from 37 percent to 57 percent. Now it is close to 65 percent. Three-fourths of the students in the public schools are Hispanic. Throughout the entire valley, home to 200,000, the trend is the same, though Latinos are not yet a majority. They came mostly from south of Mexico City, in the poor state of Michoacan. But the echo from the 1847 debate is bouncing off the irrigated hills here: they don't really belong this far north, some politicians who speak for the desert interior of the Northwest proclaim. Here is CongressMAN Helen Chenoweth again. "The warmer climate community just hasn't found the colder climate that attractive," she says. "It's an area of America that has simply never attracted the Afro-American or the Hispanic."

Ricardo Garcia came to the Yak Valley—where temperatures sometimes plunge well below zero in the winter—in 1962, by way of Texas, and the army. "I'm an American citizen, but I have not forgotten my past," he says, taking a break between radio shows at KDNA. "I was pleasantly surprised to find thousands of familes from the Tex-Mex country like myself. The attitude then was, folks welcomed the Mexican migrants. The growers would throw a big party after the harvest, and then most people would go home, back to Mexico. Now, they stay. And because of that, there is just so much tension."

Garcia helped set up the first Spanish-language radio station, in a crumbling, two-story building in Granger. They would broadcast a few hours a day, mostly giving survival information to farmworkers and trying to dispense hope to the people who had followed a harvest trail to this far northern valley, eighteen hundred miles from the Mexican border. Inside the building is a mural that shows three figures: a conquistador, a Mexican Indian, and a Chicano. Next to the mural, prominently displayed but yellowed with age, is the American Declaration of Independence. Now there are three Spanish-language stations in the valley, three newspapers, and a television station.

"There came a time when so many people just wanted to live somewhere, to settle down," says Garcia. "The talk was: we have to stop traveling and find a home. And then came the amnesty in 1986. Following that, people were allowed to bring their families in. So people stayed. But what they say around here is that Hispanics are going to take over our structures, our streets, our schools, our country. But it hasn't happened. Look . . . here is what happens. We acquire a love of country—America. I don't care what anyone says, but English is our language. We have our ties to Mexico; we are not ashamed. It used to be, you went to school here with a burrito and came home crying. Now . . . what is it? Salsa is the number one condiment in America? Salsa is bigger than ketchup! And we realize the American Dream works. There are three hundred Hispanic businesses in this valley. But still, there is so much tension now compared to twenty, thirty years ago. There are gangs. Teenage pregnancy. Families that have trouble because both parents work."

But there also is this miracle in their midst, the Virgin on the road sign at the Yakima Valley Highway intersection, and that has made the troubles seem less of a burden to many people, Garcia says.

I WENT out to see the road sign from heaven in late afternoon. Along the way, I had arranged to meet a longtime resident of the valley, an Anglo, trying to live on seven dollars an hour, working in the new Wal-Mart. He ran a department, and every year Wal-Mart promised him a raise of thirty-five cents an hour. We met in a park near a city pool that was full of Latino children.

"We hate them," he blurted out, very suddenly, and then said I could not use his name. "Everyone here hates the Mexicans, I'm sure. They have no respect for the people who've always lived here. They're dirty. They steal things at the store. All the time. I mean you really have to watch them. And they're dangerous. Just the other day, in Pasco, there was a murder, some Mexicans killed a guy for no reason. There was never any crime around here. Now this valley is going down the tubes. I don't recognize it."

I tried to argue with him. Little Sunnyside was going through the brutish initial stage of the immigrant cycle; the Irish, the Italians, the Chinese, every nationality had gone through the same thing, from delinquent to doctor. In a generation's time, they would be living in tri-level homes and whining about new arrivals from foreign lands. Besides, the West would fall apart without its Latino work force. Look what happened in Jackson Hole. How many apples would get picked if the blue-eyed boys of Sunnyside were all the muscle available in the valley? Just today, I had read in *El Mundo,* one of the valley's Spanish weeklies, that farmworkers had won a 20 percent raise—to six dollars an hour.

"Almost what I make," said the Wal-Mart manager, frowning. "You watch," he added. "Watch what happens at the rodeo. These people are different."

AT THE road sign shrine, I found two women praying in Spanish, and some plastic flowers at the base of the aluminum-and-wood structure. They were Mixteca Indians, from Oaxaca, and spoke only a few words of

English. It was waffle-iron hot on the pavement. I went to get an iced coffee at the drive-through espresso booth, a block or so away.

"Business must be terrific since the . . . miracle," I said to the woman inside the caffeine hut, a young Anglo.

"Nope. Just the opposite. It's gone down some."

"But you've had huge crowds here."

"They aren't the kind of people who pay two-fifty for a latte."

At the road sign, I sucked on my iced coffee and tried to see Our Lady of Guadalupe. There was a bit of color, a kind of rainbow, which the engineers said came from an antioxidant coating. I stared for a long time, waiting for a face, a movement, as the two Mixteca Indians prayed. The coffee helped. But after an hour in the hot sun, I could not see the Virgin. I left for the rodeo.

IN TOPPENISH, site of the sixty-fifth annual Rodeo and Pow Wow, the streets were packed for the biggest celebration of the valley. Saloons were full. Restaurants were jammed. RVs and tents circled on the grass. Heeeee-yeeeah! Kids blew off fireworks from the reservation, illegal everywhere else, but just part of the background here. Horses trod through town, trailing turds. The streets smelled of burritos, barbecued ribs, beer, smoke, and horseshit. Even more than Sunnyside, the neighboring town of Toppenish shows its cultural confusion—equal parts Indian, Anglo, and Latino. In a slump ten years ago, the town came up with the idea of doing to itself what many a person with a head full of cheap beer has done in dives along Seattle's waterfront: gotten a massive tattoo. In this case, the town covered itself in murals. The first one to go up was called *Clearing the Land* and showed a tough-looking homesteader and a horse ripping what few trees there were in the Yakima Valley out of the ground, with tipis in the background. Once the wall-painters of Toppenish got started, they couldn't be stopped. Now, it is the Illustrated Town, with every blank wall in town, brick or plywood, covered. The walls show Indians and whites in respective iconic poses—farming, fishing, or riding horses in a cloud of dust. One depicts the 1855 treaty, in which the Yakamas gave up twelve million acres, almost one-fourth of the state of Washington, in return for their 1.3-million-acre reservation. Governor Isaac Stevens, the dwarf alcoholic who pressured the Yakamas into signing the treaty, has never looked taller. In all, there are twenty-nine murals, with stagecoaches and thundering herds of horses almost jumping off the walls. But nothing of the Latino West.

At Los Murales Restaurant—"cuisine of northern Mexico"—I had a Tecate beer and tried to cool off. The place was jumping, but not a hint of trouble. At the rodeo grounds, I saw some teens, Latino gang-banger wannabes with pants that showed their butt cracks, trying to imitate the white teens, with pants that showed *their* butt cracks. They were part of the American birthday show, in their way, though possibly clueless as to what it was all about.

I fell in with the cowboys for a time, smoking a cigar while they chewed tobacco. The rodeo queen, Jamie Mahaffey, strutted the grounds, her blonde curls cascading halfway down her back, cowboy boots polished, smiling to kids eating curly fries. One of the youths made a remark, and she kept smiling, even though it was not the kind of thing people in small towns are expected to say to rodeo queens. I watched the horses before the competition. I liked the Appaloosas. The animals jumped around in early evening, looking sublimely incorrigible. Rodeo, of course, is a term coined by vaqueros long ago, and many of the riders setting up for the evening were Hispanic. And the horses also descended from the herds brought to New Mexico by the Spanish. I found a seat in the half-empty stands. A mariachi band, ten pieces and men in sequined uniforms and sombreros, set up on stage and started playing. They drew a quick crowd. The music made me feel good, songs for the weather and the desert, and I could imagine myself in old El Paso a hundred years ago. I looked out beyond Lost Horse Plateau, toward the sunset, to the big volcano of Mount Adams, the second-highest peak in the Northwest, 12,270 feet. The glacier dome, a rose-colored blush, seemed to settle in for a seat by the rodeo. It was in the mountains around Adams that William O. Douglas, the only Supreme Court justice ever produced by the Yakima Valley, had one of his great epiphanies. "I felt at peace," Douglas wrote. "That night, I think, there first came to me the germ of a philosophy of life: that man's best measure of the universe is in his hopes and in his dreams, not his fears; that man is a part of a plan, not a fraction of which he can ever understand."

Not more than fifty yards from where I sat, Yakama Indians had set up their tipis. Because they lived east of the Cascades and roamed the broad Columbia Plateau, the Yakamas were buffalo hunters, some of them making the long trip to Montana. In the old days, it took about fifteen tanned buffalo hides to make a traditional tipi. Today, on the powwow grounds, the Yakamas used lodgepole pine for support, as was typically done, but have long gone over to canvas for the wrap. The Indians sold jewelry and cedar carvings, frybread and smoked salmon. Many of them wore T-shirts with a single word on the front: Dignity. And now, even as the mariachi band played, as Queen Jamie with her bouncing blonde curls flirted with the tobacco-spitting cowboys dressed in shirts of American flags, the Indians began to chant and play drums, low and rhythmic, in a circle in front of the tipis. In the rodeo grandstand were campesinos with blistered hands and freshly washed scarves around their necks, and big-bellied Anglos with cowboy hats, and girls in cutoffs, giggly and summery. All the sounds came together in the evening with the smells and sights, the cheatgrass giving way to Mount Adams, and the Appaloosas young and unfettered. The West of Wonder was in place again.

BEFORE I left the valley, I went back to the road sign to try one last time to catch a miracle. The rodeo and powwow had played to record crowds, and it had gone off without a hitch, the sheriff's deputies said, unless you count the people arrested for drunkenness or the half-dozen folks treated for sunstroke. I would be disappointed if you could not fill a sheriff's ledger in the valley with such notations. In my last visit to the road sign, I was alone. It was early, and the light was sharp, right on the back of where everyone else said Our Lady of Guadalupe had made her visits. I saw, more than I had seen before, the rainbow outline of color, and if I had really tried hard—maybe if I had had a triple-shot espresso at the Homestake Drive-Thru—I could have seen a face. But I was not disappointed. In ten years' time, maybe less, I knew I might look at a road sign in one of these valleys, on a day when other things seemed flat, and see the Mother of God. It was inevitable.

CHAPTER 14

Frontier

American River, California

> This is how the New World looks, this is what is happening
> in the vital madhouse of Eden, the vanishing Lotus Land.
> —Wallace Stegner,
> *All the Little Live Things*

A t one point the leading minds in Europe believed that California was an island with an unapproachable coast populated by single-breasted Amazons. For much of the 1990s, the leading minds in America thought California was dead, a still life of flakes and brutes with only the ground truly alive, and then in a terrifying way. So perhaps the way to find California's place in the West is to go somewhere that is vaguely consistent. On a day when it is 104 degrees in the Sacramento Valley and the urban ozone looks the way a bee sting feels, the snowmelt of the Sierra makes sense. Water and wonder, the two elements the West needs in order to stay healthy, are the magnets of the Range of Light. Through all the dreams, disasters, and schemes of empire-builders under five different flags, California has had its source of liquid renewal in the Sierra Nevada Range.

So to the Sierra we go, my friend Jim Wilson and I, and a handful of Californians new and old, logical and looney. We wade into the middle fork of the American River, pushing a raft into the stream, and then we are held captive by the current—a tether to the ages of California. We are two thousand feet, perhaps a little higher, above the stifling valley, the interchangeable Taco Bells and Shopkos, the California of walled compounds and toxic auto culture, and only fifty miles or so away by direct line, and yet we have escaped it entirely. I'm stunned. Nobody would call the American River a wild stream by the standards of, say, Idaho's Salmon or Oregon's Deschutes. Most of modern California history has coursed through it or been touched by it. Carrying mustard-colored flecks from the granite tables of the Sierra, this river lured the first crush of Americans, and now feeds the $25-billion machine of California agriculture. The people who lived in the river valley six thousand years ago left milling stones behind, their only record. In a flash, nineteenth-century argonauts rerouted and turned over the river, yanking it from its gravitational home, scraping the bottom bare. They burned and cut down all the trees, killed or drove out all the wildlife, and knocked down the banks with hydraulic cannons. By 1882, it was "treeless, mud-laden, filthy and fishless," as Myron Angel wrote.

But after it was fleeced and stripped bare, the American River was left alone, given over to the jet stream in late winter, and springtimes when thirty-five feet of snow would melt and rush downhill. It is clean, swift, and alive today at a time when whole forests have been felled for writers of California's obituary. Into the current we go, a bit less hesitant to face what the Golden State has become.

When we stop, I climb a rock and jump into a pool; it could be the west slope of Colorado. When we hit rapids, the spray covers us and makes everyone laugh; it could be the Green River in Wyoming. When we slow to a dead drift, nobody talks, because we all feel the same thing, the soft embrace of a valley. Not two days ago, the water around me was in a north-facing cranny of the High Sierra, snowbound. And several days from now, the water will be spit out of a sprinkler in a desert cul-de-sac in Moreno Valley, in homes protected by lasers and armed-response, a covenant-bound conclave where neighbors sue each other over oddly-placed basketball hoops. It is a quick ride from the Geography of Hope to the cliff of fear. But then, no place on earth has risen and then gone to the brink of ruination so quickly as California, a state that much of the West has disowned, speaking of it in the past tense. It is not us, they say in Utah, New Mexico, and Oregon, feigning sympathy, or more often openly expressing horror. The unlivable cities. The unbreathable air. The undrinkable water. The unaffordable houses. The tribal politics. The drive-by plastic surgery. The facile weather. The crimes against nature. The crimes against each other. The traffic. The natural disasters. The man-made disasters. The sickos with guns. The sickos with Ph.D.'s. The half-baked ideas. The fight song of the U.S.C. Trojans—a dial tone is more appealing. It is not us, not the West, they say in Arizona, Montana, and Idaho, speaking as if California had long ago been cleaved at the border west of Nevada and south of Oregon, set adrift with a history all its own, on a course no other Western state would ever follow. Downriver, then, to see.

THE STATE MOTTO is Eureka, and the state symbol is the grizzly bear. The last bruin was seen in 1922. The motto, curiously, remains, spoken in myriad languages and dialects. The greatest single movement of people in American history was the heave-ho, east to west, from 1849 to 1851. It was concentrated, then, during the Gold Rush, but it has never stopped. In 1900, barely a million people lived in California. The state grew to five million by 1930, about the population of present-day Colorado; ten million by 1950; twenty million in 1970, surpassing New York as the most populous state, and thirty million in 1990, surpassing all of Canada. It will have fifty million by 2025, if current projections hold, roughly equal to the population of Italy or France. Nearly one out of every eight Americans lives in California, the world's seventh-largest economy. Within a few years, there will be no ethnic majority in the state, only a stew of all races and nationalities, each one a minority. In a year, three thousand immigrants move to California from England, twelve thousand from China, twenty thousand from Vietnam, ten thousand from Iran, forty thousand from Mexico, and nearly 800,000 come from other states of America. At what point do they become Westerners? Arrival, perhaps. Eureka, remember, means "I have found it."

The highest mountain in the contiguous United States is in the southern Sierra, 14,494-foot Mount Whitney, a mere eighty miles from the lowest point in the Western Hemisphere, Death Valley at 282 feet below sea level. One-fourth of the state is desert. One-fifth is taken up by the largest mountain range in the West. The coastline is eleven hundred miles long; the northern shore looks like Maine and the south resembles the Mediterranean. The biggest trees in the world and some of the oldest living things grow in California's misty redwood-and-sequoia zone to the north; the hottest spot on the planet is in the Mojave Desert to the south. It is all so sublime and diverse—breathless in the sheer force of its beauty—because it is still in the active process of being shaped. The Pacific Plate is moving north two inches a year relative to the more stubborn and anchored North American Plate, and the pressure from a mobile earthen crust floating atop a molten core has produced thousands of smaller faults and cracks. In one earthquake alone, the Lone Pine temblor of 1872, the Sierra rose twenty-three feet; in the San Fernando quake of 1971, the San Gabriel Mountains grew by six feet. An address, in California, is never permanent.

"THIS STATE would be paradise," says one of our rafting companions, a native Californian, trailing a foot in the current. "If only a few people lived here. Human beings have fucked it up so bad it may be beyond hope." I imagine Ishi, the last surviving member of the vanquished Yahi tribe, felt the same thing when he came out of hiding near Lassen Peak in 1911, only to live the next five years as a curiosity with a heartbeat at the University of California's Museum of Anthropology.

I have had similar feelings, flying north in an Alaska Airlines jet after covering a race riot, an earthquake, a mass suicide, a mass murder, a calamitous mudslide, flood, or firestorm, a media farce around a celebrity trial, a political campaign where the candidates are never seen except on television. On the ground, California can seem like America at its worst, a poisoned civilization in the grip of a slow choke. From the air it is the best of the West, cracked and sunbaked, uplifted and wind-buffed, groomed and cultivated in the valleys, the rocky shores stroked by the Pacific, San Francisco a perfect match for its perfect setting, Half-Dome gleaming in Yosemite, Shasta holding the late light at fourteen thousand feet. But that is like loving someone only for their looks, the bond broken as soon as he or she speaks. Besides, California was never an Eden lanced by a sudden surge of humanity, as Ishi's blinkered emergence from the pine forest would indicate. The coast, from the Baja tip to the Pacific Northwest—the original California, as named by the Spanish—had the densest population of natives anywhere on the continent, perhaps 300,000. They spoke at least eighty different languages, lived with cycles of drought and fire, fought with each other, slaved and raided. They were Miwoks and Modocs, Chumash and Yokut, Ohlones and Mojave, and they seem to have had as much trouble with heaving ground, flaming volcanoes, and sliding mountainsides as later residents did.

Today people lament the exurbs built in fire zones and flood plains, the cities straddling fault lines. But from the very beginning, Californians set the standard for defiance of their native ground.

AS IF guided by jinxed divining rods, the Spanish had a remarkable ability to find the worst and most unstable places to establish their outposts of harsh religion and slave-labor agriculture. As in the New Mexico *entrada* in 1540, the Spaniards crossed into California with the usual clanking parade of padres, cannons, gilt-skirted horses, bawling cattle, and sweaty soldiers looking for plunder. In 1769, the Portolá expedition entered the basin that is now weighed down by Los Angeles. They were greeted by the California equivalent of a Bronx cheer: a heart-stopping earthquake. It shook the ground for nearly a minute. Traumatized by the movable terra, the Spanish said Mass the next day, begging for help. In response came three more earthquakes—aftershocks, but big ones, the kind that can bring down Target stores. The following day, same thing. "This afternoon we felt new earthquakes, the continuation of which astonishes us," wrote the expedition's diarist, Fray Juan Crespi.

The basin was watered by a good little river, forested on its banks by willows and cottonwood, the brush full of ripe blackberries and blossoming roses. Antelope sprang from the shadows, and grizzly bears gobbled berries. Condors with a ten-foot wingspan, vulture-like and prehistoric in appearance, cruised for carrion. But though it was full of life, southern California also showed considerable signs of nature at its less pastoral. The grass was blackened from fire; logs were strewn along the river, evidence of floods. The Spanish did not take the cue. They proceeded to establish a mission, one of twenty-one such outposts along a five-hundred-mile length of the California coast. Most of them were placed directly atop what they did not know was one of the most fragile areas on earth—the San Andreas Fault zone. In the sand-speck of time since the Spanish arrived, it has produced 118 major earthquakes.

At Mission San Gabriel a settlement arose that soon acquired a reputation for moral sloth and easy violence: Los Angeles in its first years, a shack town of single-story tar-roof adobe buildings and heat-slowed cattle. They named one of the nearby rivers the Rio de los Temblores. At Mission San

Juan Bautista, the fifteenth in the chain to be built, the Spanish may have started to get the message. They constructed particularly strong adobe walls, three feet thick, and a red-tiled roof was designed to withstand a good shake. Nonetheless, it was sitting squat over the 750-mile-long break in the earth's crust that is the Fault. In one month alone, October 1800, there were six earthquakes a day. Twice, the mission had to be rebuilt. The European introduction to California was baptized in earthly tumult. And nothing has changed. From Mission San Francisco de Asis rose a city of rowdy Americans and anxious Chinese that tumbled during the biggest displacement of the two big plates ever recorded: the 1906 quake, in which the ground slipped twenty feet horizontally, and 490 city blocks in San Francisco were destroyed.

"We burn down a city in a night," one Californian noted after the 1906 quake, displaying the trademark resilience. "And build it in a day." Just before Game Three of the 1989 World Series came more plate slippage, more chaos and tragedy, and T-shirts, all over California, proclaiming what everyone knew by now: "Nature bats last!"

No matter how much the earth opened up and broke apart, the Spanish friars were undeterred. It had been nearly two hundred years since Don Juan de Oñate had sacked Acoma in New Mexico, after the Pueblo natives refused to bow to Spanish demands of church and state. This time, the Plus Ultra banners were left in Mexico, and the friars spoke as if going out to teach children the wonders of the world. Still, the larger lessons of Acoma were lost. And so here was Western history, supposedly in its early stages, but actually quite far along, already repeating itself. The mission leader, Father Junipero Serra, rang a little bell as he moved about, hoping to attract heathens to his side. "I saw something I could not believe," said Father Serra upon his first encounter with California Indians in 1769. "They were entirely naked, as Adam in the garden before sin."

Nude Californians in their native habitat matched, in one respect, Spain's image of the area. For nearly 150 years, the best maps of the Americas continued to show the Island of California, not too far from the Island of Japan. It was not pure ignorance. A book written in 1510, a novel by Garci Ordóñez de Montalvo, told a story of a land inhabited by very large, black, single-breasted women. They had only one breast because it made them better warriors, adept at archery; a pair would get in the way. They hunted men and fed them to goblins. Gold was ubiquitous. And over this island kingdom ruled a woman, Queen Califia. The very name California is a product of fantasy.

By the first year of the American Revolution, 1776, the Spanish had made it clear that they were in California to stay. They put down a mission and small garrison at San Francisco, preaching to the Ohlone children who played near a waterfall on what is now the corner of 18th and Valencia streets. Most of the missions had cemeteries outside their walls and frescoed houses of worship inside. Within a generation's time, the graveyards were much fuller than the churches. Spain wanted volume baptisms, a source of cheap labor, and a military presence. The church kept good records, which showed that the friars got the numbers they wanted: during the mission era, fifty-four thousand natives were baptized. But there was a more telling number, related to the cemeteries. Indian contact with whites anywhere in North America usually resulted in mass death by disease. In California, the story was the same, but only more horrific. During the initial mission era, about sixty thousand were lost to diseases to which they had no immunity. And then, during smallpox epidemics of 1828–29 and 1838, nearly half of the remaining California natives died.

At Acoma, the Indians stayed put on their rock perch, despite Spanish harquebuses and waves of aggressive priests. In California, the missionaries yanked the natives from their villages, trained them as laborers in the agricultural fields, and tried to eradicate their religions. "For the slightest thing they receive heavy floggings, are shackled, and put in stocks, and treated with so much cruelty that they are kept whole days without a drink of water," wrote one observer, a priest at the missions, Father Antonio de la Concepción Hora.

How these missions came to be bathed in the soft light of romanticism, cast as Mediterranean outposts of multicultural order and pre-gridlock California good life, is one of the great examples of Western historical alchemy. But if serial killers like Billy the Kid could become lasting icons, if Utah's authoritarian theocrats could be polished into tolerant freedom-lovers, then forced-labor posts like San Juan Bautista could be seen as health spas with a spiritual side. California, after all, is the state that came up with the term "alternative lifestyle advocates" to describe homeless alcoholics. The first real Western novel, the book that set the tone for all the dime paperbacks and movies that were to follow, was written by a bona fide member of the Eastern Media Elite—Owen Wister, author of *The Virginian*. He was a Philadelphia socialite and a Harvard man. In California, the mission image overhaul was accomplished by another outsider, Helen Hunt Jackson, daughter of a Calvinist theologian in Amherst, Massachusetts. Jackson lived for a time in the Plaza Hotel, not far from the crumbling Mission San Juan

Bautista, while writing *Ramona,* the late-nineteenth-century novel that would make early Spanish mission life seem like an extended holiday at a seaside resort. Just as writers of nature deserve credit for helping to create national parks and protected wilderness areas, so must writers of wish-fulfillment fiction be given their due for foisting on the public the dominant myths of the West. Shaking those stories is said to involve embracing a graduate-seminar version of the West, depressing and bleak, with abundant shame and obloquy for all races and religions. But simply looking anew at a somewhat forgotten piece of ground, in the era that followed the missions, will do wonders for a pilgrim in the West.

WE ARE deep in a multiple-green fold of the Sierra, shadowed by high cliffs of oak, pine, fir, and chaparral—cleared every thirty years or so by fire, another California constant. Every inch of ground, on a slope so steep it is nearly impossible to get a foothold, is covered. The American River canyon is full of birds darting back and forth, squawking and fishing. I don't recognize many of them.

"They're tropical birds," says another of our rafting mates, a sometime ornithologist. "This place has two hundred thirty different bird species in the canyon. It's one of the biggest refuges in America for tropical birds migrating from Central America."

We float on the laziest stretch of water, in the siesta part of the day, day-dreamers skipping out on the toils of Wednesday. Oars are in the raft. The current, such as it is, controls destiny. Around a bend, we come upon a pair of extras from *Deliverance.* Property-rights wackos, says the ornithologist, who has run into them on many a trip; they are a haunt in the rot of ghost towns left from a time when ten thousand people lived in the canyon. They curse the government for designating part of the American River as wild and scenic, their lives held together by the dream that one day irrefutable evidence will be found linking the United Nations, the Sierra Club, and an electronic signal in the back of speed-limit signs. I say make them part of the scenery, grandfather them into the wild-and-scenic law. Every wilderness needs an indigenous predator.

The banjo music in my head passes, and then we approach a family on the beach—two kids and their mother—playing with what looks like a frying pan.

"Watcha' doing?"

"Panning for gold," says a little girl. "Look . . ." And she shows me a few shiny specks of whatever-she-wants-to-believe-it-is in the bottom of the pan. Prospecting with a frying pan is a reflex reaction in this part of California—the Gold Country, they still call it, the setting where the "strange disease of the heart" that Cortés spoke of was epidemic.

"Wanna try?"

"Sure."

I swish gravel around in the pan like an omelette in the forming stage, standing knee-deep in the American River. The heavier stuff, the gold flecks from the blocks of the Sierra, dust from a solid formed 150 million years ago, is supposed to linger in the bottom—if you're lucky. It is fun and diverting for a few moments, and then a little bit of the fever kicks in, the lust. You look at this sloth of a river, this heaven of a canyon, this breach in the mountain as . . . motherlode! Every wash in the pan a potential strike. Every scrape at a sandbar a chance at early retirement. The American River was the source of the California Dream, and it set a pattern for all others. If you heard about it in feudal China, or hopeless Sicily, or incomprehensible New York, the promise was so simple: come to the American River, no matter your standing or background, and maybe in a month's time, or half a year at the most, free yourself from a dismal fate.

A million people died in Ireland at the time of the Gold Rush—one-eighth of the Emerald Isle's population, killed by famine. Little wonder that so much Gaelic was heard around Sutter's Mill. If they could read, they had seen headlines such as this, which ran in 1849:

EL DORADO
OF THE
UNITED STATES OF AMERICA!

And this:

THE DISCOVERY
OF
INEXHAUSTIBLE GOLD MINES
IN
CALIFORNIA

From Canton and from Guangdong Province came the first significant immigration of Chinese to America—twenty-five thousand arrived in California in 1852, most of them men with peasant backgrounds. They worked the mines that had already been abandoned by earlier argonauts, or set up merchant shops in Sacramento and San Francisco. A few of them made astonishing finds. At a place called Chinese Camp, a chunk of pure gold weighing 195 pounds was discovered. Nearly two thousand free blacks and a handful of runaway slaves made it to the Sierra foothills—some getting rich, most others getting harassed. From the Sonoran district of Mexico, entire villages were emptied of their men, the people heading for a territory that had been ceded to America nine days after the American River gold discovery. The Treaty of Guadalupe Hidalgo was signed just before Mormon merchant Sam Brannon, in a brilliant bid at self-enrichment, walked through the streets of San Francisco holding a little vial while shouting, "Gold! Gold from the American River!"

In Oregon it is still said that at the fork of the great wagon trail west, those who could read went north to the Willamette Valley; those who could not went south to California. But in a few years, nearly two-thirds of the men of literate Oregon abandoned their homes for California's goldfields. Nearly half of all Gold Rush migrants came from New England, a region ragged and depressed in an early downcycle of the Industrial Revolution. Young, bearded, rangy-looking men, they were not paradigms of Yankee stability. In daguerreotypes, they stare back with take-the-goddamn-picture looks, anxious to get back to the desperate task of ground-scraping for a jackpot.

Some saw the frenzy as an appalling greed-fest, and this view has developed into a consensus way of looking at the mad scramble above Sacramento. "Our countrymen are the most discontented of mortals," wrote Louisa Clapp, one of few women to venture into the goldfields. "They are always longing for the big strikes." The historian Patricia Limerick similarly sideswiped the Gold Rush, dwelling on poor gastrointestinal health and how the camps were such a pit. The "disease of California," one doctor is quoted in Limerick's account, "was diarrhea." So much for Eureka.

But early on at least, it was pure West—the throwing together of races and backgrounds, the utter disregard for established order, the chaos of opportunity in a wild land. "They fairly reveled in gold, whiskey, fights, and fandangos, and were unspeakably happy," wrote Mark Twain, whose career was jump-started in California. It was all over in less than four years. By 1852, human hands and a strong backbone were quaint anachronisms in the California goldfields. Earth-gouging hydraulic machines, channeling river water and scraping out canyon sides, replaced gold pans, and small prospectors gave way to wage crews.

From the disorder and violence, the potluck of dreams, came the rough outline of what California would eventually become: the world's first truly polyglot state. So, for all the latter-day hand-wringing about what a debasing free-for-all the Gold Rush had been, it did produce something that the West is still known for manufacturing—a society from scratch. Not orderly, certainly. It was something new altogether, with America's fatal faults of gun violence and money obsession at play with some of America's best attributes, opportunity and open land. California's population rose from fourteen thousand in 1849 to 250,000 in 1852, at which point the state had more immigrants than any other place in America—and arguably, the world—a blend of Latinos and Anglos, blacks and Chinese, Russians and Swedes, and Indians with superior immunity to foreign diseases. In fifty years time, five flags had flown over parts of California, representing Russia, Spain, Mexico, the Bear Flag Republic, and America. In 1850, more than two dozen languages were heard in the stores and bars and rivers of the Sierra foothills. It would take another century and a half for California to revert to that form.

Now, at the millennial snapshot, when there are more Koreans in California than any place outside of Seoul and more people of Mexican ancestry in Los Angeles than in any community other than Mexico City, the Golden State is seen by some as a tremulous new world where everyone is a minority. At Hollywood High School, eighty languages are spoken. But the modern state may be simply a more crowded, somewhat more refined, version of California in its El Dorado exuberance.

DURING the interim, from motherlode to obituary, came the fanciful attempt to graft a midwestern society onto the most Western of states. And here again, California set a pattern that other Western states would follow. As odd as it now seems to find Lake Havasu trying to be Olde England in the Arizona Desert, with a community of former Californians living around a transplanted London Bridge, consider what the great-grandparents of those Lake Havasupians tried to do. In the 1850s, Yankee settlers imported entire frame houses to California, shipping them in a kit around Cape Horn. They came with gables and picket fences to a place where people lived most comfortably behind mud and mortar. A duplicate of Boston's Faneuil Hall was built in downtown Los Angeles in 1859; brick for brick, it was a copy from across the continent.

Working with timber and white paint would prove to be the easy part in the imagined society. After building the railroads and many of the roads, and providing labor that no other people would in the Sierra goldfields, the Chinese were excluded from owning mines, from testifying against whites in court, and from citizenship. The days of *ku li,* bitter toil, were over, but only the physical part. At one point, the state constitution read that "no native of China, no idiot, no insane person, or person convicted of infamous crimes," could be a citizen. The challenge must have been establishing proof of idiocy. Mexicans were chased out of the cities and deprived of their *ranchos,* even as novels and songs were created around the story of their pastoral lives in California. After passage of the Anti-Alien Act of 1913, Japanese immigrants were prohibited from owning farmland. By 1895, Charles Fletcher Loomis would write: "The ignorant, hopelessly un-American type of foreigner which infests and largely controls Eastern cities is almost unknown here." By 1910, over 60 percent of the people who lived in California were from the Midwest. It was a warm Iowa, a looser Minnesota, a less gothic Indiana, a prettier Michigan.

The *Wizard of Oz* was written by one transplanted midwesterner, L. Frank Baum. He had to close his eyes to imagine Dorothy's Kansas, because for all the flatland cultural export, California did not look or feel like the Midwest. Still, it is where the imagined West took root, quite literally. The Spanish brought in palm trees, planting them around the missions. Soon they were the signature tree of California. From Brazil came jacarandas, flowering purple in April, some even holding their color as blocks of Los Angeles burned in the 1992 riots. Trees of heaven, so-called, were brought over by Chinese who wanted something to remind them of home. The first oranges were planted by the Franciscans in 1805. Beginning in the 1890s, garden societies organized eucalyptus crusades, planting the Australian imports on formerly treeless hillsides. The eucalyptus grows well in California; it also has taken to the hissy fits of nature indigenous to the state. In a fire, as many neighborhoods in Oakland's hills found out not long ago, a eucalyptus will heat up and then explode.

WILD ONIONS and garlic, acorns crushed into fine meal, and chinook salmon—such was the food eaten over the centuries by people living in the middle-fork canyon of the American River. Onions and garlic are plentiful this summer in the valley; I had them in a salad two nights earlier. We drank old-vine Zinfandel, a taste of the foothills. Wonderful. But the king salmon of this part of California have joined Ishi in the museum. Still, what is so startling about this float is seeing how a little ribbon of California life has healed. I had studied pictures of the late-nineteenth-century American River: Kuwait after it was torched and bombed in the Gulf War may have looked better. But the river just could not be killed. Tiger lilies and columbine, sugar pine and rhododendron—there is enough left of California before the pave-over to get a sense of the balming effect it had on people.

But we are now close to the pinkish air, the whir of autos above the canyon racing to warehouse stores, the nexus between the California where the land breeds optimism and the California where one out of every nine people lives behind gates and lasers. And again, I wonder how it all could have gone so quickly from one extreme to the other. When the gold streams were played out in the last century, people pulled their noses from the gravel and found new riches in the basic elements of California life. The Sierra air, said Twain, was the same air that the angels breathed. A person had to leave the state in order to die, he wrote without sarcasm. "What a land! What mountains! What blue skies!" said Alice H. Ramsey, another writer, after clearing Donner Pass and shouting exclamations into the setting sun, not long after the turn of the century. "Clear sparkling water! Our hearts lept within us. None of us had ever seen the like—and we loved it."

A Scottish immigrant, arriving in California after walking more than a thousand miles from Indiana to the Florida coast, sailing to Panama and then up the West coast, fell deeply in love. Stepping off a steamer in San Francisco in 1868, he asked for directions out of town.

"But where do you want to go?" a stranger replied.

"To any place that is wild," John Muir answered. He was a wiry man of twenty-nine, endowed with ceaseless curiosity and springy legs. Flat broke, he hired on as a sheepherder in the Sierra, bound for the headwaters of the Merced and Tuolumne rivers. He was indifferent to the sheep, but he took to his companion, a St. Bernard. He got so sick of eating mutton he could not sleep for the turbulence in his stomach. But one dawn he came to a ridge on the west side of Indian Canyon—"every feature glowing, radiating beauty"—and his stomach problems were forgotten. It was a mystical intro-duction to Yosemite for the most loyal friend the valley would ever have. Muir could not contain himself. "I shouted and gesticulated in a burst of ecstasy," he said, an exuberance that startled his dog.

More than thirty years later, the former sheepherder was back in Yosemite with a barrel-chested dandy in spectacles—President Theodore Roosevelt. There is no state in the West that T.R. did not touch.

"An influential man from Washington wants to make a trip into the

Sierra with me," Muir wrote. "I might be able to do some good in freely talking around the campfire." Muir was world-famous by then, a friend to the likes of Ralph Waldo Emerson and Jack London, who lived in Oakland, where Muir's father-in-law had an orchard. His writings were largely responsible for the establishment of Yosemite National Park in 1890. And his foot-long beard made him look like an American Tolstoy. Though sixty-four, he was nimble as ever, the kind of man who loved nothing so much as a good earthquake for stimulation. One night in Yosemite, when the moon was nearly full, the ground suddenly groaned, boulders tumbled, and rock walls shivered. Muir felt like a sailor on a ship tossed by the high seas. "A noble earthquake!" he yelled out. "A noble earthquake!" He called the experience "thrilling," perhaps the first time such an adjective had ever been used to describe California's ongoing labor pains.

The president had asked for four days of aerobic talk with Muir in Yosemite; he requested only that there be no roof over their heads, nor Capitol Hill gibberish among them. "I want to drop politics absolutely for four days and just be out in the open," Roosevelt told Muir. In May 1903, they scrambled up to the granite summit of Glacier Point for a view of the falls. They dodged a crowd of politicians and hangers-on at a dinner planned in their honor down below, opting to eat camp chow near the sunset-gold walls of El Capitan. Another night, they slept under a sequoia tree with a trunk wider than the table reserved for the president's cabinet meetings. T.R. loved the West down to its driest canyons, its wettest forests, its ugliest spiders. But he was also a bait fisherman, a trophy-bagger. Nature was utilitarian. He had been influenced by Gifford Pinchot, founder of the modern Forest Service, who railed against the "massacre" of Western logging but had little use for a tree falling in a forest with no one around to hear it.

"Wilderness is waste," said Pinchot, a wrestling companion of Roosevelt's. The same thing was said about the undammed Colorado River. And the same thing is said, today, about the roadless heart of central Idaho. Muir the mystic had gone much further than any of the founders of modern conservation; humans needed the wild, yes, but as something to keep the soul alive—especially amidst the clutter of twentieth-century America. "Thousands of nerve-shaken, over-civilized people are beginning to find out that going to the mountains is going home," said Muir, "that wilderness is a necessity, and that mountain parks and reservations are useful not only as fountains of timber and irrigating rivers, but as fountains of life."

He urged people to look beyond the postcard scenery of the West, to feel the brunt of a "big, bossy well-charged thunderstorm" in Montana, to experience a snow dump in the Wasatch range of Utah, to linger at a mountaintop in Yellowstone just beyond sunset "to get one more baptism of light."

The president and the immigrant emerged after four days in Yosemite, sunburned and smelling of smoke. Not long after the camping trip, Roosevelt issued an executive order adding more than a million acres to the fledgling national park and forest reserve system. It took a self-taught naturalist from Scotland and a blueblood from Long Island to save much of the West from Westerners. Muir's comment about the needs of nerve-jangled urbanites has proven prophetic; the number of people going to Yosemite has risen to a point where one year's worth of visitors equals the population of Los Angeles.

The California that gave such a charge to Muir had started to fade in the last decade of his life. During the infatuation stage of his love affair, he had written that "the whole state of California, from the Siskiyous to San Diego, is one block of beauty." But by the time Muir was in his seventies, the state had commenced on a binge of transformation, looting its national wealth, and he had stopped speaking in exclamations. Hetch Hetchy, in the temple of Yosemite, was buried by a dam to provide water and power to San Francisco. The entire Central Valley, nearly five hundred miles long and fifty miles wide, was made into an agricultural factory, flooded with subsidized water drained from the Sierra, filled with chemicals to produce ever more uniform fruits and vegetables, drained of anything wild. What had been "level and flowery, like a lake of pure sunshine," was now "ploughed and pasteurized out of existence, gone forever." To the north, the country of redwoods and Douglas fir forests, "once divinely beautiful, are desolate and repulsive, like a face ravaged by disease," he wrote.

California's transition from garden to garrison was somewhat premeditated. Many people knew they were trashing the place. Nowhere on earth was blessed with a greater wealth of natural resources than the Golden State, wrote the state's leading educator, Edward Hyatt. "And nowhere is it being squandered with such a careless hand." His book on conservation was widely read in the schools in 1913. Not that it had much effect. That same year, water that Los Angeles had taken by stealth and fraud from the Owens Valley to the north, came pouring into the San Fernando Valley. Los Angeles, with 300,000 people, did not really need the water. But six private investors who had purchased sixteen thousand acres in the arid ranch land of the San Fernando Valley, just over the Hollywood Hills, saw it as their own motherlode. With water, the dusty valley would accept the spill of a half-million new people, and anyone who owned the land could become unspeakably rich. Among those who had a big piece of the valley were the publisher of the *Los Angeles Times,* General Harrison Gray Otis, and his son-in-law, Harry Chandler. Young Chandler, suffering from a lung ailment, had come to Los Angeles for his health.

The artery that remade California took six years to build. On November 5, 1913, men in suits and women in full dresses lined the last sluiceway of the project, just above the empty, treeless basin of the San Fernando Valley. There were speeches under the hot sun, a heralding of the great metropolis that would grow just below. At last it came time for the water czar, William Mulholland, to turn the valves, opening the faucet that would remake a national forest into a skeletal grove in the eastern Sierra, dry up peach and apple orchards, and allow the biggest city of the West to feel free of the restraints of nature. "There it is!" said Mulholland. "Take it!"

John Muir died on Christmas Eve, 1914; he had spent his last days walking in the Mojave Desert. California eventually created the world's most elaborate hydraulic system, a total of 465 dams in all, plugging every river of the Sierra but one. Most of the water drained from the Sierra, about 85 percent, goes to agriculture, and feed for livestock is the greatest single crop by acreage. Large parts of the Golden State were replumbed for cattle—in tune with the cow-centric West.

The year of Muir's death, Model T automobiles were being produced at the rate of one every three minutes, and nowhere were they more popular than in California. By 1940, the first freeway was built in Southern California. The region had developed the world's largest electric transit system, trolleys linking over fifty communities in four counties. But from the time constructions crews started pouring concrete for a culture on wheels, the trolley days were numbered. The Big Red cars of the Pacific Electric were dumped in the 1950s, the transit system torn down. Smog settled in, a signature sight. Greater Los Angeles grew into the biggest city in the world, in physical size. Later, it was surpassed by another irrigation creation, Phoenix. By the end of the century, the average Californian was spending more than 450 hours a year inside a car, and 40 percent of the land of Los Angeles was given over to the storage and movement of automobiles. The California Dream—a dream of all the West, at that, a desire to live close to nature—was dying, said most Californians in a statewide poll. "We have lost our sense of who we are as Californians," the state's preeminent historian, Kevin Starr, would declare in the 1990s. "It's almost scary."

Even the architects turned on their creations. One of the chief financiers of mindless sprawl, the Bank of America, issued a report that said California was killing itself with cancerous growth. Sprawl had "shifted from an engine of California growth to a force that now threatens to inhibit growth and degrade quality of life," the bank reported. Mark Twain said people had to leave the state in order to die; now they were leaving in order to live. One of those who fled in the 1990s, heading to Oregon for cleaner air and open space, was Otis Chandler, the former publisher of the *Los Angeles Times*. He bought a ranch in the juniper tree country east of the Cascade Mountains, a place that looked not unlike the Owens Valley before his grandparents in Los Angeles helped to turn it into a land choked by dust clouds.

WE FLOAT until we can go no further. The American River Canyon narrows ever-deeper in the Sierra foothills, but the water pools up, and we bump into cables, concrete, wires, and warning signs. We are left at the edge of a deep gouge in the bedrock. Here, just outside the town of Auburn, the political powers of the Sacramento Valley have deigned to build what would be the last big dam of the West. The promise of the dam, say its promoters, is that it would allow nearly a million people down in the Sacramento Valley to be out of harm's way for good. A guarantee, in other words. The floods that buried so much of the valley in the past would be no more. And just upriver, farmland rich with silt would be carved into new gated communities where random encounters would be outlawed. Slackwater from the dam would bury every stretch of the river we had just floated, and much more: the Indian stone milling sites, the tropical bird nesting areas, the deep pools and frothy rapids, and all the Gold Rush locales— forty miles of canyon in the cradle of California history. Most of it would be under more than a hundred feet of water. A small price? Perhaps. But people without history, as the Lakota saying goes, are like wind on the buffalo grass.

They started blasting away river rock down to the core, pouring cement, and rechanneling some of the water in the 1970s, as the big dam got underway. But then came a sudden squawk from the California that the Portolá Expedition met in 1769. Nature bats last! An earthquake measuring 5.7 on the Richter scale rumbled through the Sierra foothills; its epicenter was forty-five miles from the dam site. A previously unknown fault ran just beneath the American River Canyon. Building a 508-foot dam that would hold more than 50 billion gallons of water on a cracked chip of earth might, indeed, save residents of the Sacramento Valley from winter flooding; it might also kill them in an earthquake. Construction was halted, after $225 million had been spent. It has never been resumed. But the project is alive again, thanks to Western congressmen in control of natural resource decisions, people who see only one view of the land—the Unfinished West.

DOWN IN the valley, out of the river canyon and into the brain-swelling heat, I walk along the top of a levee that keeps the river from spilling onto Sacramento. In the middle of the day, temperatures are well above 100 degrees. I am with Butch Hodgkins and some of his fellow engineers at the flood control authority. Butch has a graying crew cut, leathery face; he looks like a Californian bookmarked by the early Beach Boys period, now stuck in middle age. Walking atop the earthen barriers between the river and city, Butch and his boys press their case. All this part of California wants, he says, is one last dam. One last time to hold nature at bay, one last time to let new houses rise in a valley prone to epic floods, one last chance for California to start anew. His tone is desperate. In the state Wallace Stegner called home at the time of his death, how did some people become so afraid of the native ground of hope?

I thought of something Alvin Josephy, the chronicler of the Nez Perce, had said back in Jackson Hole, when we had gathered to consider what the West of the next hundred years would be like. In the 1950s, Josephy had gone up in a plane with Bureau of Reclamation officials. They swooped low over spectacular canyons, wild and untouched. Caught up in the mission of the bureaucrats who remade the West, Josephy shouted above the propeller noise and pointed down: "Here's another great place to build a dam!"

It has been an awful decade for California, perhaps its worst. Ralph Waldo Emerson's line—"California has better days and more of them than any other country"—seems to apply to the other extreme as well. But every Westerner should look at California's story; as it turns out, it is their own history and the fount of most of their follies, a mirror across the Sierra. Radically altering the land, living on phony myths, ignoring the best features or trying to kill them. And it is Western glory in its own fine way: a new society, with a tolerance of fledgling souls, embracing the possible. What is different is that California has done it all faster, with more excess and greater consequence than any other Western state. To believe that California is dead, then, is to believe that the West is dead, or soon will be. I cannot.

When Josephy told that story about looking for dams in God's country, everyone in the audience laughed. In one generation's time, a noble mission has been transformed into utter absurdity. And so now across the West, the corrective is underway, the compass pointing back to a land closer to the authentic. Water is being diverted from forced farms in the arid lands and returned to nature. Indian tribes, erased from much of the map a hundred years ago, have not just survived, they dream anew, and not the dreams of a ghost dance. A new Western ethic may be taking hold—the idea of letting this land be itself. We could not agree on much that November night in the Tetons, except this: subduing the wild is the one sure way to kill the West. Seattle clings to desperation salmon runs, Reno celebrates the horses that run loose just outside the city limits, and Albuquerque looks to three-dimensional petroglyphs for life beyond the banal. Why? Heritage.

IN THE American River, I could only see just ahead of me, never around the next bend. The water from the Sierra that we rode through a slice of old California flows until there is no more land, until the West comes to an end. At the edge of the continent, a small redwood forest named for Muir lives nonetheless, hugging the Pacific fifteen minutes from five million people. To the south, some of the ground that rattled the Portolá Expedition is a five-acre park, Pershing Square, in the oldest part of Los Angeles. Office buildings are stuffed with lawyers within sight of neighborhoods where not a word of English is spoken. Running through the square, in its latest upgrade, is a zigzagging earthquake crack; fake, of course. Custom and culture: Los Angeles, true to the West, is not afraid to laugh at itself. And those trees of heaven, brought to this world by the Chinese, grow in cracks of the cement in parts of California. They tolerate smog. Yes, the West ends here. But the frontier begins.

Acknowledgments

East to West, this book had many helpers. In Italy, for perspective, company and Chianti, I am indebted to the Sunday afternoon gang at Bryan and Marina's. In New York, transplanted Westerner Katie Roberts pushed and inspired, for more than five years; there is no better trail guide at the *New York Times*. Joseph Lelyveld gave the gift of time. Carol Mann did her usual matchmaking job. Sonny Mehta, Ash Green, Melvin Rosenthal, and others at Knopf are owed much gratitude for the alchemy of putting ideas between covers. In New Mexico, Frank Zoretich and Katherine Robbins were invaluable. Jim Wilson put up with all my side tours in Nevada, California, and Utah; I don't think he minded. In Seattle, Joni Balter, Sophie Egan, Matt Rudolf, and Skip Berger reminded me of the important stuff. In Wyoming, the Snake River Institute brought together some of the best minds of the West, and gave me a starting point. In Oregon, Fishtrap did the same thing. In Idaho, my brothers Kelly and Danny kept me in the river long enough to get it.

Selected Bibliography

Abbey, Edward, *Desert Solitaire*. Ballantine, 1968.

Ambrose, Stephen E., *Undaunted Courage: Meriwether Lewis, Thomas Jefferson and the Opening of the American West*. Simon & Schuster, 1996.

Backes, Clarus, ed., *Growing Up Western*. Alfred A. Knopf, 1990.

Bass, Rick, *The Ninemile Wolves*. Random House, 1992.

Beal, Merrill D., *I Will Fight No More Forever: Chief Joseph and the Nez Perce War*. University of Washington Press, 1963.

Benson, Jackson J., *Wallace Stegner: His Life and Work*. Viking, 1996.

Berger, Bruce, *The Telling Distance: Conversations with the American Desert*. Breitenbush Books, 1989.

Bishop, James Jr., *Epitaph for a Desert Anarchist: The Life and Times of Edward Abbey*. Atheneum, 1994.

Bordewich, Fergus M., *Killing the White Man's Indian: Reinventing Native Americans at the End of the Twentieth Century*. Anchor Doubleday, 1996.

Brooks, Juanita, *Mountain Meadows Massacre*. University of Oklahoma Press, 1950.

Brown, Kenneth A., *Four Corners: History, Land and People of the Desert Southwest*. Harper-Collins, 1995.

Clarke, Thurston, *California Fault: Searching for the Spirit of a State Along the San Andreas*. Random House, 1996.

Conaway, James, *The Kingdom in the Country*. Houghton Mifflin, 1987.

Douglas, William O., *Of Men and Mountains*. Harper & Brothers, 1950.

Dutton, Bertha P., *American Indians of the Southwest.* University of New Mexico Press, 1983.

Ellis, Richard N., ed., *New Mexico Past and Present: A Historical Reader.* University of New Mexico Press, 1971.

Fahey, John, *The Inland Empire: Unfolding Years, 1879–1929.* University of Washington Press, 1986.

Fletcher, Colin, *The Man Who Walked Through Time.* Vintage, 1989.

Fradkin, Philip L., *The Seven States of California.* Henry Holt, 1995.

Harden, Blaine, *A River Lost: The Life and Death of the Columbia River.* W. W. Norton, 1996.

Hepworth, James R., and Gregory McNamee, eds., *Resist Much Obey Little: Remembering Ed Abbey.* Sierra Club Books, 1996.

Hill, William E., *The Oregon Trail Yesterday and Today.* Caxton Printers, 1992.

Holbrook, Stewart, *Far Corner.* Comstock Editions, 1973.

Houston, Pam, *Cowboys Are My Weakness.* W. W. Norton, 1992.

Jones, Florence Lee, and John F. Cahlan, *Water: A History of Las Vegas.* 1975.

Josephy, Alvin M. Jr., *The Nez Perce Indians and the Opening of the Northwest.* Yale University Press, 1965.

———, *Now That the Buffalo's Gone: A Study of Today's American Indians.* University of Oklahoma Press, 1982.

Kay, Jane Holtz, *Asphalt Nation: How the Automobile Took Over America and How We Can Take It Back.* Crown, 1997.

Kittredge, William, *Hole in the Sky: A Memoir.* Alfred A. Knopf, 1992.

———, *Owning It All.* Graywolf Press, 1987.

Leopold, Aldo, *The River of the Mother of God and Other Essays,* edited by Susan L. Flader and J. Baird Callicott. University of Wisconsin Press, 1991.

———, *A Sand County Almanac.* Oxford University Press, 1949.

Lewis, Jon E., *The Mammoth Book of the West: The Making of the American West.* Carroll & Graf, 1996.

Lewis, Meriwether, and William Clark, *The Journals of Lewis and Clark,* edited by Bernard DeVoto. Houghton Mifflin, 1953.

Limerick, Patricia Nelson, *The Legacy of Conquest: The Unbroken Past of the American West.* W. W. Norton, 1987.

Lopez, Barry Holstun, *Of Wolves and Men.* Scribner's, 1978.

Maclean, Norman, *A River Runs Through It.* University of Chicago Press, 1976.

Malone, Michael P., *The Battle for Butte: Mining and Politics on the Northern Frontier, 1864–1906.* University of Washington Press, 1981.

———, and Richard W. Etulain, *The American West: A Twentieth-Century History.* University of Nebraska Press, 1992.

———, William L. Lang, and Richard B. Roeder, *Montana: A History of Two Centuries.* Revised ed. University of Washington Press, 1991.

McNamee, Thomas, *The Return of the Wolf to Yellowstone.* Henry Holt, 1997.

McPhee, John, *Assembling California.* Farrar, Straus & Giroux, 1993.

———, Basin and Range. Farrar, Straus & Giroux, 1986.

Miller, Kathleen L., "The Temple Block: A Core Sample of Los Angeles." *Journal of the West*, April 1994.

Moulton, Gary E., ed., *The Journals of Lewis and Clark*. University of Nebraska Press, 1986.

Muir, John, *The Eight Wilderness Discovery Books*. The Mountaineers, 1992.

————, Wilderness Essays. Peregrine Smith Books, 1982.

Neuberger, Richard, *Our Promised Land*. Macmillan, 1938.

O'Brien, Robert, *This Is San Francisco: A Classic Portrait of the City*. Chronicle Books, 1948.

Peterson, Levis S., *Juanita Brooks: Mormon Woman Historian*. University of Utah Press, 1988.

Power, Thomas Michael, *Lost Landscapes and Failed Economies: The Search for a Value of Place*. Island Press, 1996.

Raban, Jonathan, *Bad Land: An American Romance*. Pantheon, 1996.

Reisner, Marc, *Cadillac Desert: The American West and Its Disappearing Water*. Penguin, 1987.

Rieff, David, *Los Angeles: Capital of the Third World*. Simon & Schuster, 1991.

Robbins, William G., *Landscape of Promise: The Oregon Story, 1800–1940*. University of Washington Press, 1997.

Roosevelt, Theodore, *The Winning of the West*, vols. 1–4. Putnam's, 1889–1896.

Runte, Alfred, *National Parks: The American Experience*. University of Nebraska Press, 1979.

Russell, Sharman Apt, *Kill the Cowboy: A Battle of Mythology in the New West*. Addison-Wesley, 1993.

Sellars, Richard West, *Preserving Nature in the National Parks: A History*. Yale University Press, 1997.

Simmons, Marc, *The Last Conquistador: Juan de Oñate and the Settling of the Far Southwest*. University of Oklahoma Press, 1991.

————, *New Mexico: An Interpretive History*. University of New Mexico Press, Albuquerque, 1977.

Simon, Ted, *The River Stops Here: How One Man's Battle to Save His Valley Changed the Fate of California*. Random House, 1994.

Solnit, Rebecca, *Savage Dreams: A Journey into the Hidden Wars of the American West*. Sierra Club Books, 1994.

Starr, Kevin, *Americans and the California Dream*. Oxford University Press, 1973.

————, *Inventing the Dream: California Through the Progressive Era*. Oxford University Press, 1985.

————, *Material Dreams: Southern California Through the 1920s*. Oxford University Press, 1990.

Stegner, Wallace, *Beyond the Hundredth Meridian: John Wesley Powell and the Second Opening of the American West*. Houghton Mifflin, 1954.

————, *Mormon Country*. Duel, Sloan and Pearce, 1942.

————, *This Is Dinosaur: Echo Park Country and Its Magic Rivers*. Alfred A. Knopf, 1955.

————, *Where the Bluebird Sings in the Lemonade Springs*. Penguin, 1992.

Swartout, Robert R., and Harry W. Fritz, eds., *Montana Heritage*. Montana Historical Society, 1992.

Tirrell, Norma, *Montana*. Compass America, 1991.

Turner, Frederick, *Of Chiles, Cacti, and Fighting Cocks: Notes on the American West.* Henry Holt, 1990.

Twain, Mark, *Roughing It.* Penguin, 1981.

Utley, Robert, *The Indian Frontier of the American West.* University of New Mexico Press, 1984.

Wharton, Tom, and Gayen Wharton, *Utah.* Compass America, 1993.

White, Richard, *It's Your Misfortune and None of My Own: A New History of the American West.* University of Oklahoma Press, Norman, 1991.

Wilkinson, Charles F., *Crossing the Next Meridian: Land, Water, and the Future of the West.* Island Press, 1992.

Williams, Terry Tempest, *An Unspoken Hunger: Stories from the Field.* Vintage, 1995.

Index

VINTAGE DEPARTURES

THE EMPEROR'S LAST STAND
by Julia Blackburn

The story of the deposed emperor Napoleon holding court amid the shabbiness and paranoia of an island prison is interwoven with a history of St. Helena itself and with a personal account of the author's own voyage in search of Napoleon's ghost.

"Dazzling . . . startlingly imaginative."
—*The New York Times Book Review*

History/Travel/0-679-73937-8

AMONG THE THUGS
by Bill Buford

From a vandalous ride on the English railway to the full-blown riots in Turin and Sardinia, Bill Buford gives us a terrifying record of his passage through an alternate society: that of England's soccer thugs.

"An unflinching look into the festering soul of England . . . a great read."
—David Byrne

Sociology/0-679-74535-1

PECKED TO DEATH BY DUCKS
by Tim Cahill

In this grand tour of the earth's remote, exotic, and dismal places, Tim Cahill sleeps with a grizzly bear, witnesses demonic possession in Bali, and survives a run-in with the Throne of Doom in Guatemala.

"Tim Cahill [has] the what-the-hell adventuresomeness of a T. E. Lawrence and the humor of a P. J. O'Rourke." —*Condé Nast Traveler*

Travel/Adventure/0-679-74929-2

THE ROAD FROM COORAIN
by Jill Ker Conway

A remarkable woman's clear-sighted memoir of growing up Australian: from a sheep station in the outback to the stifling propriety of postwar Sydney; from untutored childhood to a life in academia; and from the shelter of family to lessons of independence and tragedy.

"A small masterpiece of scene, memory." —John Kenneth Galbraith

Autobiography/0-679-72436-2

BURY ME STANDING
The Gypsies and Their Journey
by Isabel Fonseca

Fabled, feared, romanticized, and reviled, the Gypsies—or Roma—are among the least understood people on earth. Now a diaspora of twelve million, their culture remains largely obscure. But in Isabel Fonseca they have found an eloquent witness.

"A revelation: a hidden world—at once ignored and secretive, persecuted and unknown—is uncovered in these absorbing pages."

—Salman Rushdie

Current Affairs/Travel/0-679-76743-X

BAD TRIPS
Edited and with an Introduction
by Keath Fraser

From Martin Amis in the air to Peter Matthiessen on a mountaintop, some of the best-known writers of our time recount sometimes harrowing and sometimes exhilarating tales of their most memorable misadventures in travel.

"The only aspect of our travels that is guaranteed to hold an audience is disaster. . . . Nothing is better for survival."

—Martha Gellhorn

Travel/Adventure/0-679-72908-9

FALLING OFF THE MAP
Some Lonely Places of the World
by Pico Iyer

Pico Iyer voyages from the nostalgic elegance of Argentina to the raffish nonchalance of Australia, documents the cruising rites of Icelandic teenagers, gets interrogated by tipsy Cuban police, and attends a screening of Bhutan's first feature film.

"[Iyer] writes the kind of lyrical, flowing prose that could make Des Moines sound beguiling." —*Los Angeles Times Book Review*

Travel/Adventure/0-679-74612-9

SHOOTING THE BOH

A Woman's Voyage Down the Wildest River in Borneo

by Tracy Johnston

A heroic and entertaining tale about a woman's harrowing ride down the treacherous rapids of the Boh River in central Borneo and through the uncharted realm of middle age.

"Funny, candid, riveting. . . . I enjoyed this book immensely."

—Joe Kane

Travel/Adventure/0-679-74010-4

RIDING THE WHITE HORSE HOME

A Western Family Album

by Teresa Jordan

The daughter and granddaughter of Wyoming ranchers tells the stories of her forbearers—men who saw broken bones as professional credentials and women who coped with physical hardship. She acquaints us with the lore and science of ranching, and does so with breathtaking immediacy.

"A haunting and elegant memoir."   —Terry Tempest Williams

THE ENDS OF THE EARTH

*A Journey to the Frontiers of Anarchy—
from Togo to Turkmenistan, from Iran to Cambodia*

by Robert Kaplan

Traveling from West Africa to Southeast Asia to report on a world of disintegrating nation-states, warring nationalities, metastasizing populations, and dwindling resources, Kaplan emerges with a gritty tour de force of political journalism.

"An impressive work. Most travel books seem trivial beside it."

—*Washington Post Book World*

History/Current Affairs/0-679-75123-8

Printed in the United States
by Baker & Taylor Publisher Services